RONALD BLYTHE

The View in Winter
Reflections on Old Age

ALLEN LANE

ALLEN LANE
Penguin Books Ltd
536 King's Road
London SW10 0UH

First published 1979
Reprinted 1980

ISBN 0 7139 0738 X

Set in Monotype Ehrhardt by
Western Printing Services, Bristol

Printed in Great Britain by
Billing and Sons Ltd

For Marion and Colin Benham

ACKNOWLEDGEMENTS

Many people helped me with this book but I am especially grateful to: Father Christopher Bryant, s.s.j.e., Mrs Adelaide Fox, the Librarian and Staff of Ipswich Central Library, Mrs Anne Islet, Major S. Ozanne, s.a., the Reverend D. G. Richards, Mrs Irene Turner, Dr Ursula Hamilton-Paterson and the late Mr Douglas Saunders.

My thanks are also due to the publishers and individuals who have kindly allowed me to quote from the works of the following poets: W. H. Auden, 'Old People's Home' from *Collected Poems*, Faber & Faber, 1976; May Wedderburn Cannan, 'Rouen' from *In War Time*, Basil Blackwood, 1917; Frances Cornford, 'Childhood' from *Collected Poems*, The Cresset Press, 1954. By permission of Barrie & Jenkins; Walter De La Mare, 'A Portrait' from *Collected Poems*, Faber & Faber, 1970. By permission of the Literary Trustees of Walter De La Mare, and The Society of Authors as their representative; Ruth Fainlight, 'Losers' from *Twenty-One Poems*, Turret Books, 1973; Ted Hughes, 'Winter in the Village' from *Season Songs*, Faber & Faber, 1976; Philip Larkin, 'Next Please' from *The Less Deceived*, Marvell Press, 1955, and 'The Old Fools' from *High Windows*, Faber & Faber, 1974; Wilfred Owen 'À Terre' from *Collected Poems*, Chatto & Windus, 1971. By permission of the Trustees of The Owen Estate; Palladas, 'We are Born every Day' from *Translations from the Greek Anthology* by Robert Allason Furness, Jonathan Cape, 1931. By permission of the Trustees of the Estate of R. A. Furness; Pindar, 'Human Life', translated by H. T. Wade-Gery and C. M. Bowra, in *Pindar: The Pythian Odes*, Nonesuch Press, 1928; Isaac Rosenberg, 'Break of Day in the Trenches' and 'Dead Man's Dump' from *Complete Works*, Chatto & Windus, 1949. By permission of the Literary Estate of Isaac Rosenberg; R. S. Thomas, 'Penances' from *Selected Poems, 1946–1968*, Hart-Davis/ Granada, 1973; Tyrtaeas, 'How Can Man Die Better' from *The*

Oxford Book of Greek Verse in Translation, edited by T. F. Higham and C. M. Bowra, Oxford University Press, 1938; W. B. Yeats, 'Among School Children' from *Collected Poems*, Macmillan, 1971. By permission of M. B. Yeats and Miss Anne Yeats.

Introduction

Our earthly time allowance has rapidly shot up from an average of forty years to an average of seventy years plus within the experience of all the old people alive at present. Nothing comparable to it has been known before. Although it was accepted that the body had been programmed to last for the classic three-score-years-and-ten, until now there was an all too eloquent proof that very few bodies ever did, and for a man to 'see his time out', as they used to say, was exceptional. We counter this fact by declaring that one was old at forty in those days. Yet one was not, at least not in the sense of cumulative time, which is what defines actual old age. A vast number of men and women became toil-worn and disease-marked in middle age to a degree no longer seen in Western society, but however exhausted and unhygienic their flesh, it was unlikely to have been senescent when the grave claimed it. Apart from the minority whose mortal clock – the workings of which are still a mystery – went the full round, most were not involved in the ageing process and seemed to have lived without thought or preparation for it.

It is one of the essential ways in which our forebears differ from us. Their knowledge of the destruction of the physical self was quite unlike anything we understand by hospital visits or by simply walking down the street. If a Renaissance or Georgian man could return he would be as much astonished by the sight of two or three thousand septuagenarians and octogenarians lining a south-coast resort on a summer's day in their preponderantly white and palely coloured clothes, as he would by a television-set. Astonished and maybe shocked. His was a world where it was the exception to go grey, to reach the menopause, to retire, to become senile and to acquire that subtle blend of voice, skin and behavioural changes which features so largely in our long-lived times. Because of its customary incompletion, life for him operated from a quite different premise. For one thing, it contained a precariousness which we, for all our nuclear hazards, no longer feel. For another, it conditioned a man to accept his cut-down or halved time-scale as that against which he would need to plan his education or craft training, his work and his children's future, and to think of reaching seventy in quasi-religious terms. To be seventy or eighty was to be as 'full of years' as a multi-centenarian Old Testament prophet.

Another contrast between old age then and old age now is that we place dying in what we take to be its logical position, which is at the close of a long life – when our ancestors accepted the futility of placing it in any position at all. In the midst of life we are in death, they said, and they meant it. To them it was a fact, to us it is a metaphor. It secretly disturbs us to see old people talking and behaving as if they were in the midst of life. We ask ourselves, 'How can they . . . with so little time to go?' But to love and travel and fight and bluster in the face of death, as it once confronted the early middle-aged, was thought brave and admirable. It meant that people were once, for all their fatal illnesses, vital, capable and very much alive up to the edge of their graves. It was said of the seventy-year-old Elizabeth I, when death came to her, that she was a lady surprised by time. But she was old and this was gallantry.

The manner in which death suddenly announced itself to the average mortal was indeed a surprise and the subject of a poignant literature. The common fate of a brief life bred apprehension, swift-moving ambition or piety, according to one's character, but because the majority of men knew no other life it had a normality which is now outside our comprehension. So altered are we that it sometimes seems that we are reaching the stage when we may have to announce ourselves to death, and may find its avoidance of us hurtful and neglectful. In hospitals up and down the land lie the finished lives which appear, as it were, to have been 'cut dead' by death. It is as though one needs a special strength to die, and not a final weakness. Yet weakness is what characterizes the old most of all. And so, in its less extreme state, is there a power in this unique weakness which sustains age and makes it as positive a time as youth or maturity? One of the reasons why the old suffer is because the non-old dislike the notion that they are vital still. 'How well old people come to know that peculiar look of suppressed disgust which their obstinate concentration on some restricted sensual pleasure excites in the feverish idealism of the young and in the impatient pragmatism of the middle-aged! What is their wisest method of mental defence against the shameful discomfort caused by this look?' wrote John Cowper Powys when he was seventy-two.

We talk and think and generally preoccupy ourselves with this new fate of an old age for everybody. But we never say, as we might with any other general advancement, 'How wonderful it is that by the year 2000 everybody will be more or less guaranteed of a full life!' Instead we mutter, our faces thickened with anxiety, 'Just think, in twenty years' time half the population will be over sixty.' We rarely add that any blame for an imbalance must be shared by the young for not having babies or that when *we* reach sixty our energies and hopes and intentions are as likely to carry us forward into the welcome decades to come as much as the next old man's.

The economics of national longevity apart, the ordinariness of living to be old is too novel a thing at the moment to appreciate. The old have been made to feel that they have been sentenced to life and turned into a matter for public concern. They are the first generations of the full-timers and thus the first generations of old people for whom the state, experimentally, grudgingly and uncertainly, is having to make special supportive conditions. This book listens to them talking. Except for a few spiritual travellers – and the most heroic of these confess to weeks and months and years when the static element in old age makes it impossible for them to advance an inch in the heavenly direction – all movement in the talk is backward to youth and childhood. The skill and determination with which the aged are able to return to their first memories is only equalled by the world's eels slipping back to the Sargasso Sea. They find pace in childhood but none in maturity remembered and little in the present. So they embark, along with any willing ear, for the beginning, where things still move fast and are bright and clearly defined.

The most irreconcilable aspect of agedness is the destruction of progressive movement, that hard fact of having come to the end of the journey when custom and instinct still insist that one can, and should, go on. When the old say, as they so often do, 'I simply can't go on,' they are stating their major frustration, not announcing a coming to terms with death. Few are nervous about the nearness of death, although what time remains often becomes very precious and sweet in spite of the harassment by disease and arthritic pain, unhealing skin and multiplying discomforts. Many old people, talking within months or weeks of their deaths, became exceptionally alive and were greedy for every sight and touch. Some were full of arrangements about the disposal of possessions. A few dropped the mask by which the world – and this could include their families – had known them and confessed to what they really were. These masks were primarily those of orthodoxy hiding the married homosexual, the church-going unbeliever and the heretic in the political party. More of a conspiratorial than a cowardly attitude was revealed in the reasons for wearing masks; all the world being a stage, it appears that there are far more people who get their dramatic kicks by operating its conventions than is suspected. The old, too, revealed conversions to a host of well-nigh forgotten causes and loyalty towards vanished concepts. These ideas lie about in their natures and in their thinking, an ineradicable tincture acquired half a century or more ago in the Empire, on some grim farm, in the ritualistic Mess, via Douglas Credit or early Hollywood, Toc-H, the Left Book Club, the British Union of Fascists ('Ah,' said the eighty-year-old Henry Williamson gently, going through his snapshots, 'the S.S. . . .') and never quite disappear. Men are usually converted to notions and creeds for which they have an innate disposition. Listening to the nonagenarian who had opened her heart and mind to the teachings of Maria Montessori, one saw the highest example of such a predisposition.

Many of today's old people had such rough starts, such small scraps of education, wages and possessions generally, that they feel they are ending their days in clover. 'Manage' is a word they much use and having 'managed' then, they manage now. They describe penurious and exhausting working lives without rancour. They are proud if they never cheated, and they are proud if they did and got away with it. But some find that now is the deprived time. They are aware of ceaseless depredation and of everything being snatched from them or placed out of reach, and of being narrowed and lessened and ground-out of their very personality. They are shaken by the extent of their impoverishment, both spiritually and materially, and are disturbed when such guardians of their riches as a loving family or a good doctor are powerless to prevent it happening. Tolstoy dealt with this terrible dismantling of the ego in his story *The Death of Ivan Ilyich*, in which a middle-aged man who has acquired everything necessary for his social identification among the successful and the conventional, has to watch himself stripped down by cancer until all that is left of him is a scream. Constantly, as one talked to the aged, one felt this struggle to say who they *are*, not just who and what they have been.

And then there are the relinquishers and abdicators who drop the reins of their own accord, who sometimes acquire new friends because they don't insist on close relationships, and whose main action seems to be stretching out an irreverent arm and sweeping the clutter off the board. This category of old person often welcomes solitude, which is thought perverse and awkward of them by the family and by the welfare authorities. Many old people, however, simply want what they have had. They want it badly, and there is never much diminution in the strength of their hankering for what has been, for all the convenient talk about the merciful failing of desire. Old age is not an emancipation from desire for most of us; that is a large part of its tragedy. The old want (but their sensible refusal to put such wants into words suggests to us that they have given up wanting) their professional status back, or their looks, or their circle which is now a lot of crossed-off names in the address-book, or sex, or just a normal future-orientated existence. Most of all they want to be wanted. It crashes on them like a nightmare, the leaden fact that they are eighty, and that now it is often not so much a matter of their being incapable of having some of the things they want, as there being laws and conventions preventing their access to them.

Perhaps, as the young begin to realize that they are likely to be 'old' for twenty or more years, radical changes will effect what the aged want and could still have. Certainly, we are likely to see retirement-refusal, and a lifting of one of the last big sexual taboos, that placed on sex in old age.

The hope that sexuality itself would wither away and not add its desperate frustrations to agedness has long since been turned into the quite unfounded assurance that with age we naturally become asexual. What evidence we have to the contrary we manipulate to prove the social desirability of a sexless old age and to advocate the controls needed to achieve it. We tell the old, if you do not conform to this negative ideal you will be either ludicrous or indecent, that people will be frightened of you and think of you as pitiful or as a nuisance, for you are engaging in what is next to impossible or unthinkable. Thus the wistful legend and the rules of convenience which it has spawned. These rules and attitudes are among the very last to be overturned by our society in its urgent need to understand the realities of ageing. But the notion that the old are beyond sex still governs most public and private systems to house them and, outside, in countless ordinary situations such as going to the pub, the cinema or on holiday, the elderly man or woman finds it prudent to conceal any interest in what takes his or her fancy. We approve of this and are grateful to old relatives, friends, neighbours and even old strangers for this disciplined concealment. But we prefer not to know that among the most important reasons why the old guard their eroticism from the risk of having it mocked or judged is not because they believe it to be shameful or unnatural at their time of life, but to protect something which has in the past brought them so much love and delight from contempt. For all our new caring and planning, to be old today is to be contemptible. Why? Because to be old is to be part of a huge and ordinary multitude, a section of society so fast-growing in its needs and demands as to create another kind of helplessness in the young and middle-aged, making them feel guilty and resentful. The reason why old age was venerated in the past was because it was extraordinary. Among the few ways an aged individual can escape from a vast problematical category into his own distinctive personality is via his genital primacy, even if it means little more at this stage than living in what has been called 'a kind of after image'.

Proof that overt sexuality in the aged is all part of the sexual legitimacy which accompanies us from the cradle to the grave, so to speak, lies in its ability to disturb society as it does. We may prohibit it or ridicule it, but when we become involved with it, however peripherally, it is always a bit of a shock to find in it something neither old nor age-defying. As was said at the first symposium of the Boston Society for Gerontologic Psychiatry nearly twenty years ago, when the whole subject began to be demythologized, 'The conflicts concerning sexual thought and behaviour that are so clearly seen in younger people survive in the old. In many of the aged, conflicts concerning sexual expression are long-standing. However, many people who during their youth and middle years were able to achieve relative comfort about sexuality became uncomfortable with their erotic desire in a culture that either forbids or denies it its reality.'

'The fact that the idealized sexual standard of the culture emphasizes the firm bodies of youth may also reactivate oedipal conflicts in the aged,' it was pointed out by two of the delegates, Dr Zinberg and Dr Kaufman. 'The passage of years has not made forbidden sexual interests any easier for the person to tolerate [and] we know full-well from our patients that it is not only the children, but also the parents, whose sexual interests and defenses against them are activated by the processes of development. This *ronde* does not stop until death. The shame experienced by the old man as the result of a forbidden sexual impulse that may or may not be repressed sets up reverberations in his younger physician and family . . . This rondelay of point and counterpoint is complicated by the cultural attitude which makes it extremely necessary for both sides to deny that it is taking place. When feelings are so urgently repressed, the result is often more rather than less activity . . .'

However, the aged are not only expected to continue to suppress what they were obliged to suppress most of their lives but also that conventional sexuality which, until they became old, was an acceptable or even a welcome aspect of their personalities. It could include a permissible and admired sexual display on the dance-floor and the beach, the wearing of attractive clothes and hair-styles, and the playful sensuality which doesn't feel obliged to conceal itself in the conventional body-contacts of hugs, handshakes, kisses, etc. All this, should it still exist, has to be subject to a new discretion. Not the least tragic aspect of old age is learning how to provide false evidence in such matters. Old men and women will continue to do so for their own safety's sake until society rids itself of its inhibitions on the subject.

Modern geriatric psychiatry speaks of the old being wounded in their narcissism, a poignant term and one which eloquently compresses the whole business of what we once were, and what we must inevitably become, should we see our time out. To be sexually prohibited, even if it is only in some ignorant, unwritten and folk-belief sense, is a gratuitous addition to this hurt. The natural checks of old age lie in sublimations and in the slowly dying organism itself, not in such repressions. In any case, they are only a surface thing, for the old learn how to prevent too great a wounding of their narcissism by healing forays into the past, where there can still be found much of what is necessary to maintain a self-acceptable image of themselves. Such an image is bound to have its bright sexual facets, for, as A. L. Vischer says, 'It is difficult to renounce a thing when we know its value and the delight which it affords and when our memory of it does not fade but even calls for repetition.' He adds that in a period in which youth, physical beauty and the achievement of sexual ecstasy are the standard grist of every popular newspaper, glossy magazine, song, film and advertisement, 'it is not surprising that the subject of sexuality is not so easily exhausted by the older generation'.

At present there is much in our treatment of the old and our attitudes towards them which is scandalously similar to that which governed nineteenth-century attempts to solve the 'intractable' problem of the poor. They are not *us*, is what we are often saying (politely and humanely, of course), and there are so many of them! Such a situation can only alter when it becomes natural to say that the old *are* us – and to believe it.

The inescapability of old age is now secretly for many the new predicament. And even those who pray, and save, for a long life have the feeling that by eating and behaving in the way which they believe will encourage longevity, they are tempting fate. Some comfort is gained by seeing 'old Mr Smith, who is wonderful' at eighty-two, and by avoiding the sight of old Mrs Everard, who *was* wonderful at eighty but who now lies, year after year, under a tidy white hump of hospital quilt which is almost as still as her little green mound will be – though when? That is her quandary, the slow-motion departure.

To be a potential candidate for the Tithonus situation is the great dread of the aged. The possibility haunts the latter years of retirement. Tithonus was a beautiful young man who so delighted in being alive that he asked Aurora, goddess of morning, to make him immortal. She did, but as it had not occurred to him to request perpetual youthfulness as well, he simply became an old man who could not die. Eventually, taking pity on him after listening to his repeated prayer that he should be freed from his never-ending dissolution, the goddess turned him into a grasshopper. Not, presumably, the burdensome insect of Ecclesiastes, which some have interpreted as an image of the withered, useless genitals of an old man, nor yet the swollen-paunched locust of the modern translators of the same passage, but the leaping, chirping creature whose alacrity is the antithesis of fixed senility.

Tennyson's finest poem is based on this legend. In his 'Tithonus' we hear the voice of all those old people who have long passed 'the goal of ordinance' and who yet are cursed to open their drugged gaze on morning after new morning. The poem is the most eloquent case made for those whose last fate it is to be toyed with by time, to be mutilated and mocked by it. If the Mrs Everards of the proliferating geriatric wards could utter, it would be against every new morning. Nor is this longing to depart confined to advanced senility in its tragically comprehending moments; old men who still appear to be enjoying life will suddenly chill the talk by inquiring the way to death as matter-of-factly as they might ask the way to Totnes. A man of eighty-four, widowed and with more pain and difficulties than might have been supposed from his delightful conversation, turned to a contemporary as they were leaving a party and said, 'I'll tell you what I *really* want to know. I want to know how one gets off the hook . . .'

In today's Tithonian situation, the request is for the longest possible spell of the conditions we enjoy during the early years of retirement. Life is good and buoyant then, and we want it to last. With a new house in a new place and, subsequently, a new circle, there can come a new energy which breaks into new interests, often with more forcefulness than that which inaugurated our working days, for we still retain the poise given us by the seniority of the work from which we have just retired. Under modern conditions, too, the sixties to the early seventies are often very healthy years. As Montaigne observed, 'The greatest vice the sages see in us is, that our desires incessantly grow young again; we are always beginning again to live. Our studies and desires should sometimes be sensible of old age; we have one foot in the grave, and yet our appetites and pursuits spring up every day.' We now take this perennial resurgence of appetite and pursuit to be a blessing, though the fact that it drives us along with some of the same zest as that which sent us on our travels when we were young, or prospecting for fresh jobs, experiences, etc., has to be reckoned with. If, as seems likely, chronic unemployment brings increasingly reduced working lives for the employed, retirement will begin so early that men will enter it without being toil-worn, and possessing latent energies which are going to demand from a very long 'old age' an expression which is at present not catered for at all by society in its planning for the superannuated community. As for the workless – or even the under-worked – man, how does he 'retire'?

It is now increasingly accepted that the first decade of retirement is not old age. Senescence, though visible enough during these years, is not devastatingly apparent. People often live with it very comfortably. They put their feet up intellectually as well as physically and turn the worries of the world off. They promote a heightened sense of well-being with 'little treats' and exude stability and permanency. They do a vast amount of unpaid voluntary work and are always 'on the go' in directions which do not tire them in the deep psychic way in which bringing up children and the exacting demands of a career once tired them. The Tithonus of retirement, though so near to him, cannot conceive the Tithonus of the geriatric ward. His prayer is that he will live long but not *that* long. He says, quite often, 'I told my doctor – he's become such a friend – "Doctor, don't let me become a cabbage. Whatever you do, you will tell me, won't you, if you see it beginning to happen, if I do funny things?" I don't mind what happens to me now so long as I don't become a cabbage.' A cabbage? Why not a rose or an apple? Because a cabbage has come to symbolize the most tightly furled and withdrawn member of that vegetable kingdom which the medieval mind placed lowest in the hierarchy of organic things. However, a man cannot become a cabbage. What he becomes – sometimes – is a very slow-dying man.

None of the talkers in this book displayed cabbageness although most confessed to the horror that they one day might. It is clearly modern man's ultimate dread. The voices speak for that sprawling new commonwealth of the aged which is here to stay and whose citizenship we are all likely to take. They are a mixture of villagers, scholars, craftsmen, city-dwellers, priests, miners, rich and poor who, while in the process of telling how it was *then*, drop the curtain to reveal a little of how it is for them now. Has any previous group lived to witness such an outmoding and abolition of the social and moral tenets of its youth, such immense advances, such losses and such a transformation of the common scene? Is it any wonder that with so many contemporaries dead and so many signposts obliterated, a lot of thought and energy goes in to repeating who you are, both to the young and to yourself? 'You need only claim the events of your life to make yourself yours,' wrote Florida Scott-Maxwell at eighty. Small events tend to have the greatest claim to be remembered. Seldom do the very old deal in the epic. They specialize in flakes of colourful minutiae, as if they know that, when they are dead, it is not great deeds from their maturity which will recall their individual tones but the way they described a day on the river long ago. What they are saying in essence is, 'There are records to tell you when I was demobbed, married, honoured/disgraced, sacked, promoted; but *I* want to tell you what I now want to hear about myself. Those matters which haven't been entered on my passport, in the school register, on the call-up papers, because I *must* be more than I am officially!'

When people are old it isn't just egotism and a senescent liberation of the libido which speeds them down the autobiographical routes at such a determined pace. It is the compulsion to piece together a true self from all the fragments which have no place in the official file. 'So you see why I had to leave Cardiff that September,' concludes the old woman. 'So you see, I was quite a boy!' says the old man with satisfaction. You don't see – not exactly – but the talkers do. They see themselves as no one sees them any more. But if not seeing very clearly, you feel, and that is important. To be able to arouse more than that solicitous feeling which we reserve for the over-eighties is a triumph for the old. A breakthrough. It causes them to hope against hope that the next step can be taken, the step which leads to some aspect of them which can be loved, for, as that eloquent Swiss geriatric apologist Paul Tournier flatly declares:

I have come to the conclusion that there is one essential, profound, underlying problem, and it is that the old are not loved. They do not feel themselves to be loved, and too many people treat them with indifference and seek no contact with them . . . I think of the multitudes of retired

people who hold aloof, who do know that people are concerned that they should have, as we say, decent living
conditions, but who know that no personal interest is
being taken in them.

Staring directly at the new bureaucracy which is taking more
and more charge of his expanding needs (the average cost of
looking after a seventy-five-year-old is seven times that of
the state treatment for a worker), fixing his unfooled eye on
the professionally kind rest-home entrepreneur, and even on
the dutiful middle-aged daughter, the aged man or woman
can repeat with Jean-Jacques Rousseau, 'These people do
not love me.'

Unable to love the old, we approach them via sentiment,
duty and an eye to our own eventual decline. We make sure
that they are housed, fed, medicated and facing their favourite
channel. We see ourselves in them and they see – what is it
that the aged see? Down on a young arm? God in majesty?
The world's superstructure collapsing? We care for them
without real interest and believe that they must be unhappy
because we would not be happy to be old. Yet a recent Age
Concern survey proved that old people are far happier than
their image suggests. This survey says that only seven per
cent of them feel lonely most of the time and that only eight
per cent feel that they have nothing to look forward to. What
half the old people interviewed had to admit was that no one
relied upon them any more, and that a third would have gone
on working if they had been allowed to. At the moment their
annual cost to the main social-welfare programmes is
£10,000m, or a third of this budget. So far we have given the
old both what we believe is good for them and what will keep
them apart from the rest of us, but in 1979 the Government
is taking the unusual step of publishing a White Paper on
what the aged say *they* want. It could be the beginning of a
revolution as the number of the old increases – twenty-four
per cent more seventy-five-year-olds-plus in 1986 than now –

and it demands a more participatory role. It has to be remembered that the old have votes.

It is surprising how many post-war gerontological studies, both European and American, examine the ageing process as if it had no previous literary or even scientific history. As though ageing had to reach today's proportions before it was sufficiently intriguing to stand alongside love, death, sex, adventure, faith, art, work, war, etc. in the gamut of written human experience. Simone de Beauvoir decries most literary conceptions of old age up to the nineteenth century because they leave out the old age of the majority, the common people, and only describe that of the privileged classes, thus giving a false idea of its personal and social effects at any period. She writes:

> The picture is blurred, uncertain and contradictory. It is important to realize that the expression 'old age' has two very different meanings throughout the various pieces of evidence that we possess. It is either a certain social category which has greater or lesser value according to circumstances. Or for each person it is one particular fate: his own. The first point of view is that of the law-givers and moralists; the second that of the poets; and for the most part they are radically opposed. Lawyers and poets always belong to the privileged classes, which is one of the reasons that their words have no great value. They never say anything but part-truths and very often they lie. The poets are the more sincere, however, since they express themselves more spontaneously. The ideologists produce conceptions of old age that fit in with the interests of their class.

All this is most questionable. The fact is that if centuries of poets, playwrights and novelists have not gone to the subject of old age as often as they have to those of love, adventure, crime, power, etc., they certainly have not dodged it. If one includes journals, autobiography and

biography, the literature of old age will be seen to be immense. But somehow, perhaps because we care less to think of
it existing as a collective comment than we do about the
assembled knowledge we possess on every other aspect of the
human condition, there is a feeling that it has been ignored
or avoided. Or that it is fresh ground which we have got to
brace ourselves to explore. And while we know that the mass of
the people do live and die with the minimal reference to their
ever having existed, what is said in the literature of old age is
as generally applicable to them as to the privileged classes.
Shakespeare, Shirley, Gray, Hardy and many other writers
use the ultimate sameness of the fate of rich and poor like a
repeating clock in their work. The fate of Lear was the arche-
typal fate of many an old peasant whose children were greedy
for his farm. His abdication of all that he was in the interests
of the young was only different in degree to that of the clerk
giving up his desk, the craftsman his bench and the miner his
lamp to pressing successors:

> To shake all cares and business from our age,
> Conferring them on younger strengths, while we
> Unburden'd crawl towards death.

Lear, too, makes the most ignored of all human requests,
that one should be allowed to remain within the circle until
the very end:

> If you do love old men, if your sweet sway
> Allow obedience, if you yourselves are old,
> Make it your cause . . .

It is Lear also who connects an emancipated libido with
geriatric collapse – 'When the mind's free the body's delicate.'
In these and in statements throughout the play four centuries
of every condition of men can see their final selves. When they
look up now to the eyes running the bank, the shop, the pub,
the church, the daughter's home, what is it that they repeatedly
read in them but,

> O, sir, you are old;
> Nature in you stands on the very verge
> Of her confine.

Or, if the old dare to show that they can still keep up with things which are strictly preserved for the young, is the sharp reminder given to Falstaff any different from that given by society today?

> Do you set down your name in the scroll of youth, that are written down old with all the characters of age? Have you not a moist eye, a dry hand, a yellow cheek, a white beard, a decreasing leg, and increasing belly? Is not your voice broken, your wind short, your chin double, your wit single, and every part of you blasted with antiquity? And will you yet call yourself young? Fie, fie, fie, Sir John!

To know one's place is now the chief duty of the aged, to refuse the placing a crime.

Chaucer would have none of this. He probably wrote *The Canterbury Tales* when in his forties. In this masterpiece, which the critic Stephen Medcalf has called the humour of the sublime, a rollicking picture is given of the old participating in anything they fancied, with beneficial or farcical results. If one was like the old woman in 'The Nun's Priest's Tale' who reared chickens – including Chanticleer and Pertelote – and was content with her lot, her diet kept healthy by a narrow purse, her body exercised by hard work and, now and then, a jolly dance, there was little to fear. No gout, no apoplexy and nothing ridiculous or repellent for the world to condemn. But if one was self-deceiving, like two of the five husbands of the Wife of Bath, old men who tell themselves that she has married them for their passion, then one was simply unrealistic. Both old husbands had plenty of opportunity to discover that she 'never had much for old bacon' yet were unable to see themselves in this category, and so the Wife gives them belltinker, more for their vanity than their inadequacies. As she ages, she is scandalously honest about her passion for a boy named Jankin, the sight of whose legs at her fifth husband's funeral besots her. She weds Jankin and enjoys him, once she has managed to stop him reading books, which are his real lust. But soon he dies like the rest, this being an instance of ripeness annihilating greenness. The Wife adores living and gets better and better at it, storing up experiences on which to nourish her old age:

> But, Lord Christ! When it all comes back to me, and I recall my youth and gaiety, it tickles me to the roots of my heart. To this day it does my heart good that in my time I've had my fling. But age, alas! that cankers everything, has stripped me of my beauty and go. Goodbye, let them go, and the devil go with them! What's left to say? The flour's all gone, and now I must sell the bran as best I may. Even so I mean to rejoice!

'The Merchant's Tale' tells a very different old-age story. It is about a bachelor knight named January who, at sixty, the same age as that when Chaucer himself died repudiating his genius for what he called 'lascivious lay' and repenting his *Troilus and Cressida* and all the delights which trespassed against the purity of Christ, decides to get married. Unlike the impotent old men of the other Tales, January is sexually vigorous and has woken to the realization that it is now or never. His only worry is that his old age may turn out to be so blissful and successful that Purgatory won't provide its traditional 'happy release'. His bride is a teenager named May, and January is immensely kind to her and is as active in bed as a lad. But as Chaucer, with his deep understanding of the life cycle, shows, the performances of age, however sturdy, are not the performances of youth. For one thing, they are unaesthetic – 'God knows what May thought in her heart when she saw him sitting up in his shirt with his nightcap on and the slack skin round his neck ashake.' Also, when January wants May he cannot wait and when January takes May, it is at a price. Something snaps in a body which should be past this compulsion and the old husband becomes blind. Enter, unseen, the inevitable cuckold, Damien the young squire. At first the shocked realization of what Damien is doing to May makes January very clear-sighted, but soon his wife is able to convince him, in the way in which the old are always finally manipulated by those who still care for them but who are no longer able to regard them as whole people, that in future he might often imagine such foolishness. Thus, having sown the seeds of uncertainty in the old, she is free to carry on as she likes. Her moral reasoning behind her adultery is that it is more unnatural for January and May to be bedded together than it is for young lovers to seize their chance. 'The Merchant's Tale' is psychologically fascinating because in it Chaucer allows that often the old do possess the capabilities of youth and a zest for living, also tenderness and warmth, but that none of these things are of value when youth itself is there to supply them.

Some old people are so entirely absorbed in an interest which unites the intellectual and the sensual that time ceases to threaten, question or mock their actions. When Gilbert White made the last entry in his Journal in June 1793 – 'the ground is as hard as iron' – there isn't the faintest forewarning of what was to happen a few days later, when he would be lowered into it. He was just continuing what he had begun twenty-five years earlier with 'Horses are still falling with the general disorder. It freezes under people's beds.' He is an example of those who pay scant attention to ageing. Other than a mention of his getting a bit deaf in his fifties and, on the day before his last entry, that he had been 'pulled down' by the 'wandering gout', there is no indication of his going on to be seventy-three, a great age for that time. His final letter concludes, 'The season with us is unhealthy,' and somehow the sentence does suggest that he could have been thinking of something other than the weather, which was bitter, or that he had just heard of Louis XVI's execution.

White had integrated himself with the movements of two calendars, the simple movement of a rural parish and the infinitely complex movement of the natural year. Because he had to act on the movements of both calendars daily he became a philosopher of the present, which is why he is so satisfying. We read him less for his science than for his daily-ness. The rising sap, the state of the cucumbers and endive, the flash of the blue hawk across the wheat stubble and the sound of the nightingale in the 'harsh evening' are steadiers. If we learn to look like this that spinning yearly-ness of old age is kept in some check. Knowing that White is in his seventies when he writes such sentences as, 'My weeding-woman swept-up on the grass-plot a bushel-basket of blossoms from the white apple-tree' or 'Finished piling my wood', we are more affected than if he had confessed all the particulars of his physical and mental change as his life ebbed. He died in great pain which was a little relieved by laudanum, though only after a last week of being quite normally active and death-free. White's old age was that of the man who is too busy to dwell on it and who, outside a good deal, riding, walking, digging, often wet-through and becoming one with plants and birds and climate, gets too tired in the usual way to feel its special weariness.

Age-consciousness comes very early to some men. John Middleton Murry, when he was sixty, told a friend, 'It's very nice to be old.' He was not being facetious. He saw alterations in himself which made him decide to 'acquiesce gracefully in the beginning of the declining curve'. The first half of his life had been so emotionally strenuous, so work-stacked and so idealistically committed to this cause and that, as to leave insufficient energy for the latter half. But he welcomed this running-down of his strength and used it for purposes which would have been outside his range in his heyday. The first half of his life, the deaths of two wives from tuberculosis, a disastrous third marriage, a vast output of critical literary studies, philosophy and journalism compounded with intense relationships, such as that with D. H. Lawrence, the editorship of magazines and an active commitment to many of the important moral issues of the Fascist decades, had burnt him out. But he enjoyed making something from the ashes, and in this he shared one of the most subtle pleasures of the very old, which is the utilization of one's frailty and slightness, the knowing how short a distance one can go – and then going it. And the knowing that one need not do more because it is impossible to do more. Ever again.

Frank Lea, Middleton Murry's biographer, draws an intriguing picture of this premature and not unwelcome senescence. At twenty-five, he says, Murry had been young for his age, at fifty, old for his years. 'Even physically he appeared to have shrunk, to have turned small and hard-drawn, like a mummy.' The Second World War had punctured many of his hopes and his third wife had wrecked all he understood by what he called 'the true man–woman relation'. Where publishers were concerned, he was an outmoded prophet and he himself, though only middle-aged, continuously dwelt in the past. He believed that he was a literary failure because he had put more of his imagination into the man–woman relation idea than into his books, and he saw the careers of certain contemporaries, such as T. S. Eliot and Joyce Cary, as instances of the success of single-mindedness. And then at a time when most writers would have been driven by habit and the need to rehabilitate themselves to go on working, Murry retreated to a Suffolk village with a girl who was the antithesis of all his wives to lead a life dominated by St Benedict's motto *laborare est orare*, to work is to pray, which for Murry did not mean literature. He told the world that his farm was 'nothing less than the Monte Cassino of a new Christian civilization' and a 'winning back of the waste lands of the modern world', two images which proved how stuck he was with a recent past. Like some octogenarians he wants to leave the record straight, and he has to nurse both head and hand in order not to go to the grave without making a final statement, *Love, Freedom and Society*. With this book he said that his 'thought adventure'

had come to an end, and his biographer speaks of his extraordinary state of gladness that he could draw such a premature
conclusion. 'I have a hunch – nothing more – that this feeling
of mine [that he and Eliot had something important to say to
each other] is connected with my conviction that my strange
and weary pilgrimage . . . is over,' he wrote to the poet.

At sixty his face aged so much that it began to closely
resemble that of his father in his eighties. At sixty-six he said
he was 'completely unable to remember as a living fact the
hydrogen bomb'. Gardening brought on an attack of angina
pectoris and he died saying, 'I should not have asked Katherine
[Mansfield, his first wife] to go on, I should not have asked
Lawrence to go on . . .' as though he had been guilty of wishing
a long life on others. D. H. Lawrence had died at forty-five
and Katherine Mansfield at thirty-five, so, comparatively
speaking, the years had carried Murry quite a distance from
the sources of his vitality and by their terms he was aged.

Coleridge, too, experienced an early ageing, though his was
exacerbated by abuse (drugs) of his mind and neglect (sloth)
of his body. When he died at sixty-two he was a sorry wreck.
In his poetry the old terrify the young. They accost strangers
and spoil their day, like Death in medieval experience, who
links arms with youth or maiden in broad sunshine. In his
'The Old Man of the Alps' an aged father stops a traveller
to pour out a tale of personal grief just to be pitied – it is 'sweet
to pity an aged breast'. In 'The Three Graves', a poem which
enthralled Thomas Hardy, another old man, a sexton, tells a
traveller a dreadful story of a thwarted marriage, and in 'The
Rime of the Ancient Mariner' the wedding guest, a man about
to participate in one of the major celebrations of human joy,
is waylaid by age and its blighting confessions. But in his
'Limbo' Coleridge insists that even the most vacant senility is
preferable to death and the 'mere horror of blank Naught-at-
all'. Better a moonfaced old man, 'his eyeless face all eye',
conscious only of light, his head turned to the moon in order
'to gaze at that which seems to gaze on him!' for at least he is

still in 'human time'. 'In 'Youth and Age', written when he was fifty, he reads the signs and dreads them. He sees 'this drooping gait, this altered size' which tell him that 'Youth's no longer here' and that soon, if he wants to catch its attention, he can only bring it to a standstill with the terrible information which only old men can give. Coleridge's old men are Gribouillists, the term given in modern geriatric psychiatry to those who embrace the hideousness of old age and who use it to plague the rest of society.

A writer who is interested in the full range of human activity will not omit old age and even where this theme is not used explicitly for a novel or a poem, there will be pointers throughout his work to how he sees it. Sir Zachary Cope was able to diagnose that Jane Austen's last illness was the then undiscovered Addison's Disease from the fleeting yet intensely truthful and percipient descriptions of what was happening to her which began to run through her letters. And a similarly individual trail of change can be traced in the ageing writer, or in the young writer brought up against the ageing of his parents or friends. So, while Old Age as a principal theme makes up a short list when we compare it with Childhood, its existence as a literary aside is endless. And even the short list is much longer than is generally supposed and repudiates the odd idea, so often expressed, that up until now, when the cost of gerocomy has forced us to face it, the whole subject has been avoided. For as well as the acknowledged masterpieces, *King Lear*, Cicero's *De Senectute*, Sophocles' *Oedipus at Colonus* and Swift's appalling tirade, written when he was fifty-five and the most hate-bearing statement on ageing that we possess, there is a range of comment upon and experience of the last years of life which, when we add it up, omits nothing.

In his *Acharnians*, Aristophanes shocks his age-despising, youth-adoring audience by siding with the old. Brecht in his *The Unworthy Old Lady* takes a similar theme to V. Sackville-West's *All Passion Spent* and describes an aged woman refusing

to fit into the role which society has created for her and causing
consternation by what the world regards as her waywardness –
i.e., an insistence on experiment, change and lack of supervision. In *Endgame*, *Krapp's Last Tape* and *Happy Days*,
Beckett sees the impotence and helplessness of the old as part
of that half-appalling, half-comic individual solitude and
ineffectuality which can enclose a man at any age. In Dante's
Il Convivio, the old are weary ocean-worn barks making
harbour, in Yeats's poems they are incorrigible – 'Why should
not old men be mad?' – or they have strange remembrancers
such as grave-diggers 'who thrust their buried men back in
the human mind again'. Philip Larkin sees an old woman discovering some sheet-music (just as today's young will come
across some pop album sixty years hence) and finding that
'The glare of that much-mentioned brilliance, love' had not
fulfilled its promise when she felt the 'certainty of time laid
up in store' and that it 'could not now'. Larkin, in a number of
poems, says be your age. Don't look forward because,

> Always too eager for the future, we
> Pick up bad habits of expectancy.

And don't look backwards because it is futile:

> You cannot always keep
> That unfakable young surface.
> You must learn your lines . . .

R. S. Thomas finds the old often undeserving of the kindness and consideration with which it has become the social
ideal to surround them:

> Here; every farm has its
> Grandfather or grandmother, gnarled hands
> On the cheque-book, a long, slow
> Pull on the placenta about the neck.
> Old lips monopolise the talk
> When a friend calls. The children listen

> From the kitchen; the children march
> With angry patience against the dawn.
> They are waiting for someone to die . . .

A truth which can nowadays only be whispered about the old is that they can be boring, cruel or disgusting, and that they can make the middle-aged ill.

Almost as tentative and unexamined a subject as old age and sexuality, is that of the octogenarian and the emotional effect he – or more likely she – has on his child. If there is a taboo on old age and sex, there is certainly a very strong natural and social stricture on what middle-aged sons and daughters can say when confronted, maybe, with a decade of geriatric care and nursing. The dread that this may happen is often so overwhelming that it begins to eat away at the respect and affection which the children have for their parents long before, or if, they show signs of senility. It is not just a reluctance to take on a burden which causes this corrosion but the emotional shock and resentment at the reversal of the roles. Many people suffer from a kind of indignation when they see what looks like an abdication of parental care in their mother. No longer capable of exercising it, she becomes in effect not entirely their mother. It feels as though she has freed herself from them but they, in contrast, are imprisoned by her. Even if a parent enters an old people's home (where, though it is hard to accept, there is often greater happiness and affection than can be found in the family) the middle-aged children can still suffer from this strange sense of imprisonment. On the other hand, a son or daughter will care for their aged parents with the utmost devotion and even find pleasure and fulfilment in this duty, dreading the day of release. But whatever the direction such a relationship takes, it is one of the most difficult to discuss, and we still know too little of the effect of longevity on younger people who are now having to spend years in close contact with it.

Even 'angry patience' is achieved at a cost. In Prosper

Mérimée's *Lettres à une Inconnue* the correspondent is frank about her dutiful visits to an aged godmother who is 'a cross-grained old woman who ought to die'. It is to make certain that she inherits an exquisite service of Sèvres china. So she puts up with 'a querulous, selfish old creature who has not a lovable quality in her whole disposition' only to find that when this 'useless tyrannical life ends' her godmother hasn't made a will and all her possessions go to a distant relation who has never so much as called on her. But the young will endure the vulgarity of the old because they are vulnerable as well as powerful, though this does not prevent a mounting distaste, and perhaps, with full-span lives having become the norm, people may need to learn how to be aged as they once had to learn how to be adult. It may soon be necessary and legitimate to criticize the long years of vapidity in which a well, elderly person does little more than eat and play Bingo, or consumes excessive amounts of drugs, or expects a self-indulgent stupidity to go unchecked. Just as the old should be convinced that, whatever happens during senescence, they will never suffer exclusion, so they should understand that age does not exempt them from being despicable. To fall into purposeless-ness is to fall out of all real consideration. Many old people reduce life to such trifling routines that they cause the rest of us to turn away in revulsion. Sometimes we should say to them, 'How can you expect us to be interested in this minimal you, with your mean days and little grumbles?' This slide into purposelessness must not be confused with the ability of the old not to take life all that seriously, for this has its virtues and assets. To appreciate the transience of all things is one matter, to narrow the last years – and they can be numerous – down to a dreary thread is another. One of the most dreadful sights in the country of the old is that of the long rows of women play-ing the Las Vegas fruit machines. Had Dante heard of it he would have cleared a space for it in Hell. It is symbolic of that specially self-indulgent mindlessness of old age which is its most intolerable aspect.

Proust illustrated how even the limited movement and interests of extreme old age could enliven the day. Few dramas can be as minuscule as Aunt Léonie's in *Swann's Way*, yet hers remains tiny without being trivial. This ancient woman has turned her small obsessions to good account and has made some of the less admirable foibles of old age, hypochondria, domestic tyranny, nosiness, etc., into something which is life-supporting not only for herself but for her family and the neighbours. Aunt Léonie is a trial but she isn't a bore. She sits behind a curtain and spies on the town, sips Vichy water and uses her prayer-book like a drill manual. She is beadily absorbed in life and her personality is so unfractured that those who know her don't have to adopt charitable attitudes when they discuss her. On the contrary, her sayings and doings are collected and prized, like the first words of a baby: '"I do not ask to live to a hundred," my aunt would say, 'for she preferred to have no definite limit to the number of her days.' No one, whether doctor, daughter, grandchild, priest or friend, thought of her as a problem or as anything less than she had been at any other stage of her life. Age had added comedy to her attributes, that was all. She was allowed the amusing notion 'that there was something broken in her head and floating loose there, which she might displace by talking too loud' and her little lies about never 'sleeping a wink', her tedious rituals and avid gossip. Her amnesia is respected and when she apologizes for it to her maid, saying that she is wasting her time, Françoise replies that her time 'is not so precious; whoever made our time didn't sell it to us.' Nobody thinks that it is a pity that Aunt Léonie isn't either younger or dead. She is as much enfranchised to make what she can of life in her eighties as she was when she was eighteen, and she doesn't need to conceal her eccentricities any more than a child does. A child will badger, will fantasize and will demand special assistance, and so will the aged. In Aunt Léonie's family first and last words are significant and are reported. Similarly, just as her parents entered into her childhood games, so do her relations enter into the spirit of her final playtime, her 'little jog-trot', as she calls it. The marked difference in pace entertains them. They relate it without damaging her integrity for, like the poet W. J. Turner, they discover that

> The young are serious but the old are not frivolous,
> They see what they saw in the days of their youth,
> Yet all things appear to them in different proportion . . .
> The young are impatient, but the old are not desperate,
> Though they see in the distance the rock which divides.

One of the reasons why old people make so many journeys into the past is to satisfy themselves that it is still there. In his seventies, Thomas Hardy returned emotionally and geographically to convince himself that he was once in love with his wife. And he was eighty-eight when he published *Winter Words*, which opens with a Tithonus-like demand to Dawn to explain what she is 'doing outside my walls', and which includes a number of 'look back' poems. Sandwiched between a poem in which he tells the Dawn that he must no longer look back on love or attempt to love again, and one which attempts to get inside the mind of his best friend at the moment of his suicide, Hardy has placed his reflection on his eighty-sixth birthday, 'He Never Expected Much'. In it he accepts a certain colourlessness in his life and a certain injustice. Finally, in 'He Resolves To Say No More', Hardy refuses to let Time roll backward or forward in his poetry. What he has seen and what he sees ahead he'll keep to himself. He has spent a long life revealing past and future, now he will be silent. The silence of old age is unnerving. We expect the aged to speak and when they do not we are devastated.

Sometimes the old check on the marks they made when they were young. Even a signature on a tree, or like the name which a boy carved inside a Suffolk belfry when he was eighteen and which he climbed the stairs to look at when he was ninety and near to having it repeated on a stone below. Often there is an

intensely resurgent interest in the long journey just when it
looks like coming to an end. It is reminiscent of Rousseau's 'I
only began to live when I looked upon myself as dead.' He was
a young man recovering from Ménière's disease, from which
Swift also suffered. Rousseau's *Confessions*, written in late
middle age, were as accurate a retracement of his steps as he
could manage. He is more truthful than most men about their
ability to say what actually happened to them, and says that

> memory often failed me or furnished but imperfect
> recollections, and I filled up space by details supplied by
> imagination to supplement those recollections . . . I loved
> to expatiate on the happy moments of my life, and I some-
> times embellished them with ornaments supplied by tender
> regrets. I said things I had forgotten as it seemed to me
> they ought to have been, and as perhaps in fact they were . . .
> I sometimes lent strange charms to truth.

Restif de la Bretonne, a literary ancestor of Genet and known
in his own day as 'the Gutter Rousseau' – *le Rousseau du
ruisseau* – both because he had as great a passion for pavements
as his nick-namesake had for wild nature and because of the
candour of his writing, carved every important happening of
his life on the walls of the Ile Saint-Louis. He carved the record
of an event immediately after it occurred, symbolically
using a key to scratch the paragraph of personal history to
which he added a Latin commentary. Havelock Ellis says that
Restif turned this beautiful Parisian district into his personal
temple, incising his life into its stone parapets. This was one
version. The other lay embedded in his quasi-autobiography
Monsieur Nicolas which Schiller placed alongside Cellini's
Life as a masterpiece of self-statement. But when Restif was
a filthy old man, thought by some to be the greatest writer of
the eighteenth century and by others its major pornographer,
it was not to the printed but to the carved word that he made
pilgrimages to see what really had happened to him. After
the Revolution, he would be glimpsed, late at night, making

the rounds of his carvings, knowing that the energy which had produced them was part of that same force which had produced the events which they described.

Wells, Dickens, Tolstoy, Ionesco, Colette, Michelangelo, Gide, Maugham, Hemingway, Milton, Eliot, Amis, Spark – the list is present wherever and at whatever period one looks in literature – have all said something about age. But the subject has a way of being fugitive, of being little seen even where it is profusely represented, as it is in Larkin's *Oxford Book of Twentieth-Century English Verse*, for example, where there is a startling range of old-age poetry.

Few writers in the past needed to consider the dangers and blessings of being pensioned-off, or its effect on a previously work-regulated life, because such things hardly ever occurred. Charles Lamb in *The Superannuated Man* is able to deal with such a subject as a novelty. Even so, his picture has an accuracy which is relevant to contemporary retirement. He tells of a fifty-year-old clerk who has worked in a Mincing Lane counting-house since he was fourteen and who is beginning to show signs of physical collapse. This clerk has averaged a ten-hour day, six days a week, for thirty-six years, working mostly in candlelight and, like 'animals in cages', had grown doggedly content. It is only when he starts to disintegrate that the clerk realizes that the routine breaks from this dim tread-mill, Sundays, Christmas and an annual week in the country, have neither refreshed nor re-created him. On the contrary, Sabbatarianism has introduced a repressive 'weight in the air' which has actually stopped him from enjoying himself. As for the week in Hertfordshire, no sooner has he begun to relax there than it is time to get back to the City. The reader can contrast a future prospect of excessive leisure with a time when it was minimal.

One day the clerk's employers summon him for what he thinks is the sack, being conscious that his work is not what it used to be and that, try as he will, he cannot get back to his old standards. Instead, to his amazement, he is retired on two-thirds of his wages out of gratitude for his past achievements. His feelings are mixed. He is 'stunned, overwhelmed' and he wanders about idly 'thinking I was happy and knowing that I was not' and realizes that 'I had more time on my hands than I could ever manage.' He warns others of his fate and tells them not to retire all at once as the strict switch from a work routine to no routine is dangerous. He sees a young man at his desk and using his hat-peg, and it is a kind of death. Although he knows that walking the City in work-time and feeling the sun and not candles should be paradisial, he uncomfortably compares 'the change in my condition to passing into another world'. Soon, the fifty-year-old clerk turns into the un-needed, unnecessary man we see on the public seats in parks and libraries today. 'I am no longer clerk to the Firm of, etc. I am Retired Leisure. I am to be met with in trim gardens. I am already come to be known by my vacant face and careless gesture, perambulating at no fixed pace, nor with any settled purpose. I walk about; not to and from . . .' This chilling Beckett-like confession comes only after the work-denied man has paid his conventional tribute to the retired state. It includes the ironic statement that 'had I a little son, I would christen him Nothing-To-Do; he should do nothing. Man, I verily believe, is out his element as long as he is operative.' Charles Lamb, an office-worker all his life, is listening to the corporate sigh of that vast army of nineteenth-century clerks, chained from school to grave to their ledgers, who cannot imagine drawing a line on employment.

Literature is also full of examples of old people who are the victims of transience. A. L. Vischer, describing our experience of transience, says that

> the desire to stay where we are and the desire to press forward are two distinct categories of human life. We participate in both and both are capable of proving a source of good or evil for old people, depending on the attitude which they adopt and on how they put their attitude into

effect. A positive experience of transience can release powerful forces which may act as an incentive for us to make the most of our remaining days.

But many people stay where they were, long years ago, not because they have made up their minds to do so, but because what happened then was seismic, turbulent and thrilling. Having been part of a great political or artistic or scientific upheaval, they only realize that they are no longer in the avant-garde when, in advancing years, they sense a solitude and a silence and, looking around, see that they are alone. These old men are the victims of transience. Biography is full of examples of their plight. It is a strange thing to be left behind by later generations whose moral or material advance is due to the heart-and-soul battles of one's own youth. And stranger still to be battling on when the cause has been won and forgotten. Worse, to find that although the cause was a correct one, and of benefit to oneself and to the world, it is now slotted into the general orthodoxy with no very great addition to the sum of human happiness.

Edward Clodd, the folklorist and disseminator of Darwinism, was in his twenties when the great debate on evolution began and forty when he abandoned Christianity for the Rationalists. At this period he was a kind of scientific Theist who was constantly ill. In fact, such was his continuous stress and exhaustion that he did not expect to see his fortieth birthday. On the day he was able to convince himself that God did not exist he began to grow well and happy. At fifty, while admitting that 'the future has not the potency of the past', he was transformed into the robust figure who, to his huge circle of intellectual friends, epitomized man released from his superstitious chains. He exuded well-being and joy and, like many Victorians, he did three people's work, managing a joint stock bank, churning out a stream of books and articles, and maintaining a complex social life. His friends included Thomas Hardy, Edward Whymper, George Meredith,

George Gissing and Holman-Hunt. As he got to know them, and scores of other intellectuals besides, he discovered that most of them far from shared his total emancipation from religion. Huxley still retained some theology in his library, Hardy was seen in church, one of his guests was caught praying and Gissing had a priest present when he was dying. It seemed never to have occurred to Clodd that while most of his friends were artists, he was fundamentally a propagandist. That, in Jacquetta Hawkes's phrase, he lived in flatland while they retained some of the vision of creatures who could not live without symbol and ceremony. In *Boon* H. G. Wells said that Clodd ('Dodd') had banished God from the universe but he hadn't actually got rid of him, and thus he had constituted himself a sort of alert customs officer of a materialistic age . . . and slept with a large revolver under his pillow for fear of revelation.

As he aged Clodd's sense of purpose faded, chiefly because it required a tough response from the leaders of those who did not share it. Neither could his mid-nineteenth-century mind comprehend twentieth-century mathematics and scientific theory. At eighty he wrote, 'I am like Milton's angels, "in wandering mazes lost . . ." How one sighs for Huxley to make the thing luminous!' The reference to Huxley throws up another complication for the kind of old person 'who has known everybody' – his constant bereavement. Also, Clodd's faith in human progress had been battered by the casualties and political cruelties of the First World War. Yet at seventy-four he could not bring himself to think that life was over and had married a second wife, a young scientist who, when she was in her eighties, was to kill herself rather than further endure old age. At the time of this marriage, Clodd read Havelock Ellis's *Psychology of Sex* and wished 'that it had been published when I was a younger man when so much that one would have been the better for knowing was not talked about'. At this period he felt that 'man must be his own Redeemer' and that the only place for Jesus, should he be on this planet during the twentieth century, would be 'on the Committee of the Fabian Society'.

He was eighty when he published his last book, *Magic in Names and Other Things*. A year later, condemning Wells's belief in the moral advance of society, Clodd declared, 'Today all the forces of disintegration are in full play.' At eighty-three the deaths of friends and acquaintances were so multitudinous that they poured into his little house by the North Sea like an icy storm. He had eczema, was less able to walk but still read omnivorously, though he found himself disturbed by the new explicitness regarding both sex and spiritual philosophy in the learned journals. When he was eighty-seven he had a slight stroke followed by aphasia. At eighty-eight his eyes and speech began to fail and he became bed-ridden, and then just a few months before his death in his ninetieth year, he began to walk once more. A few days before his death he read and re-read Arnold's 'Dover Beach' and 'Empedocles on Etna', and noted how all values alter when one is ill. During the final period he returned to the scientists of his youth and was delighted and relieved to find a critic condemning Freud as 'a dangerous lunatic'. In March 1930 his bronchial asthma returned, brought on, he believed, by the dreaded Suffolk coast east winds. He remained fully conscious to the end, repeating, 'I die, I die.' Edward Clodd retained intelligence and appetite for life into extreme old age but neither could cope with the amazing new fare which they had helped to initiate, and it was as a victim of transience that he matched the thud of the sea on the Aldeburgh shingle a few yards from his death-bed with Matthew Arnold's 'melancholy, long, withdrawing roar'.

It is the nature of old men and women to become their own confessors, poets, philosophers, apologists and story-tellers. My method, if method it can be called, in listening to a few of them, some friends, some strangers, was to hear what they had to say with an ear which had been mostly informed by what someone called 'the low-lying literature of old age'. No single conclusion can be deduced from them or it. Old age is full of death and full of life. It is a tolerable achievement and it is a disaster. It transcends desire and it taunts it. It is long enough and it is far from being long enough, as the poet Ruth Fainlight says in 'Losers':

> Assume nothing at all.
> Even to hope you might live for ever
> Brings the end too close.

1 · Winter in the Village

And the seventh sorrow
Is the slow goodbye
Of the face with its wrinkles that looks through the window
As the year packs up
Like a tatty fairground
That came for the children.

Ted Hughes, 'Winter in the Village'

Two kinds of people grow old in the village, those who were young in it and those who came to it for the purpose of growing old in. The native and the transplanted. The new old people will say that they have retired *to* the village, and not that they have retired *from* the city, a small point but one in their optimistic favour. It suggests that they have come to the country to live, not to die. The indigenous old farming people don't use the word retired, they say they have given up work, though this is a too definite description of their state because for a decade or more after they have become pensionable they are apt to potter about on the fringes of their previous tasks, nor do they move out of sight of everything they have seen for a lifetime. And so at first, although their years run parallel, the emotions of the two superannuated groups have little in common. Also, a new old villager will arrive with a clean slate. No one is ever likely to discover in much detail what gave him that look, this manner, those ideas. He and his wife have come fully fashioned out of the regiment, the business, the foreign climate, the profession, and have to be taken at face value. Not so the old farm-worker, his widow or their employer. The village will understand in elaborate and intimate measurements what it took to produce their admirable or funny old ways. But later, when both groups are very old, they are drawn to

each other in their common senescence. Contemporaries who
started out upon the rural road from the opposite ends of the
earth, so to speak, are now in close touch, in thought if not in
person. Everything that can be learnt of an octogenarian
neighbour is of interest.

The village is inclined to be more flattered by having people
retire to it than commute from it. It is the difference between
accepting it for its pleasures and making it a convenience. The
new old people will sing its praises. What a find! Nobody
chooses where to live without justifying the choice. Once
arrived, the émigrés work fantastically hard, often astounding
the locals with their energy. They plan reducible gardens,
make bread, sail, join half a dozen societies and get put on
committees, entertain and behave as though life is beginning
instead of ending. White-haired and sun-tanned, they look
bursting with health. 'A man's ageing and his decline always
takes place inside some given society,' says Simone de Beauvoir. 'It is intimately related to the character of that society
and to the place that the individual in question occupies
within it. In itself the economic factor cannot be isolated from
the social, political and ideological superstructures that contain it.' But with the mainly middle-class town to village
retirement, and such conveniences as private transport, central heating, sophisticated shops around the old market cross,
and television, plus the international standards often to be
found in the local music festival, the excellent county library,
etc., many people age in social conditions which are quite
unlike those of their actual background. Their retirement
reflects achievement and is a successfully perpetuated holiday,
whereas the old age of the old villager can be an unnatural
idleness amidst scenes ineradicably associated by him with
timekeeping and doing.

Another thing. The new old resident's choice of the village
will almost certainly involve his concept of abidingness.
Having spent his working life witnessing to the world that he
was a modern, flexible being who relished progress, a large

part of the impetus which directed his post-toil days to the countryside is made up of his conviction that it is better to live where progress does not exist. He will tell himself that he has worked hard in some alien sphere for this reward of a natural home. He will stare over the valley and see the houses folded in the fields and the church tower casting its reflection where the lane twists, and he'll say that, the march of the Klee-like pylons apart, he is seeing what the Tudor farmer who built his house saw. This sense of perpetuity nourishes him and, at seventy, makes him feel sane and strong, and himself part of the everlasting.

The old age of the countryman is quite another matter. In the first place he will never have held this drastic and romantic retirement change in view, and only near the very end of his life might it dawn on him to wonder whether it is a good thing for him to die where he was born. What is more likely to occur during his seventies and eighties is a dimming of the trans-formed fields and houses and faces of the last two decades, and a clearer sight of all that preceded them. Far from abiding, it will seem to the aged villager that all he once possessed is either lost or altered. Looking around, often he can't believe his eyes. In a way, he hasn't needed to move because his sur-roundings themselves have passed through such a transition that it frequently strikes him that he isn't where he was anyway. In fact he is a bit puzzled and out of his element in church and pub and field where little is still done and said as they were for centuries before. God is you, not thou. There is scampi in the tap, Long Acre, Redmells and the Hoist Land have been ironed-out into a vast barley slope called No-name. The churchyard is the school register carved in marble. Two hundred horses have vanished without hoofprint. Another language is spoken. Coins, once so precious, feel valueless. A boy on a motor-bike is the dead spit of Charlie, killed on the Somme. One walks with a stick along the road which mother patched with flints from the uplands. Everything has its duality, nothing remains of the untouched and serviceable ancient dimension as a singular force, and all the early beliefs, habits and work methods lie like abandoned implements on the clay, concealed by new growths, both main sowing and catch-crop, but imperishable all the same. One isn't necessarily strengthened and revitalized by falling back upon a superseded code however much more fitting to one's years it may seem to be. One could be putting oneself out of reach.

Knowing nothing of its pain and complexities, the new old people in the village love everything which they can discover about the rural past and are moved when they discover it clamped like ivy to the heart and soul of a neighbour. It never occurs to them that, for some individuals, local ties are local shackles, and that these aren't likely to get any lighter in senescence. 'We choose many things by a tribal truth, many more that we like,' wrote Florida Scott-Maxwell when she was eighty-two, 'but there is a truth in the very pit of one's being that opposes tribal good. What honest heart denies that many delights are based on the premise that others will not, even cannot, do what you do? Sometimes it is because you feel the need of doing something in your own way, sometimes it is the sheer delight of being lawless that you crave; or, more likely, because you are drawn to the charm of the exceptional.' Old country people especially like to recall the moments when they tricked or triumphed over the hard and fast pattern. They often see tradition as the frozen surface of a winter river on which, careful not to crash in that penny-pinched climate, they would chance a private arabesque or two. Unlike that of their grandchildren, their culture was not future-orientated and they are grounded in fatality. Never possessing much in the way of future-shaping thought because of common-sense recognition of the economic limits to what might be hoped or prayed for, the ordinary countryman born at the turn of the century is psychologically separated from those born fifty years later by the smallness of his expectations. Sentimentalists like to describe all this as contentment and to read contentment in the hard, strong, brown old faces which so often are weathered masks hiding collapse, fear and wonder. What is going to happen? What has happened? More, usually, than anyone supposes.

Young village people, with their taken-for-granted 1970s windfall of gadgets, education, travel and funds, are so time-divorced from their grandparents as to find them mysterious. The geriatrician M. Grotjahn, writing of a comparable division between the generations in the United States, declared that senescence in America is even more a cultural artefact than it is a biological reality and that the aged are 'in the eyes of the younger generation the representatives of the dark past'. Even with a smattering of social history, plus training in modern farming practice, it is sometimes strange to be with these earlier versions of your own flesh and blood, still hearty and digging the garden most likely, and realize the grim facts of their recent servitude. Grotjahn says that their American immigrant equivalents felt more apologetic than proud of their age and tried to keep up with the younger ones, for whom they constituted a tragic group which he called 'the hidden relatives'. The old men and women in the village make no effort whatever to keep up. They live at their own rate in what remains of their own ethos. What they possess of the generally accepted standards of modern living did not begin to surround them until they were late middle-aged, and they are super-imposed on the simplicity of their cottages like decorations on a very plain cake.

Another previously unknown phenomenon which has altered rural old age is the superfluousness of its experience. Going to an old shepherd, ploughman or craftsman for the purpose of gathering history or speech patterns is one thing, but recognizing him as the repository of essential agricultural knowledge is another. Passing on the little-changed things from generation to generation across the centuries was the task of old men, who knew that they had the key to the happiness and prosperity of their children's children in their shaking hands. Far from being the singers of obsolescence, as they so frequently are now, the old men from the fields became the teachers by the hearth. Since no one likes the world to know that many of the things by which he gained his reputation can be taught and learnt in a day, the old men would spin out their information until there was consternation about their taking it to the grave. Thus drama and importance could sustain the ancient ego. But there still remained a mass of people in the countryside from which nothing was required, nothing asked, except brute strength. When time drained this, old age would appear in its most mocking, most terrifying guise. Illiterate, economically embarrassing to the self-supporting parish, the fate of the common labourer and his wife in old age was to be punished by society for daring to grow old. The visiting officer called and they left for the workhouse, sometimes in a cart, often walking, their eyes averted. They had transgressed. They had gone on living when they were beyond value. There they were parted, often after half a century of marriage, and were only to see each other now and then by application to the Master who, estimating if they had a bit of go left in them, set them to tasks. And so they'd scrub and peel and chop their paths to the grave, via the infirmary. All the old people in the 1970s countryside witnessed this. It was a commonplace up until the last war. It is such experiences viewed against the £19.50 a week pension-book lying on the telly which give the contemporary village octogenarian his edge.

In what he admits was an extremely difficult analysis of the performances of ageing men in various occupations, Dr Alex Comfort says that by their mid-sixties, twenty per cent of men employed in industry will have changed or be about to change their job and that by seventy, the same percentage will have become physically incapable of working at all. He found that figures vary considerably in different occupations and that farm-workers 'naturally survive longest because they have the greatest choice of activities' – an interesting point. What he doesn't take into account is the fact that the old ex-farm-workers of the 1970s represent a large proportion of the

1920–30s villagers who lacked the initiative to get off the land, or who belong to a special village group which stays faithful to its home acres, come what may. These stay-at-homes certainly do show a high longevity figure in some villages.

Of the 194 people who died in a typical Suffolk village during the last sixty years, 10 were in their nineties, 47 in their eighties and 55 in their seventies. A complete analysis of these death ages since the First World War also shows the transformation in infant mortality: an average of one child-death a year between 1917 and 1933 and a total of only two child-deaths between 1934 and 1977. The chart gives the pattern.

Men:

Teens	20s	30s	40s	50s	60s	70s	80s	90s	
–	1	3	3	9	18	31	21	4	+ 16 children

Women:

									Total =
1	3	4	–	12	12	24	26	6	194

Thus of the 194 who died, 112 lived to be old, that is over seventy years of age. And of this number, 57 lived to be very old, that is into their eighties and nineties. All these old people were born during the reign of Queen Victoria, the first one in the year of her coronation, the last, who died in 1976 aged ninety-six, in 1880. They were farm-labourers and servants, country craftsmen and farmers for the most part, and nearly everything they did in the way of toil and nearly everything they believed in by way of philosophy has been up-dated almost out of recognition. The old people still living in the village spent two-thirds of their days in the same working-thinking climate of these departed nineteenth-century inhabitants, and part of their problem is having to both decline in, and go on living in, what is virtually a post-revolution situation in the social sense.

They remember the dead easily. Give a name and they flesh

it out, recall gestures, sins, skills, voices. Of the 112 old people who died, 47 died in winter, 17 in spring, 25 in summer and 23 in autumn. Leonard, Annie, Arthur, William, Mary, Ethel, George, Elizabeth, Charles and Frederick was what most of them were called, although Sarah and John weren't far behind and there was a fanciful sprinkling of Manora, Ocean, Joel, Enos, Jeremiah, Ruby, Georgiana, Herman, Ny and Marsha. 'That Joel,' says Mrs Wilkes, scanning her window for meals-on-wheels. 'I set in schule along o' he. What did he look like? You may well ask!'

There are some forty inhabitants over seventy in the village now, of whom the doyen is the ex-tailor-postman, a regal giant in his early nineties with taut back and large feet, a skin the colour of ripe sloes and a scathing independence of manner. Twice a day he leaves his house, pitched tall and thin by the busy roadside, to walk to the pub for company's sake. In the winter he advertises his presence in the black lane with the merest spark of a torch. His cottage is the epitome of every old rural widower's home with paint, curtains, garden and glimpses of rooms all faded to the point of disappearance. No more definition. The medieval wall-paintings in Grundisburgh church have fresher tints than the tailor's thirties chintzes. He has no television and no visitors; his entertainment and his society are things he goes to in the little bar. He is sardonic. 'See you tomorrow,' they call out. 'Will you now?' answers the stick-straight old man who was lifting the latch, as they called it, in the nineteenth century. They also called it 'using the house'. He uses Brandeston Queen, they'll say. 'Which house did you use then?' 'When?' 'When you were fifteen.' 'When I was fifteen – what are you on about?' He looks pleased.

Some of the old people in the village obediently involve themselves in 'senior citizenry', join Forget-me-not clubs, and go through the social motions expected of their generation. Others don't and won't, and are thought wilful because they never join in. Once a week they collect their pensions at the village post office. Once the postman stole all the pension money, burying it in a hollow tree, and hitting himself on the head to prove he was robbed. Too much TV for a twenty-five-year-old. The pension money was instantly discovered because the first place you look for loot in a village is a hollow tree, particularly an oak.

About half the old people live alone and are nerve-racked by a mixture of threats and possibilities. For one old woman it is lorry-drivers who pull up on her verge and eat half a cut loaf of sandwiches and call out, 'Hi! Hi!' She bolts both front and back doors fast. Others hear steps in the garden or breathing in the orchard. The soldier's widow, who is eighty-five, has developed a policy of laying herself open, as it were, to every emergency of these strange, last Edward-less days when her breath thunders in her throat and she seems to be cooking lunch when the church clock strikes five and people wave but who-is-that? *'Who is it?'* she calls, half pleasure, half terror. She is too deaf to hear an answer anyway and smiles through the kind talk. One night the soldier's widow woke with a start and was convinced that it was her death-night. It was late September and the village was all long shadows under the moon. She leapt from her bed and opened every door and window for Death. At six she closed them and put the kettle on. 'What does it *feel* like to be nearly a hundred years old?' the shepherd's widow was asked. She was stout and sane. 'Well, you wake up in the morning, you say to yourself, "What, still here!" and then you make the tea.' Florida Scott-Maxwell put it perfectly: 'When a new disability arrives I look about to see if death has come, and I call quietly, "Death, is that you? Are you there?" So far the disability has answered, "Don't be silly, it's me."'

Many hamlets and villages have only old people left in them, which is something which could not have happened before. Bit by bit since the war the young have had to go where the work is, with the result that the village school, shop, pub and even the church have become uneconomic and are closed down. A bus may run to these villages of the old once a week, though often there is no public transport at all and the aged inhabitants are lucky if one of their number still runs his car and can get them to the surgery or post office in the market town. There are no children's voices in these villages and no bells on Sunday, nothing but distant tractors driven by strangers and the ignoring aeroplanes. They are a new way of abandoning the rural old who are left stranded among distant beetfields in Domesday foundations which can no longer support village viability.

In contrast to such places and as disturbing in the opposite sense, there are the villages which have taken-off into the future under the pressure of estate developments and their attendant public services. In these the indigenous old spend the last years of their lives in scenes of scrapping and renewal. The brightness and energetic spread of the new village makes them feel shabby and weak. There is in such places much congratulation and community pride in 'what is being done for the old' but often its recipients feel not so much cared for as overlaid, and they long for the caring of the earlier community, ramshackle though it was.

On the whole, the countryman believes that a conversation about old age is a conversation about the past. He is more his own historian than an analyst of his final self. He worships habit, not looks for explanation. His strictly observing today, what got him through yesterday, gives him confidence in there being a tomorrow. Like the poet Crabbe's country clergyman, habit with him is all the test of truth. Simone de Beauvoir goes so far as to state that habit in the old brings about a crystallization similar to that which Stendhal describes when he writes of love. It is 'the past brought to life again, the future anticipated'. Aged contemporaries in the same village have such an overlapping past that often theirs is a corporate habitual behaviour and where there are a score or two old folk in a little place one can still feel the strong, underlying rhythms of its earlier power. They are attuned to what has been, not to what is. They can't remember when they stopped adjusting the past to accommodate what the present is teaching. Their politics are static, halted at some advanced point which is now so far behind as to be useless. So is their mainly nominal religious faith. The current ethical and social debates of their own nation, as conveyed by radio and television, and the local press, are so far-flung from the position they once took up on certain matters as to sound as if they were being relayed from the Gold Coast and so it is comforting to go right back to the years when one did not hold an opinion at all, to childhood itself. No amnesic barrier denies access to this magic realm where they were shaped and moulded, and they will hurry any willing ear in its direction. It is the actual geography of boyhood and girlhood which the old long for, and with a longing like that of Peter Abelard for his new Jerusalem:

> We for that country must yearn and must sigh;
> Seeking Jerusalem, dear native land,
> Through our long exile on Babylon's strand.

A. L. Vischer calls this longing for the scenes of childhood the passive phenomenon of old age. 'In the first half of life people imagine that they can be happy wherever they are, but later on they often feel an urge to revisit the places of their birth.' For the two groups of aged village people, the locals and the retired settlers, finding the native place can be an equally imaginative process. Even if you were born and bred in the place, so much has happened to it and yourself over the past seventy years that to resort to it involves memory, rather than a stroll. Hence the child's view of the beloved landscape. For many, says Vischer, youth has constituted their one great experience. Listening to the old confirms this. Regression is the *sine qua non* of ageing, wrote Martin Berezin. There is no choice left for the aged person except to retreat to previous libidinal positions.

A Nice Little Blaze:
the District Nurse, aged eighty-four

Poor old things, poor old things! They weren't what they are now, I can tell you! Of course, they hadn't got the food, you know. They didn't get the living that they get these days. They say they're badly off now, but they're *not*, you know! But when I looked after the old people before the war in the villages round here, they had nothing at all. Nothing.

There were the poor old cottages with next to nothing in them, and all so cold. They used to go and chop sticks. You'd see them, the old ones, men and women alike, pulling sticks out of their gardens or out of the hedges along the lanes, pulling sticks, picking up sticks, to make a bit of a fire. They had a mite of coal but not much and they'd measure it out, a scrap today and a scrap tomorrow. So one of the things they'd enjoy was a bit of a blaze from sticks. They liked to make the kettle whistle. 'There!' they'd say, 'I'll make you whistle!'

It was all very simple. Usually there wasn't a penny in the house. Nothing left from the days when they'd earned money because just look what wages they got! So when you got old there was nothing. You sat about and thought, and you crept around looking for a bit of kindling to make a blaze. Your children would give you a look and so would the rector. There weren't any old people's clubs or that sort of thing. You were given various things at Christmas, a few logs, a packet of tea, a calendar. And blankets were lent you when the weather turned. Yes, at one time in this village there were blankets to *loan out*. Oh, yes. I don't know who they actually belonged to in the first place. They came to me, the nurse, these blankets and I was told to loan them out where they were wanted. There were some old people who didn't have any blankets at all, and I'd let them borrow one or two. I went to cottages where there was nothing upstairs. Poky bedrooms nearly empty and, oh, so cold! Poor old things then.

I had to visit the big young families and the old shrunken families, and make reports. One young family had fifteen boys and girls in two bedrooms with one of the boys tubercular. He was supposed to have slept alone. Well, where *did* he sleep? I asked each time I went. Well, he slept here, he slept there – always in little holes away from the rest, they'd say. But he didn't and I knew he didn't, poor lad. He slept cuddled up warm with his brothers and sisters, T.B. or no T.B. I didn't lay the law down whether for the young or the old. Anyway, it was a waste of breath. In the village conditions of those days I just helped people get through. I saw them through, the young and the old. And that is what these aged men and women were doing when I called on them, just getting through – the day, the week, the rest of their lives. They didn't grouse about being hard-done by or pretend to be happy. They simply stuck to things like getting through the night and getting up to make a bit of a fire, and staring out of the window. That was something you saw plenty of, old faces pressed against the window glass and staring out all day long. They're staring in now, aren't they – at the telly! Half of them don't even know what the weather is outside. Few of them even had the wireless then – in the thirties, this was – but they might have the lend of a paper or a book like *Woman's Weekly* or *Home Chat*, and pass it on. If they could read. Many of them couldn't. So they'd look out of the window a lot, these ones. They'd have worked well into their seventies, like as not, so there wasn't all that time left to be idle and alone in. They'd go behind a bit then and everybody expected them to.

When I first came here in the twenties, lots of old people were neglected, really neglected. Even when they were still living with their families they would get dreadfully dirty. And you'd get this peculiar thing where a son or a daughter couldn't do anything for them. Intimate, I mean. Father was father and mother was mother. You couldn't touch them. They sat about and stank. And some of them were right tartars and families would long for them to die. I know it was a help when I arrived on the scene, and washed them and changed them and stripped their beds. It was quite an operation but it could work wonders. If father was an authoritarian then I could be a bigger authoritarian in his house! 'The little nurse' is what they called me. I was only a girl to them but I did come in my Morris Seven and sometimes with my own soap and flannel! That counted. It's surprising what counts.

But other old people were gentle and good. Full of prayer, I suppose. Some of them had worked ten to twelve hours a day for nigh-on seventy years, and with nothing in the world to show for it except a bent back. Not a penny in the teapot bar what came from the five-shilling pension and a skimpiness of things on the bed and up at the windows. They'd have dad's old khaki coat to give the bed a bit of weight and they'd treasure that. The old, old mothers'd lay there in the big feather beds in which they'd had their children. They got so they couldn't turn them or get the chamber-pot down the garden to the privy. Their bedrooms would be sweet and close and cold. Oh, that smelly cold! To have a fire in the bedroom grate meant you were taken bad. Lots of old people died in the big bed watching a cheerful little fire. When the fire was lit, people would say, 'He's going.' And if the family was fed up with the old person who had died they'd always say, 'It was a happy release.' And I knew they meant it for themselves. But there!

Lots of old widowers muddling through. Old horsemen like poor old Mr Edwards. He used to look like Father Christmas. Right up to his death, I attended him. Washed him, tidied him every day. He used to look for me – these old village folk did a lot of looking. 'I'll come and give you a look,' they'd say, and they'd walk, slowly, slowly along the field path, calling to their friends over fences, 'I thought I'd come and give you a look!' Mr Edwards had worked hard as had they all! They worked until they couldn't do anything. That was the whole matter then. They'd scrap on and on and they kept their jobs until they just couldn't get to them. I can see them now, trudging along with a stick, getting to the farm, and having little rests, and breathing hard, and wiping their wet old eyes with those red hankies. It wasn't the money alone. Most people then didn't like to stop working. It didn't seem right. It was, well, shameful.

Old Mr Deaves down in the council houses now, his parents worked like that. When they stopped I had to look after them. Their poor old feet – corns and I don't know what. Nothing had ever been done to them. Mrs Deaves went lame and couldn't ever get out. I would find out what people like her had been living with – enduring half their lives – and try to change it. Very few had false teeth, just the odd stumps. But they *did* live a long time. They ate sensible things from the garden. Just plain things. Lots of bread and cheese. Lots of women still made their own bread. It was most extraordinary how they'd struggle to go on and on until they couldn't.

They all spoke of the workhouse, and they weren't 'a-gooin' there'. That they weren't! Oh, no. We called it the infirmary but they called it the 'wuk'us', and how they hated it! How they hated the very sound of it. Nothing would drag them there on no account, they said. This would be in the early thirties, like. Infirmary or not, you still had to work if you could when they got you there. Chopping wood, cleaning big old floors. If you were on your feet they kept you on the go. Sometimes the old people would go in for a bit and then they'd come out for a bit. They'd suddenly arrive back home with the door-key. They'd find their cottage all wet and their gardens grown up, and they'd set-to and sweep up, and light the sticks in the grate.

I can remember visiting the workhouse at Blythburgh when I first came this way to nurse and I was disgusted. I went there to see someone. It was about 1928. I saw them, sitting on hard old chairs in the huge bare room. Men and women I knew, and strangers, in the bare room, passing a word or two, maybe. Some of them were doubled-up, all twisted and listless. You'd never think to look at them that they'd spent all those years in the beautiful fields. It was summertime when I went to the workhouse called Bulcamp at Blythburgh and I was young and so it seemed sadder. A woman I knew had to inspect these Suffolk workhouses and she told me that Bulcamp was the worst place she'd been into. How dreadful it was! When I saw Bulcamp I saw that I had to do everything to keep my villagers at home. They were frightened stiff at the bare mention of it.

The old people came at the end of my day's work. It was maternity first and these old 'uns last. That was how it was arranged. The old weren't only cottage people; I had the care of them in the houses, the rectory, the Hall and such-like. First mothers and babies, then my old men, waiting for me and looking out. Poor old things! Who remembers one of them now?

An Incorrigible Idyll:
the Crossing-Keeper's Son,
aged seventy-nine

This is the happiest time of my life – that is, and I tell yew straight! I wish there was twenty-four hours in the day. Wuk hours, awake hours. Yew can keep y' sleep; plenty of time for that later on. I niver thowt I'd come to this. Mother [wife], she say, 'Come yew on now, dinner's ready. That's on the table, look!' But when I'm makin' these hare things on my bench in the shed I'd as sooner not come. Time's a funny thing, yew know, a very funny thing. I'll tell y' somethen – that don't fare to be no time at all since I was a little ol' boy. That all seem to be some time yisterday. I come out with tales and sich-like about that time to mother and she say, 'Why don't you write a book?' I could tew! But that would be tellin'! 'If I keep my health,' I tell her. I keep fair to middlin' so I marn't grumble. Grumble – I should think not indeed!

Now I'll tell yew somethen, I was a bad boy and I'm glad ont! Don't ask me why. You're not sorry later, spite o' what they say. Glad, that's what yew are. Glad! Glad yew done it, glad yew worn't an angel. Yew hear 'em goin' on about morals in the olden days and morals now, but what do they know about it? Yew ask me. Mother, she shake her hid at the thowt of it. Giver har dew, she's allus bin a good soul. But I was merry enough, wholly merry in me day. An' that day seem only some time yisterday. I goo over it all in my mind, seein' it all so clear-like, and relishin' it, if the truth be told. Why be sorry when you're glad? Don't make sense, do it?

Where to start? There was this hare mill in Constable's country, that was the start. Start there. Start when I went to schule in Lawford. Father was on the line – a ganger. On the railway, father was. Good wuk then y' know – the best. Well, jist afore the Fourteen War father he fancied a lighter job, so that's how we come up here to Marlesford. So I went to Hatcheston schule. I had four year at schule all towd. That was because I fell off a hoss 'n cart and bruk me legs an' all manner o' things. I was eight or ten an' lay there on the couch indoors. Doctor Bree, he come and done what he could and I niver went to no horspital.

Well, father'd set beside me evenin's-like and he'd whittle away at things. Things he was makin', see. He was that cliver with his shutknife and could tarn his hand to any mortal thing. It was a pleasure to see it. So there he'd set, in his ol' chair – father's chair, we called it. That wouldn't dew to let him ketch yew with your arse in it, that that wouldn't! I would love to know where that chair is this minute, that I would! I should know it no sooner I seed it. Silly fule, I give it away years agoo. The chair father made. I see him makin' it, an' I give it away! Pity. Father's chair – fancy me athinkin' o' that now! But that's how it is when you're an old un, it all kind-a starts up agin, the long agoo. As plain as lookin' out that winder. So this ol' chair. Father'd set in it by me, carvin' things and restin' the wood on the arm. He'd carve and wuk things on that arm till that was all but cut threw. Only on that one arm – th' other was perfect. That was father's bench, that chair. Snares, he'd make. I lay there on the couch larnin' the carvin' and the snares, apickin' it all up, gittin' like father, gittin' father's skill.

That's why I'm happy now and no mistake. I've known father set in a wheatfield and bend them ol' straw things, them dollies, up quick as lightnin'. Rum thing, worn't it? They were man's wuk then, o' course. I niver heard o' gals dewin' it. It was fellers like father that made the ol' straw things. He'd put ships in bottles, too – all that manner o' thing. So I got my craft from father.

They was hard times. I'm not sorry about anythin' I did to make 'em easy, that I haint! A few didn't o' course but I did. I reckon I deserved a larrupin', but there yew are! If us all got what we deserved we'd be rich an' pore an' one thing an' another. So there y'are! So git back to the tale – I love a tale, so do mother.

When I left schule I was twelve and I used to goo round with the shepherd. I was allus fond o' sheep, I don't know why. So there was this shepherd and he was a man with a catapult. He'd knock a pheasant down – *zonk!* We used to make lead bullets, him and me, for the catapult. We'd set in mother's kitchen and there was this hare coco-mattin' on the floor – no rugs nor nothin', but coco-mattin'. And a ladleful o' our hot lead went all over it. Mother, how she jawed! That lead was there for life, of course it was. Crumbs, how she jawed!

I used to goo round with shepherd sometimes at night and help with his sheep. Mother made me a frock out o' drybit [drabbet]. A smock was longer than a frock and drybit was somethin' not quite so heavy as canvas. Anyway, mother made me this frock and I had a belt underneath it, and when I went out of a night with shepherd, I used to hook 'em on there. Pheasants. We'd knock 'em off a tree and they all hung around me under the frock.

And then there was pheasants' egg-layin' time. My father

wukked up and down the line that parted Colonel Rigby's park and Miss Hollender's park. Lady Hollender we called her sometimes, yew know how it is. She'd come out when we was pinchin' the walnuts an' chestnuts an' shout, 'Pick up as many as you like *but don't knock the trees about*!' There was thousands and thousands. Well, father was well-in with har keepers and the Colonel's keepers, an' he'd get a shillin' a nest for every pheasant's nest he found on either side o' the line. Or they might be partridges. Howsomedever, he'd watch out for both. Well, shepherd had an ol' wife what had an ol' pram, an' an ol' dog called Willwood, an' they three would sarnter along threw the parks, innocent as you like, till Willwood found a nest. Then that ol' dog Willwood would carry these pheasant-eggs, one at a time, one at a time, one at a time to this ol' gal and her pram with shepherd's dinner in it, and she'd load 'em up and take 'em to father, who sold 'em back to the Colonel or the Lady. And they'd put 'em under a settin' hen and rear 'em. That's bad! But that's how it was done.

You couldn't exist then if you was too good. Not if you had a family to rear. I've bin to schule many a time with a raw tunnip with jam on. I had to eat it because else I'd goo hungry. That's the gospel truth. Mother'd git a raw tunnip, peel it, slice it, dabble a mite o' jam in, and that's what fed us many a time. I've passed threw such a change. I laugh when I think about it. 'Mother,' I say, 'do yew recall ol' so and so . . . ?' 'Yew and your tales!' mother says, 'dew yew put them in a book!' We niver had much. We were born with narth'n and we finished up with £12 a week. That's the most I iver arned, that was the very highest. Now, blast me, if they don't want a hundred! We saved, mother and me. Mother's good on savin', you know. We still save, even on the pension. Mother's a manager. If yew married a bad manager in them ol' days yew knew it! But she knew how to do it. Her grandfather kept the mill, yew see. I was a-courtin' har thirteen year. Thirt . . . teen . . . year. I used to pull all the water up for har out o' that ol' well behind the pub where she lived with har aunty. I saw har brew and bake and do it all. She's the one, I thowt. Lovely, that well was but they condemned it. Ol' people thereabouts lived to be eighty and ninety a-side o' that well and niver took no harm from it. Soo that's the beginnin' o' the matter. I don't know where the end will be, do yew? I reckon we're comin' to it fast, but there it is.

When the Fourteen War bruk out I was twelve and I had to leave schule to wuk on the land to take the place of a man what volunteered. I got ten shillin' a week and the hossman only got twelve-and-a-tanner, so I didn't dew so bad like. The chap what went to war soon came back all wounded. So did others. They were killin' the people no end. No one knew what to make of it. I did all I could on the farm, charned the milk, did all manner o' things but I allus wanted to be a cabinet-maker. I crazed my father and he went to see a gentleman at Wickham Market who was a cabinet-maker, and he wanted £50 to 'prentice me. Well, naturally, father had no way of showin' £50, so that was that. All the same, from the beginnin' I was allus one for makin' things, though I've niver done so much in that line a-durin' this last year or two. That's what I want all this hare time for now to make things. I draw and paint too. All I do are recollections. I love drawin', allus have. But I was no good at schule because I niver went to schule, not really. But that's narth'n new because there's several round here who can't read and write now, an' they're sixteen, an' they've bin to schule for years and years and years! I could have done with a bit more of it. For makin' the models in the shed. When I want to reduce somethin' to an eighth, say. And I love a book. I like readin' anythin' trew. Lilias Rider Haggard, I love har books. But television I can't look at at all. I leave that to mother. 'Dad, come and look at this,' she'll say. 'Do *yew* look at it,' I say.

I set at this bench and I don't want the day to end. And it all comes back to me – when we were boys, y'know. How we used to get in the river to goo tradin' [treading] – things like that. There we'd all be, clear as clear, just as we were. We'd have an ol' hamper, a clothes hamper, and there'd be four or five on us jump in the river with it, and then we'd trade all through the weed, an' where the water pushed through we'd howd our skep. It was like beatin' for birds, except yew done it in the river. We'd trade ivery foot o' the weed an' all the eels and pike, like, used to leap in this hare skep. It'd nearly knock yew over when a grut ol' pike come in. We'd throw the fish on the bank and goo on tradin'. Stampin' the weeds and laughin'. I'd-a bin about sixteen about the last time I done it. We didn't strip. We just took our jacket off and jumped in and you'd feel the river ride up your legs cold to the crotch. Our trousers soon got dry. You couldn't goo in where the mud was deep. Afterwards we'd set and skin the eels, cuttin' round the heads fust. We'd take 'em hoom, boil 'em, then fry 'em. But we didn't eat the ol' pike – no fear! There'd be Harry and Ainger and several more. All clear as clear.

But father loved a pike. So I'd snare him one with a leather bootlace. I'd see a pike lay in the river and I'd take this long ol' leather lace and make it into a loop. Then I'd hang it from a pole and gradually, *gradually*, hold me breath, I'd lower it down right in front of him, this still, still pike. Inter the slip-knot he'd goo and out on the bank he'd come! I caught hundreds o' pike like that – hundreds! They'd be that riled!

It seems that I'm by that river a lot now. I'm a boy and I'm by that river, an' we're all there like we used to be. I can hear our talk plain as plain. 'Let's goo babbin'' – things like that. Before we went babbin' we'd goo into the yard and dig up a tinful of worms. Big worms. Then we'd worry mother to give us a bit of worsted and har big ol' darnin' needle, and then we'd thread all these worms in a string. Then we'd wind this worm string round and round our hand till that was a ball o' worms. Then we'd tie an ol' ston' or nut on for a sinker, fix the whol' thing onto a line and take it to the river. All yew had to do was jist touch bottom with it – then *zink!* – an eel's teeth were stuck in the worsted! Yew marn't take the eel off the bait in the long grass. He'd be away in a flash. Away he'd be! What we liked to hev handy was an ol' gig umprella upside-down in the reeds and chuck the catch into that. Then you'd got 'em! *Then* you'd got 'em, my boy!

I'd pass along the river at night with shepherd. There was proper hunger about – it's the Fourteen War now. And I've seen shepherd git hold o' a lovely lamb an' put his knife in the back of that's ear, an' in ten minutes that's skin was off, an' he'd hev half and we'd hev half, and that's the truth. Lamb, nice lamb. Mother salted it down; it'd last a long while. Mind you, they was hard times. Yew wouldn't credit how hard. You'd cheat on rat-tails then, let alone a lamb.

A chap I knew would git a penny a rat-tail, penny a rat-tail. And so'd I. We used to git a packet o' tin-tacks, which cost about a farden, and him and me we'd nail all our rat-tails up on the barn in sets o' dozens. All in order of length, like organ-pipes. Jist the same. There were millions of rats then, millions! You'd see the runs they made when they went down to the river to drink, and you'd snare these hare runs. About four o'clock in the afternoon, down to the river they'd goo, and do yew know what I see once? I see a rat in the snare and another rat coming back to help it by bitin' the string to let him out. Trew.

It was the schulemaster who was givin' a penny for a rat-tail. Yew niver took the rat to schule, yew took his tail. Yew chopped his tail off by layin' the rat across an ol' scythe and comin' down on him against the blade with a hulk o' wood. Flew off, they did.

Well, come night-time, I'd slip along and git half a dizen o' these tails off the barn door, cut off the bit where the tin-tack went through, take 'em to the schulemaster and git a tanner. 'Yew goo and bury them, boy,' schulemaster would say. But I didn't. I used 'em several times and they bro'ght me in several pennies. Several. Penny was a lot then, y'know.

In the winter weather I'd stay at hom and see few. If I

could git a-hold o' a ol' tea-chest I counted meself happy. I used to rub it all down and make it smooth, and I'd fix a paper pattern on from *Hobbies*. Then I'd cut all round it. Used to take hours. And all in the same room with mother and the dust flying everywhere. Yew drilled your hole and threaded your saw through, an' cut an' cut. Cut careful.

Twenty year ago I started making these hare brass things, ploughs, churches, furniture and the like. At fust I'd make 'em and give 'em away but now I keep everything. And I use anything. Rubbish. Odds and ends. Weldin' wire, ol' fardens, bits of switches, handles, brass buttons, copper bolts, any mortal thing. I don't copy anything, I make what I remember. I tarn wood. I paint the fields. As I say, I've niver bin so happy in my whol' life and I only hope I last out. I've bin a bit of a lad and when I'm workin' I see it all so clear, so clear. I can smell that river and I can see us all so clear.

Better to Travel: the Farmer, aged seventy-seven

I don't find retirement difficult – not really. I was farming and I wouldn't have retired in the ordinary way, but then I was so ill that I practically had to. Otherwise I would have gone on for years and years. Perhaps longer than I should have done, and making things more difficult than was necessary. So, yes and no. The only retirement feeling I have is one of relief. I feel that I can go off whenever and wherever I like and be independent. I like to be out, I like to be away! Away, away! Or just out gardening. Here, there and everywhere, that's me. I don't stay in, I get out. I'm always out. I like to be out. Being out keeps me free, so I'm out whenever I can. I feel I'll live if I'm out.

I love to get in the car. Then away, away! No one to ask, nothing to stop me. When I was a lad I used to do a lot of bareback riding. I had my donkeys and my ponies, and a galloping horse. I would jump bareback on to a horse in the evening and would ride flat under the trees so that I missed the boughs. On and on. The Lord knows where I was going. But on and on, galloping on.

I've always liked some form of transport. I went in my first car when I was four. It was one of those beautiful old-fashioned things which were rather like a tub-cart, with seats in front for the driver which were turned-out at the turn of the century. How they lasted! When I was thirteen father bought his first Model-T Ford in Hertford. He'd never driven before. But he just paid for it, got in and drove it away. The garden-boy used to look after it. Father hardly knew about it having to be fed oil and water. He'd just hop in and drive.

I've always had this elated feeling of movement and some-times it has been so strong that I've had a sensation of being out of the body. I know you can have dreams which give you the impression that you are out of the body but I've experi-enced this thing so vividly that I've had to acknowledge that, for a time, I really was outside. It has happened to me, both at night and in the daytime. In camp during the last war, we'd just had our breakfast and were waiting for the rollcall. It was about seven o'clock and I was just sitting there, and the sun was shining. And then, all at once, I was at home in my little workshop and looking at the shelf, and at all the different tools and things. I was free and happy. Then I remembered – *'You're supposed to be at Blandford in the camp!'* And back I was again, rushed back. The other time it happened was at night. I'd had a long drive from the main road and it was dusk, and I could see the sides of the grass, dull, lifeless and flat, as I was walking towards the house in the ordinary way. As I walked I looked left and right, first to the paddock which I had wired-off for the cow, and then to the other side, and as I looked I began to say to myself, 'What are you doing? Why are you walking up here in the middle of the night? You should be in bed. In bed – that's where you're supposed to be.'

And there I was, lying in my bed. Neither of these experiences were frightening to me in the least. They stand out hard in my memory – too hard for dreams.

I wander for days in my car now. I don't stay in, I get out. Off we go! I say. Away, away!

A Silence Falls:
the Farrier, aged eighty-two

'What you can't do in one day, you must do in two,' was what they used to say in Suffolk when the slowing-up process started. At first the dwindling and draining of strength was unbelievable. Where had it gone? How could it go? It shook you not to be able to put in the full day. You took a look at yourself, at your arms, and at the top they were the soft arms of a fat woman. You stopped for more rests, you asked yourself what was going to happen when what you could do in a day couldn't be done in a week – couldn't be done at all. Full stop. Neighbours and friends advised you to pack-up now. Don't kill yourself, they said. Have a bit of pleasure before you go. Go? Well we've all got to go, haven't we? To prove it the farrier's wife went, the girl he had married who had become the stiff, managing old woman. She had left him, and with such a finality that all the business about widowerhood seemed irrelevant in comparison. Going after fifty years, she had plunged him into an amazing situation. It was best not to try to describe it. Trying to describe it was like looking down when you were clinging to a cliff, so just say, 'My wife died.' Say no more. Whenever he had tried to reason it out he had swayed giddily. She talked and talked ('You don't hear a word I say'), she clicked needles and teeth, she shifted herself from room to room, she creaked, she rustled and had no truck with silence. You knew when she was at home all right. She was good-living and proper and always on the go, though not a scrapper – he'd give her that! And now gone for good and her hat still up on the wardrobe. Say no more.

The farrier trembles, though not with shock. Parkinson's disease keeps his gentle old flesh in constant motion. His mother, his aunts and an uncle all got the shakes. They also all lived into their eighties. The palsy appears to lap and protect him like a springy, nervous elasticity keeping off more rigorous disasters. His cup leaps about on its saucer but somehow doesn't fall or spill. Now and then the trembling builds up into a cakewalk of convulsion and you only hope you aren't pouring yourself a drink when this happens. Anyway, he'd never had to do for himself in his life before. There had been the strict division of labour, him in the forge, her in the house, she with her few flowers, he with the potatoes and things. It's a funny thing getting at her cupboards and looking out the linen. Her order is scrupulously maintained and the way he gets on without her admired. 'She could walk right back into that house and set herself down, if she could,' they say. They keep an eye, they add. The farrier is in two minds about this. When does help stop and interference begin? he asks himself. It is the question which the old ask themselves in dread. It is why they struggle on and why they are secretive. On his left wrist the farrier wears a pure copper bracelet which doesn't join to charm his arthritis away. Has it? Hasn't it been a certain cure for four thousand years? he says.

He is particular about being called a farrier and not just a blacksmith. A farrier descends from the days when the forge became specialized and divided itself into general ironworkers, horseshoers and armourers. The Ferrers and Ferriers families are all said to descend from the men who shod the Conqueror's horses. The old craftsman followed his trade accompanied by endless conversations, for the forge is the classic talking-shop of the village and more important things will be said there than in the pub. The sociability of the forge, though different, was not less than that of the bar, and whilst acknowledging

the blankness caused by his wife's death, the farrier hasn't
allowed for the generations of children crowding the traverse,
the political wrangling round the bosh, or water-trough, or
just the companionable hum of gossip in the snug muddle of
fire-new implements, tongs, pincers, pig iron, pokers, clut-
tered benches, chisels, trugs, shovels, rakes, mondrels, har-
rows, coulters and enough horseshoes for a cavalry regiment's
existence. As normal to the forge as its bellows during scringing
winter or baking summer had been the faces round the fire
and the hammers ringing through the talk. Father and grandfather heard it all before him. Their anvil, all three hundred-
weight of it, squats in the dust like an abandoned altar. Curling
diplomas from ancient agricultural shows are tacked around
the walls like votive requests and prize-cards patch the beams
with achievement. But the delicious, outrageous stench of
scorched hoof from thousands of shires, ponies and hunters
can only be imagined.

Unlike neighbouring colleagues, the farrier made no effort
to move on into the wrought-iron gate business, at least in
any modern village-craft way. He is a man of his father's day.
If you ignore the electric bulb, his forge is essentially the same
as that in the Caxton woodcut or in *The Boy's Book of Trades*
of 1888. One day, surprised more than usual by age, he let
the fire out and closed the rickety doors. Mallow, burdock
and spear grass shot up from the road's edge and locked them
tight.

'Was it hard to give up?'

'Hard?' the farrier is puzzled. 'It was the *time* to give up,
wasn't it? The *time* had come, hadn't it?'

His nature is unexamining and non-analytical. He isn't
nostalgic because, now in his early eighties, his thinking is
that of the old days themselves and innocent of any sense of
advance – or retreat, for that matter. He sits all day and every
day in the small, polished brown interior of the average old
countryman, hoping for a visitor. German, American, British
and French shell cases shine on the mantelpiece. On to the

British one the farrier has soldered his Royal Artillery Cap-
badge, *Ubique*. His talk is much of the wars, France in the
first, village scandals during the second. Although reduced to
an almost translucent silveryness of skin and bone, and
swimming blueness of gaze, in speech the farrier is often
sharp and tough. He is the sloppy old dog who will give you
a nip. His talk is studded with references to the police, the
guards, the local gentry and power groups of all kinds. He is
short but early photographs show him strong, shapely and
even vaguely menacing. His body has collapsed like that of an
old weight-lifter but his outlook was carved in conservative
turn-of-the-century Empire teak and hasn't absorbed a lot
since. Borrow, in *Lavengro*, wrote, 'It has always struck me
that there is something highly poetical about a forge.' This
would be news to the farrier. His old age is unadorned prose.
He waits, he shakes, and is a stoic.

*

My boyhood seems a wholly long time agoo, I don't mind
tellin' you. Donkey's years. I'm eighty-two, so you know it
worn't yesterday. I must say, I carried on at school until I was
fourteen when others left at twelve, and then I went to evening
classes at Grundisburgh. The classes were useful to me in
sech things as land-measurin' – all sech things as that. I could
goo out and measure-up a field all shapes and sizes. It was two
nights a week. We was taught to measure-up a heap o' mang'l's
or a heap o' straw. Even thatchin' we'd measure-up. It was all
part of a lot o' things I was taught that was useless. I was
taught some sums but as for the decimal system, you had to
be a good 'un for the decimal system.

The village was less cut-off than now. We went all around.
We had to walk everywhere, of course. There were footpaths
and near-cuts, and plenty of different ways hom. I walked two
mile to school and two mile to chapel. My mother was a real
chapel woman and there was this here wonderful chapel at
Grundisburgh. It used to be crowded. I used to ha' to walk

to Sunday School, take me dinner, stay all arternoon and then to the service at night. When they had anniversaries in July it was like hittin' a race meetin'. Horse an' traps by the score. I had to goo to this chapel before I could fend for myself and on account of mother bein' a big chapel woman. But arter I left school I used to like to goo to chuch. We real chapel boys would walk to different chuches, Clopton Chuch, or Hasketon-like. But so far as any real *faith* in religion, I never did take to that, chuch nor chapel. I liked the Salvation Army meetin's. Several of us boys would bike to Ipswich to the Salvation Army meetin' and hear the singin'. I still like goin' to chuch on high days but I haven't a might o' faith in it.

After I left school my craze was to git on the railway. I was up in London when I was fifteen, stayin' with one o' my oldest sisters that had a dairy-shop there and a foreman from the engine-sheds at Strawberry Hill came to it each day, and this sister, she told him that her little brother would like to work on the railway, and that I was willin' to be a cleaner, willin' to start low and do anythin'. But there worn't any vacancies because every boy wanted to git on the railways, and the foreman said try again in three years. And there was in three months! But I didn't want it then. My father had taken me on at the forge, although I was small, and I was gittin' on well with him. I've thanked myself since that I missed the railway. I'm sure I've had a happier life.

My father was eighty-seven when he died, so I've got a year or two to ketch up with him. He could shoe a hoss almost to the end. Hoss-shoein' was my hobby – what I delighted in but I had to stop because of the shakes. I marn't blow my own trumpet, but in five year I got thirty-seven prizes and for two year I was champion o' the Eastern Counties – one year at Norwich and one year at Ipswich. When I was a boy, my father would shoe 'em for nothin' practically. He'd charge three bob for a farmhoss. At Grundisburgh they'd do 'em for half-a-crown and Charsfield for two bob! Make the shoes, take an hour to put 'em on, supply the forge coal and the iron.

My father, he was a good blacksmith. No one would stamp on his feet. When I was a boy, he'd teach me true.

Some o' the ol' blacksmiths were ignorant fellers and they wouldn't know about the anatomy o' the hoss's foot, which is important. A lot of people reckon that a hoss's foot is like a block o' wood and that you can shove a nail in anywhere. But you can't. Inside the foot there is bones and flesh, and the wall of the hoof is only about $\frac{3}{8}''$ thick, accordin' to the size o' the hoss, and to drive a nail you must be expert not to lame the animal. When I was a boy, my father he taught me like this. He heared of a lovely Suffolk hoss that had bruk a leg in a field over there and that had to be destroyed. 'See if you can git they two front legs,' said father. 'From the knees, mind.' I saw the man and he cut 'em off for me. My father, he told me what he wanted me to do. 'I want you to saw that right through, hoof an' all, so as you can see inside the proper structure o' the leg.' Then he rigged up an ol' copper across the road, on that very spot, and he boiled the other leg until all the bones were free. That's how father larnt me all he knew.

I don't know where I would have found more happiness than at the forge. It's all shut up now and I sit an' listen to the kittle b'ilin' or watch the telly. I find the time passes well enough but occasionally, well, I feel on my own. All on my own. There are some days when I don't see a soul to speak to – although there is plenty goo by. My wife, she died four year agoo. That's her picture up there. It's an oil paintin' by our kind neighbour. At the bottom right-hand corner there is a little glimpse of my forge. At the time I did properly miss my wife, and no mistake, but I had my daughters and that took it off. When you've spent your whol' life a-usin' of your hands, like I have, you don't know what to do when you can't. You really don't. I have two nice daughters and grandsons that are gittin' on well, an' a granddaughter that is at the teachers' college at Canterbury. I balance things up when I can. I've got no work and no wife, but I've got what I've done, haven't I? We've all got that, haven't we?

I do silly things. I fell from the apple-tree, so I've bin in orspital. 'The apple-tree?' said Doctor Smith when he come. 'Don't you let me ketch you up no apple-tree ever agin!'

A Formidable Acceptance: the Farm Foreman's Daughter, aged eighty-one

For many country people old age exhibits what looks like a restoration of vigour. Bodies which, in their sixties, were heavy and soft, harden once more, and voices and personalities which had grown discreet become resonant and very decided. It is old age accepting its dues and demanding homage.

Grace is the daughter of a farm foreman on the Duke of Hamilton's estate. She began work in the fields when she was six, stone-picking and singling-out. When she was twelve she went into service a hundred miles from home. There were seventeen servants kept and thirty in the neighbouring house (Lord O'Hagan's). Her cousin was the cook and between her and the general supervision, there was hardly a moment during her adolescence which she could call her own. She remembers seeing an attractive village boy at church as she sat amidst the banked rows of servants, and dropping her prayer-bork to catch his attention. They would then stare, but they never met or spoke. 'It was impossible.' The attitude towards young housemaids was exactly like that towards dogs; you never let them out of your sight in case 'something happened'. Her employers were kind and helpful to her later, assisting her to buy a cottage when the Duke sold-up his Suffolk estates. Grace bought it for £190 in 1919 and has lived in it ever since. It was the house in which her husband was born.

Matthew is eighty and looks like an ancient boy, his face soap-shined and his still-dark hair dampened to his head. Photographs from the First World War show a stout soldier twice the size and somehow possessed of a different personality. Matthew is very ill and has been for years and years. His illness has parted one existence from him, imposed another. It has left him fragile and thoughtful. His ailments are real and overwhelming, diabetes, dropsy, cataracts, and shrapnel wounds from the trenches which occasionally erupt in fiery little volcanoes of pain in all directions. He is immensely devout and loses himself in labyrinthine prayer and the Bible.

'Matthew is a real Christian,' says Grace, 'but I don't go *that* far.' When the rector prays with Matthew, she always breaks it up when she thinks they've had enough. 'That'll do,' she says. 'After all,' she adds, 'it *is* my house!' When they were confirmed sixty-eight years ago, they knelt on hassocks covered with a white cloth. Neddy Chapman, another village boy, put one knee on each of the two hassocks when he knelt before the bishop, not knowing any better. 'The bishop soon pulled him over!' Matthew and Grace also knelt on white hassocks when they were married.

Grace, at eighty-one, is a big, handsome, sturdy woman who talks a lot and worries about her 'goin' on-like'. But she is more loquacious than garrulous. She has the horsy good looks of an English lady and something of the same panache. She can be rude with style. Her parents were illiterate. She herself is a mine of tales, gossip and history, all of which were told to her by now-vanished talkers. She gives little suggestion of being old. Her smile is wide and attractive, she has skin like a girl and her hair is thick and strong. She is not over-grateful for her picture-of-health appearance; it conceals infirmities for which she would like a little sympathy.

She looks after Matthew as a mother would a little son, washing him, cutting his hair, and seeing that he is well turned-out. She also reads the Bible to him now that cataracts prevent him from doing it for himself. Her consideration for his feelings go as far as eating her cake before he joins her for tea, so that he doesn't feel deprived or left out and reminded of his diabetes. Fifty years after the war she decided that

Matthew should receive some compensation for all his shrapnel wounds and so she wrote to the Government. She spent the money doing-up the kitchen.

The house is bright and fragrant, with masses of needle-work cushions, runners, tablecloths, curtains, etc. every-where. The television-set is draped in needlework. Grace moves about in the tidy spaces between her embroidered possessions with great zest, her booming and highly articulate comments suggesting not so much a running-down of life as a penultimate realization that life has confined her. Her village is nothing more than a group of medieval farms and a church on a remote, high plateau. It has neither school, shop nor pub. Its sparseness seems to have no connection with the endless anecdotes which Grace draws from it. She adores giving information which you won't find in books but will suddenly say, 'There, now, that's enough! Come again, but not till August!'

*

I can spell better now than I could in years gone by. Nouns and pronouns, I used to think they were silly, now I think they are very interesting. I spot things now on the telly, things that years ago I wouldn't have noticed at all. You need to keep your wits about you when you get on. It don't do to be a fool, what with my husband's diet and these doctors, and strangers apt to knock on the door. I answer the telephone in the morn-ings and he doesn't answer it at all. He's a nervous man now. I get the logs and coal in but I only light the fire now and again because of the bending-down. I keep the electric-bar on a lot and I've stopped frettin' about whether I shall be able to pay the winter bill. What is it we're supposed to get – hypo-thermia? I'm not havin' none o' that. I've got him to see to. I'll ask for what I want. I can't understand people being so dumb. I've never refused a soul a little help all my life and now I say to myself I'm going to have a little help back. If I can have it for the askin', then I'll do the askin'. I 'on't go without, no more I shall! And I'll speak up for Matthew because I'm the only one that's left to do it. I don't hold back – not now.

I was shy as a child but you'd never believe it. The village was full of old people then. You never heard *them* complainin' that they'd had hard times because they'd never had no different. I don't know that I can recall any o' these old 'uns livin' alone like they do now. In those days people were nearly like people are still in foreign countries, gran'ma, great-gran'ma, auntie, parents, children – all in the one house. That was what they called 'the family' – not just your mother and father and you. We was similar to them in foreign countries – like them poor refugees, with granny and baby in the same boat. And that's how we should be still, if you ask me.

Of course you didn't have to be old to look old then. Black and old you'd be at fifty. Now they dye and look black and young till they're dead. Mother wore a bonnet when she was young – *she was married in a bonnet* – but she never wore a bonnet when she was old – that she didn't! She wore a sailor's hat. A black sailor-hat, mother had, and her hair done back tight. Years didn't make my mother go old. When my brother Jack was killed in 1917, it was then she suddenly turned into a little withered lady, and that's how she stayed. She'd never had such a tragedy in her recollection, you see, and afterwards it was all that she thought of. Jack. The war aged women like mother – I should think it did! You could watch it happen after they got the telegram. They'd got all these other children but they aged for the one that was shot. All round here you saw it. That was one way of going old.

I suppose I should mention the workhouse. Don't forget the workhouse! Chance'd be a fine thing. That was a very dreadful thing. That was why you didn't find old souls on their own – they was in the workhouse, I shouldn't wonder. Bulcamp, they used to call it. They promised us Bulcamp if we didn't behave or if we got found out, or if we got *them* found out! Young girls used to be in service in these big houses and they'd be funny things a-goin' on, and when there was trouble it would be the workhouse. Some went in to have a baby and that was where they'd finish. Truth. People don't realize that now, but it's absolutely true. 'You get into muddle, and it's Bulcamp for you!' they'd say. And they meant it! And all the old fellers and women would set at home dreadin' the day when the relievin' officer would find them and drive them off to Bulcamp. 'Good-bye, good-bye . . .'

There was another workhouse down at Chapel Lane in Wickham Market. My father, and sometimes me, used to drive an old clergyman there from Brandeston in the brom [brougham] to take the service. We should ha' saved that brom; we should ha' made money. But we knocked it all up. Those old workhouses – it don't do to think about them. But I went to an old people's hospital-like where my sister had to finish because she'd lost her husband and her children and all, and that was bad enough. No one told me they'd taken her there, I just heard. So I went to see her. She lay there and I thought, 'That's my sister.' We hadn't had a lot to do with one another but I thought, 'That's my sister' so I helped her eat. The nurse went by and she shouted, 'So we have to have a nursemaid now, do we! ha-ha-ha!' I bought her a bed-jacket and a dressin'-gown and slippers. I must have spent £20. But she never wore 'em. I spent me rate money on her. That's the thing that bothers me – goin' in to them places. I never want to finish my time in them places. I've got such a will-power I'll keep goin'. They look after you as well as they can, no doubt, but they're no place to go at the last, no place at all. Keep out of them, keep out of them, I say to myself – just as you'd ha' kept out of the ol' workhouse. Show them your will-power. I never let my mother go; I'm glad of that, that I am.

I had to look after my parents from as way back as the First War. They were allowed half-a-crown a week from my brother in the army and us girls had to keep our parents alive. That's true. I worked at the Royal Artillery Mess at Shoebury-ness and, of course, I could happen on little mites o' things

which I could send home to them, drippin' I bought from the
chef and cheese-ends, and sugar from the bottom of the sacks.
I had to pay the postage but a librarian I knew would get these
parcels out of the Mess for me. The officers had plenty – and
so did the farmers, though we won't go into that – but my
mother often used to say that if they hadn't had the little bit
what I sent they'd have starved. It's the truth. People don't
realize. They say to me now, 'Mrs Cardy, you say this and that,
you stick up for yourself.' But I've had to. I've been through
it all. The young can't understand it – how could they understand it?

Years are passing. There were nine of us and now there are
two. There was a favourite – my brother Don. Don was the
best of all. The others were kind but Don was kindest. When
the tribunal took Don from the farm for the war, my father
nearly dropped dead. The farmer said he could manage
without Don and so he had to go. A lot of the men got off but
when it came to Don the farmer said, 'If the army wants him he
must go.' 'I don't know how I shall live – takin' me sons,' my
father said. 'You'll have the half-a-crown a week,' they said.
Don came home but he went a little bit silly on account of the
shellin' and so he had to go in the Mental Home. I sent him
rusks and coconut-ice. I've kep' a little letter he wrote. I've
been through it, I can tell you! I'm eighty and I don't do so
bad – considerin'.

A Glimpse of the Duke:
the Gamekeeper, aged seventy

I am just on three score year and ten and will write down what
has happened to me in this place. On 10 February 1904 to
Samuel and Emmaretta Pipe a son was born. They already
had four children, two girls and two boys. For three weeks
this child lived at the Half Moon public house, Grundisburgh,

with his family. Very unfortunately at this time his mother died. He was taken by his uncle and aunt to be brought up as their own child although they already had four children, three boys and one girl. This baby boy who was me was called Richard Richardson Pipe. His uncle and aunt were Frank and Rose Richardson. Their eldest boy was called Frank, Albert was their second son, and Tom was their third son, and Mary their daughter. Frank Richardson was a keeper for the Duke of Hamilton at Easton and lived at Park Cottage on the borders of the most beautiful woods and farmland. A very primitive track, one mile in length, led from this cottage to the village.

My earliest memory is that of riding round in my uncle's game-bag and feeding the pheasants. I used to stand up in the bag and hang on to his shoulders. When I was five years old my cousin Mary took me to school in a push-chair. She, like all the other girls at school, wore a red cloak. These cloaks were presented by her Grace and all the girls in the village wore them. It was about a mile to school and during severe winters we were unable to go because of deep snow-drifts. Mary was in the large room and I was in the infants' room.

Park Cottage was situated close to Maids' Wood. It was strongly built of brick covered with ivy. It was always the Duke's wish to have ivy planted against any houses which he had built. Also when planting new plantations to have ivy put against each tree. His Grace loved ivy.

Our drinking water came from a pond which was at the top of the garden. In this pond were many newts, toads, and small fish. I have enjoyed many an hour on its banks, my rod a hazel sapling cut from the hedge, with a bent pin for a hook and dough for bait. They were happy, carefree days. I was very interested in birds and I had red and grey linnets in cages. They were great songsters. In October my aunt, who was sorry to see them shut up, would say, 'Let them go now, Dick,' and I would open the cage doors and out they would go, loving their freedom.

At Park Cottage we had many dogs belonging to the Duke

and Duchess. There were two St Bernards, Trimond and Una. We also had sealyhams and labradors. The sealyhams were used by her Grace for ratting parties during the threshing season. I well remember how Trimond and Una used to howl at the moon and also how I sat on their backs when I was very small. They are buried in the Dogs' Cemetery behind the church. As well as his Grace's dogs we also kept two golden retrievers of our own.

My cousin Bert was in the navy and stationed in India for two years. He was serving in H.M.S. *Highflyer*. One day we received the exciting news that he was coming home on leave. My aunt said, 'You go and watch for him, Dick, and when you see his white hat coming, you call me.' Presently I saw the white hat far away down the long lane. I shouted to my aunt, who came running out of the house with Kiss, Mary's white Persian cat. We three went off to meet him. As he drew near we saw that he had a monkey on his shoulder. It ran down his leg and received a nasty scratch on the nose from Kiss, who did not like the look of him. Bert gave him to me and he was a great novelty in the village for the next year or so. On Saturdays I used to take him to the village shop for sweets. He wore a harness with a small chain attached and in winter he wore a coat.

The Duke of Hamilton's estate was a very large one, taking in Brandeston, Kettleburgh, Hoo, Monewden, Charsfield, Letheringham, Hacheston, Parham, Gt Glemham and other villages. The seat of the Duke was Easton Mansion. There were nine under-keepers and one head keeper, George Meadows. In those days the estate was teaming with game, pheasant, partridge, mallard, snipe and woodcock. There were also thousands of rabbits which were fed on Easton Park. The Duke insisted that they should be fed in sharp weather. These rabbits were of different colours. A man was detailed off with a Suffolk horse and tumbril to feed them with turnips, swedes and other root vegetables. The Duke had two rabbit shoots each year. My uncle told me that on one occasion they shot 1,000 rabbits before lunch. The pock-marks of the shot are still to be seen today on the crinkle-crankle wall which surrounds the park near the Grove. After the shoot the rabbits were taken in a tumbril to the Model Farm where a pit had previously been dug, and they were buried. These rabbits were unfit for human consumption as they were so badly peppered with shot and, anyway, there were these signs of disease in them owing to interbreeding.

Having so much game on the estate inevitably did a good deal of damage to the crops and because of this the farms were let to tenants at reduced rents. The estate was managed by two brothers named Godley. One of them went down on the *Titanic*. Each under-keeper was expected to rear 1,000 pheasants a season and was allowed casual help from one man between 1 April and 31 October. At this time there were several osier-beds on the Duke's estate which were rented to my uncle George Pipe who employed mostly throughout the year eight or nine men in double-digging and replanting the beds with osier sets. The Godley brothers did not encourage my uncle to be in the osier beds during the shooting season as he disturbed the game, so he too was compensated fully for any damage done by hares and rabbits. He started cutting osiers on 2 February as the game season was then out. Game loves osiers and good drives were enjoyed by the Duke and his guests. They were very spectacular shooting times with bags of from 500 to 1,000 pheasants a day. Two marquees were erected near our cottage and lunches were served to the guns, loaders and keepers. The beaters were given half a loaf of bread with half a pound of cheese and two pints of draught beer.

Forty men were employed as beaters, plus a dozen boys who took up positions as blocks [stops]. There were also cartridge boys who wore velvet suits and who carried trays of cartridges for the guns. Cartridges were bought by the ton and were brought by rail to Wickham Market Station and collected by a farm-labourer with a waggon drawn by two horses. They were taken to the Mansion and put in the Gun Room. Many of the beaters came from Wickham Market Foundry and they would pick up the used brass cartridges, take them to the foundry, melt them down and turn them into trinkets. Two policemen always attended the Duke's shoots and they would eye the bulging pockets of the foundrymen in case they were pilfering game. But it was only brass cases.

At the end of the day all the keepers and loaders would be in the Gun Room cleaning their masters' guns and talking about the events of the day. They drank gin and there was laughter and chatter. My uncle could remember when the keepers all wore livery of green velvet with brass buttons and hard hats.

All this was a long way back in my lifetime but I lived it. I remember it all most particularly, aunt, Jacko my monkey, her Grace, the game everywhere, the round houses which the Duke built and all the fun we had.

The Old Man of the New Age: the Chauffeur-Mechanic, aged seventy-seven

There are people my age who have followed things through from start to finish and those who came later won't be able to say that, will they? I was born with the century and I've had to follow the century. I drove the first cars, mended the first wirelesses and bikes, and dealt with the first garages. And you'd hardly call me old – your seventies aren't *old*.

Seven boys left school when I did. I was the only one with a good character, so I went to the Hall. The old gentleman was alive then. I went into the stables. And no sooner was I settled than all the horses went and all the motor-cars came in. The Lady had a motor, the two toffs had one and the Lady also had a landaulette. She always sat outside. And then we had another big motor with a basket at the back, where the footman used to ride. Oh yes, motor, footman and all. Old Crossley was the chauffeur; he'd been there for donkey's years. But the carriages didn't go away. They stood there in their sheds for years and years until they gradually disappeared. Beautiful things, they were. We had to keep them clean although they were never used. And all the harness, the leather, the stirrups, all, all under green baize and under glass. All waiting and ready. If ten years after the motors had come someone had ordered, 'Bring round the carriage,' it could have been done in a jiffy. But nobody did. Because there were all the lovely, lovely motor-cars. All brass. Bright brass. Talbots, Wolseleys, a Starley, a Delage. It got so that I had to spend a month with the electrician – the Hall made its own electric-light – and a month with the chauffeur.

I'll tell you how I learned to drive. There was a shooting party and I had just got this car all washed and polished and clean ready for the pick-up – the guns – when a boy came out of the house to put some dirt in the dustbin. I called out, 'Come for a ride, Harry?' just as a joke, laughing, you know, but then in Harry jumps aside of me, looking pleased and excited. So what could I do? I was sixteen. I'd watched old Crossley with the gear-lever and the brake, and I told myself, 'If he can do it, I can do it.' So I reached for the pedals and suddenly there we were, dashing down the front drive! That drive was a mile long and ended at the bottom lodge, where the village policeman lived. I was driving straight to prison, I told myself, for taking the motor. And could I turn it round and bring it back? But that lovely motor had a cool clutch and four gears and a reverse, and by luck I managed them all – brought it back safe, washed it all over again, and nothing was seen or said. That was the first time I had a drive and I've been driving ever since.

I immediately got a job at another big house as chauffeur-electrician, and extra footman for waiting at table. I got 17s. 6d. a week and lived in, of course. Sometimes the Lady would come out to me towards nightfall and say, 'There's a nice play

on at the Haymarket. Can we make it, Maurice?' Then off
we'd go 100 miles in the Wolseley to London, and very little
on the roads. The Lady went into the theatre and then I'd
find a place to park and sit in the motor. They never gave you
anything. I used to find a bun and wait. They never thought
anything of you at all. You were the servant. I tell myself I'm
pleased those days are gone and then, when I look back on
them, I see that they were good days really. Life is very contra-
dictory. Anyway, back to Suffolk we'd come after the late
theatre with no heating and no windscreen. The Lady slept
in the back like a kitten in silk. Before we started, my job was
cushions here and cushions there. In bed she was behind me,
fast asleep. I was nineteen.

When I was in service I've known what it was like to work
twenty-four hours straight through, perhaps twice a week. It
was because I had to run the electric-light as well as drive the
cars. However late it was when we got back from some
engagement, the car had to be washed and polished in time
for the next day's orders at ten.

Bridge made you late. Bridge kept you up all hours. We'd
go all over Suffolk for the Bridge. Bridge could make one
work day just run into the next without any sleep for a chauffeur
who had to run the electricity. Or you'd done the electricity
and the motors, and it was near dinner-time, and the Lady
would ring because she hadn't got a footman to wait, and she'd
say, 'Hurry, Maurice, you'll have to plaster your hair down
and change and be at table.' I had all these thick curls and they
had to be wetted and flattened-out quick. Whatever the
emergency in the house, the servants all buckled-to. Whatever
the whim, you carried it out. In those days you didn't get many
rich people drive their own cars – they couldn't start 'em, you
see. And, anyway, they were used to having everything done
for them, big and small. People just got in and out of their
cars. It was all wonderfully comfortable. And all gone now,
of course. I don't know whether it's a pity or a fault! Looking
back, you can see that you were all in it together, so to speak.

It was very peculiar. For instance, I had to drive all the way to Felixstowe for *fruit*. Thirty miles once a week. They couldn't buy fruit anywhere else although it was sold everywhere else. No, it was Felixstowe for apples, bananas and pears. Nowadays I often say to myself, 'What on earth was it all about? Who on earth did they think they were?' Why do you think I left there? Because as well as driving, waiting and doing the generator, the gardener said I was to go digging. So I left. I hadn't got a job. But digging!

Soon after I bought a lovely motor-bike, an Alldays and Onions – that was the name of the motor-bike. Then I could ride to work. It was a bicycle place. It was 1928 and everything mechanical was coming in. I used to make push-bikes. We used to buy Reynold's Tubes, which were about twenty-five feet long and if, say, you were a tall man and you wanted a twenty-eight inch frame, we could make it to measure. Push-bikes to measure. You never sent away for the parts then, you just made them. But everybody couldn't afford a bicycle because the poverty was incredible. Hercules bicycles were £3 19s. 6d. and we used to chuck in a lamp and a bell free. Lots of people paid sixpence a week hire-purchase. It wasn't cheap because there was no money about. Poor! People were dirt poor, dirt poor.

Soon my guv'nor sold the bicycle business and went into wireless, and, later, into television. When we did wireless we were making crystal-sets all hours of the night. I kept mainly with the motors and stayed on in the same firm for thirty-four years. Then this last war came along and they took all my mechanics and I stayed there in the garage all alone. And some of the roughest, most thieving people from London came down here to Suffolk. I think they must have let them out of prison to drive lorries. I used to paint the lorries. I could have earned more driving a lorry than painting it, but then I would have lost my reserve and had to go into the army. So there I was, welding old Till and Stevenson buses for the searchlight base, and all manner of things. After the war, the guv'nor put me in the spray shop. It dam' nearly killed me. I wore a mask but it wasn't no good and I had nothing on my eyes. No goggles. The day he lit a bonfire and sent smuts all over a car I had just sprayed decided me. That's enough, I said, I'll have my cards on Friday. So I left and got another job and there I stayed until I drew the pension. So there you are, change, change, change.

2 · The View from the Starting-Post

What do they think has happened, the old fools,
To make them like this? Do they somehow suppose
It's more grown-up when your mouth hangs open and drools . . .
. . . Can they never tell
What is dragging them back, and how it will end? Not at night?
Not when the strangers come? Never, throughout
The whole hideous inverted childhood? Well,
*   We shall find out.*

                              Philip Larkin, 'The Old Fools'

I used to think that grown-up people chose
To have stiff backs and wrinkles round their nose,
And veins like small fat snakes on either hand,
On purpose to be grand.
Till through the bannisters I watched one day
My great-aunt Etty's friend who was going away,
And how her onyx beads had come unstrung.
I saw her grope to find them as they rolled;
And then I knew that she was helplessly old,
As I was helplessly young.

                              Frances Cornford, 'Childhood'

There no child shall ever die an infant,
No old man fail to live out his life;
Every boy shall live his hundred years before he dies,
Whoever falls short of a hundred shall be despised
. . . My people shall live the long life of a tree . . .

                              Isaiah 65: 20–22

That direct stare which passes between the young and the old is high up among the classic confrontations. It prefaces one of the great dialogues of opposites, and contains a frank admission of helplessness on either side, for nothing can be done to blot out the detail of what has been, or block in the detail of what is to come. On the one side is the clean sheet and on the other the crammed page, although the aged man knows only too well that youth isn't pristine and that some of the ugliest marks to be found on the record were made then. As young and old survey each other, there is no envy and little envy respectively. The young do not want to be old, nor do they entirely believe that they ever could be, and the old, generally speaking, do not wish to be young. Once through the gamut of time is enough for most people. What usually occurs is that an aged man finds life surprisingly sweet still and desires more agedness, but not a full repeat trip. The young and the old are also sympathetically linked by their common awareness of the burdensome nature of life, because being strong, and facing the prospect before us, can be as daunting as being weak, and facing the end of the road. In one respect, however, the old have the advantage, for with agedness comes an amazing recall of the talk and actions of youth, exquisite, painful, shaming, triumphant or whatever. The busy decades of work, parenthood and adult drives of all kinds promised to have obliterated these immaturities, and one of the shocks and sensations of old age is the completeness of their recovery. If the young could understand the intensity of this recall it would be enough to make them deliberately do things worth the recalling, a kind of burying of spring's trophies to be dug up for nourishment in the winter. So the main difference in the confrontation is that the young do not realize that they are accumulating the memories which, in old age, will often enough, alone, make them interesting and tolerable to youth. For it is a bitterness which no amount of common sense can lessen that memories are about the only thing that youth will want from age.

There are further linkings. The young and the old protest and grouse. Florida Scott-Maxwell says, 'We old are the wailers!' but then so are we young. Not much wailing goes on during our lengthy middle period. It is all at the start and finish, and it is caused by us first caring for more and more, and getting our ideals dragged down into the possible, and secondly, as Auden put it, via self-disgust, thinning blood and nipped vision, we find ourselves caring less about more and more. To be forced into either state by one's age is agony and guilt. And so the aged and the young wail from their different states of impotence, and out of great passions for which those in middle life on their more pragmatic levels have no use. They wail because they are dead serious in a world which finds them either too young or too old to take seriously. Old age sometimes recovers the seriousness of youth which middle age lost or put aside because of its inconvenience. Similarly, it can also mock the stolidity of the adult-controlled universe with words and attitudes which the young find conspiratorial. They know that just as in this universe the young are thought not to have politically, sexually and economically arrived, they are assumed to be politically, sexually and economically finished, and so theirs is often a wail to prove life and breath. It has to be remembered that some of the most radical, as well as the most reactionary letters in the newspapers are written by very old men and women, and where a little incaution is required to get things going, the aged can be as much counted upon to provide it as the young. Both have an indignant sense of being dictated to. The old challenge authority because they have exercised its pretensions, the young because they cannot believe that they will ever have to.

Physically, the old and the young are less disturbing to each other than either group is to the middle-aged. The aorta may begin to collect at seven years old those fat deposits which guarantee the gradual downhill trudge to senescence, but ageing is unlikely to shake our confidence for a good half-century

beyond this point. It is usually in their mid-fifties that many
people hear themselves referred to, or observe that they are
being treated, as old for the first time. Curious and unmanageable things can happen then which will become less curious,
and thus more manageable, later on. Such as imagining that
the demonstrative affection of a twenty-year-old is a sign of
desire, when it is actually a sign of kindness allied to an
assumption that there is nothing to fear. The middle-aged
frequently find themselves, timidly yet compulsively, like
tonguing a tooth nerve, measuring their assets against those
of youth to see what they have left, and against those of old
age to see what has to go. It is often a great deal in both cases.
There can be then a spiritual and physical drawing-back from
the old, as if they possessed some centrifugal force to drag the
no-longer young into their slipstream decay. Many still
sexually attractive men and women in their fifties, and at the
height of their careers and intellectual interests, have to disguise their loathing of old people. This repulsion can even
extend to hospitals and geriatric institutions where two different kinds of sensitivity can be seen at work, that of the young
doctors and nurses, which is non-self-protective because they
cannot conceive that what they are seeing will ever apply to
themselves, and the sensitivity of the middle-aged which is
like the formal decoration covering a tough shield. Youth on
the geriatric ward is made to feel supra-wholesome by age's
contrasting unwholesomeness. It may tell itself that it too will
have to come to it, but it does not believe that it will. The
middle-aged, on the other hand, find themselves at the source
of a time contagion and their compassion is proffered at arm's
length. The old do not fear the young but they are ever conscious of the lengths to which self-preservation in the not-so-
young will go, and they frequently fear them.

The most pleasurable and rewarding relationship in old age
is that with young grandchildren, pre-pubertal boys and girls,
with all of whom the grandparent can enter into a rich con-
spiracy of stories, embraces, secrets, bribes, teachings and

even sly battles mounted against mother, school, etc. When children are invited to discuss old age they tend to divide it into a popular journalistic 'problem' which has to be dealt with in the caring jargon expected of an enlightened person – and gran. Gran and grandad, even if they are in an old people's home, but particularly if they are living in their own house, are not connected with the 'problem'. But then in many cases gran is well under sixty when one is ten. So the child's inability to relate her to the 'problem' as he vaguely thought, or as he tenderly comprehends it via talk of pensions, special housing, television documentaries and charity advertisements, or by comparing her to an incredibly seamed and crooked neighbour in her eighties, is understandable.

All the old people spoke of *their* grandmothers as looking like grandmothers, although they were just on fifty. They half approved of their special dark, stiff clothes which insisted upon an elderly stance. The poorest countrywoman gained rank, particularly in the eyes of her grandchildren, when she put them on. Instead of indicating that she was moving towards departure these clothes announced her immutability. Here she was – for ever! The grandparental rock even now, with nothing much to offer by way of the passing on of mysteries, is too monumental a structure in a child's world for him to connect it with the rickety, grey realm of the geriatric which he already knows it is his duty to pray for, save for and which will outnumber his generation before the century is out. The most recurring pity which ten to seventeen-year-olds voiced about their grandparents was not about their agedness but that they 'had no money' when they were young. This strikes them as a savage fate. That the majority of them did not have higher education appears less socially divisive to the grandchildren than to their parents. In fact, where there have been two educated generations, a teenager is often moved and fascinated by the quite different culture of his grand-parents, particularly should it be based on something as all-pervasive as mining, fishing or farming.

Whilst increasing longevity is causing many more people to retain all four grandparents far into their adulthood, most adolescents and children have far fewer old relations than their Victorian ancestors, fifty years being accepted as old then. This was not only because big families produced numerous elderly aunts and uncles, but because of the fashion of parents giving certain close family friends 'aunt' and 'uncle' status or for covering up illicit relationships with these trustworthy titles. Much innocent incest occurred in the past, and many marriages took place within the family because actual relationships were either kept dark or simply forgotten. But a nineteenth-century child would have taken elderliness as a normal part of his home background, as frequently a considerable number of late middle-aged relatives, assisted by such things as a growing toothlessness and taboos on cosmetics and hair dyes, displayed to them the undisguised results of being seventy and eighty. Nor would he have associated these ancients specifically with death, as we tend to do our old people, for child mortality then was so inescapable a fact of life that, once having grown up or even grown old, it could make it seem that one had put a comfortable distance between oneself and death. The cradle and the grave were once terribly adjacent. Now they are accepted as being as far apart as anything can be in this life, wars and accidents permitting. And modern grandparents not playing an aged role until the very last, and this when their grandchildren are usually adult, there is now a very long stretch of life from birth to well past retirement where death, if thought of at all, is regarded as an anomaly. Thus old age is dreaded because it has become the only *normal* death-age, and children, when asked to consider it, find it hard to imagine that it possesses its own special liveliness. Their concern, when it is aroused by humanitarian arguments and social-welfare debates, is directed towards that almost impossible group, the near-dead, in which it is rare for them to discover anyone they know, including their grandparents.

An adolescent finds growing to be like his father undesirable, and growing to be like his grandfather simply incredible. The future has to be some number like twenty-one for it to belong to him in any acceptable personal sense. After that, time rolls its wastes before him with such featureless extravagance that often he cannot believe that youth will ever end, let alone life itself. For him an old man is beyond the imaginable future. He has gone as far as he can without ceasing to be and apart from this feat he is negative. If you go on living and living, you will end up with old age putting you on the spot; the young can recognize this and are intrigued by your predicament. But not because it could ever be their own. Their compassion is a detached emotion and their inquisitiveness a convention. It will remain a polite form of intimacy for years to come.

'I should like to ask you' [says Sydney Carton to the seventy-seven-year-old Jarvis Lorry in *A Tale of Two Cities*], 'does your childhood seem far off? Do the days when you sat upon your mother's knee seem days of very long ago?'

Responding to his softened manner, Mr Lorry answered: 'Twenty years back, yes; at this time of my life, no. For, as I draw closer and closer to the end, I travel in a circle nearer and nearer to the beginning. It seems to be one of the kind of smoothings and preparings of the way. My heart is touched now by many remembrances that had long fallen asleep, of my pretty young mother (and I so old!), and by many associations of the days when what we call the World was not so real with me, and my faults were not confirmed in me.'

It is a familiar confession and a dividing one. The young man in this instance, because of his impending fate, is not detached from it. To die young is to escape being confirmed in evil and also that great natural rounding-off which brings one back to the inception. The concept of life being a straight line a brief way along which youth can be 'cut off', and of life being a circle around which age will stiffly wheel until it returns to base, are the Hellenic and post-Hellenic concepts respectively. The Greeks saw life as a thread-like stretch of straight road, the first happy miles of which could be strode along in the sunshine, and the last in increasing gloom. It was part of their realism not to expect anything worth having during the latter part of the journey and for it to be accounted a blessing not to live a long time. To even have reached early middle age was, for them, a fatality of the senses and they could have said with Iras, 'The bright day is done, and we are for the dark.' They did not look forward to or wish each other a long life – 'Whom the gods love die young,' wrote Menander, a sentiment echoed by the Roman poet Plautus, who saw early death as a divine favour.

Contemporary youth is in many ways sympathetic to this attitude, more so, perhaps, than any generation of the young has been for centuries. Their chief difference is that although they worship the first part of life as extravagantly as did the Greeks, they don't want to die when it is over. Since the 1950s youth has become increasingly conscious of its own specialness and, assisted by many sophisticated industries catering exclusively for its tastes and demands, has formed itself into a multi-national club with pitiless rules. Whoever one is, if one is young there is membership. Or, whoever one is and if one is *not* young (and those who are know instinctively), there is no getting past the barrier. The young themselves have sub-divided their youth into periods so that to have taken part in some recent but discarded movement, such as flower-power, or to have been associated with a vanished pop-group cult, is to reek of senescence. Modern youth has to clamber out of its own geriatric formulae before it can see what a lot of youth there is to live beyond the pale, so to speak. Possessing as it does a clock which says that the old age of the young is thirty, it is no wonder that youth should think of old age proper simply as an academic disaster. Unlike the Greeks, the young today do not dread this disaster. What they dread most is not being young to the young, that awful day of exclusion when, somehow, they have to go on living outside the perfect category. They are hit badly then. It is a temporary blow, of course, a comparative tragedy. And age remains comparative right up until the end. 'She's our baby,' say the octogenarian inmates of an old people's home of a seventy-five-year-old, and it wasn't quite a joke. The younger woman spoke and behaved more youthfully because of it. 'The girls have gone on ahead,' remarked an old man of his eighty-year-old wife and her sister, and watching the tall, receding figures one saw them shed decades. The advantage of our times over all others is that, due to modern hygiene, limited work and incomparably improved health standards, once we no longer qualify for the youth cult, we can stay 'young' virtually until we are old. Society no longer requires the posture and attitudes of age in a grandparent or in a retired person. But when old age does come after such a protracted period of permitted youthfulness, it is often shocking.

The Greeks found any attempt to mitigate the fact of old age by the various agencies of youth, tasteless and even blasphemous. Although they did wonder what purpose the gods had in mind for inventing such a horror, for it made no sense to men. Euripides said that it was because the gods did not think like men, for if they did they would reward virtue with the gift of a second youth. R. W. Livingstone, in his book *The Greek Genius and its Meaning to Us*, says that it was not the miseries of old age which worried them so much as the loss of beauty and strength. Plato is almost alone in accepting its mellowness: nearly every other Greek writer attacks it with virulence and abuse, and even Sophocles, in *Oedipus at Colonus*, sinks to the usual execration when the chorus spits at 'the final lot of man, even old age, hateful, impotent, unsociable, friendless, wherein all evil of evil dwells'. To the ancient poets generally it is 'detested', 'dismal', 'oppressive', etc., and all these things, not because it is itself, *but because it is not youth*. One of Plato's favourite proverbs – he quotes it no

less than five times – is, 'First comes health, second personal
beauty, then wealth honestly come by, fourthly to be young
with one's friends.' It was life seen under the brightest light.
Only youth could bear it. When youth went, all that made
life worth living went with it. The so-called compensations of
getting older had no significance. If a passage in *The Republic*
can be taken to represent the common attitude, the Greeks
could even mock the old in their total loathing of all that they
stood for. An old man confesses to Plato:

> I and a few other people of my own age are in the habit
> of frequently meeting together. On these occasions most
> of us give way to lamentations, and regret not having the
> pleasures of youth, and call up the memory of love affairs
> and drinking parties, and similar proceedings. They are
> grievously discontented at the loss of what they consider
> to be great privileges, and describe themselves as living
> well in those days, whereas now, by their own account,
> they cannot be said to live at all! Some also complain of the
> manner in which their relatives insult their infirmities,
> and make this a ground for reproaching old age with the
> many miseries it occasions them.

Plato blames such distress – and much else – on the Greeks'
worship of the physical. To be worshipful the physical had
to be ideal, i.e. young. An irrational element entered this
worship when the physical did what it must in its nature do,
decay. Seeing what unhappiness this worship must lead to,
Plato shocked his contemporaries by inveighing against the
physical itself, whether young or old, as an object of undue
concern. Livingstone describes how Plato's vocabulary swept
along in 'metaphors of detestation' against the body, and was
listened to as a great heresy by his circle:

> Young or old, the body is the oyster-shell of our
> imprisonment, the fetter in which we are chained, the
> quack that cheats us. It wastes our time with outcries for

food, hampers us with diseases, betrays us to lusts, terrors, phantoms; distracts us into the quest for money, and thereby involves us in disputes, factions and wars. Even if we are at leisure and betake ourselves to some speculation, the body is always breaking in upon us, causing turmoil and confusion in our inquiries, and so amazing us that we are prevented from seeing the truth.

The metaphysical factor has entered Western consciousness and man as a beautiful animal stops admiring himself in the hard light of morning. He sees his flesh now as grass, green and running before the wind, then sere and falling before the blade. When the drying-up is accepted as being no more unnatural than the growing-up, the pathetic note is sounded. Livingstone says that Plato destroyed the unity of uncorrupted body and soul which to the early Greeks was Man because he detected in its golden concept the stain of an alloy. This stain was senescence. And so Plato divided the spirit from the flesh. Flesh must always be transient, the spirit need not be. And so there was a way to survive, even a way to stay glorious. From this point it could be said that life ceased to be a straight road along which a man walked from dazzling morning to loathsome night, and became instead a circle which brought him back to where he set out from. With human life caught up in the immutable rounds of the stars and seasons, youth lost its divinity and old age its anathema. Life's journey came to be seen as all of a piece and, set against the aeonic wheeling of the years, slight and ephemeral even at its most protracted. To be eighteen, to be eighty, what was it but to be momentarily whirled into and out of physical existence by Time? It was the total existence which provided the vital interest, not any fraction of it.

Pindar always addressed himself to the young when he wrote of old age, though with a special earthiness. He wrote for the athlete, or the male at his zenith, and reminded him that 'heaven allots two sorrows to man for every good thing'.

He thought the greatest human misfortune was Moira or the fatedness which prevented a man, whether young or old, from directing his own affairs. It was an outlook which would intrigue Hardy and Matthew Arnold. Pindar wrote:

> Who, in his tenderest years,
> Finds some new lovely thing,
> His hope is high, and he flies
> On the wings of his manhood;
> Better than riches are his thoughts.
> But man's pleasure is a short time growing
> And it falls to the ground
> As quickly, when an unlucky twist of thought
> Loosens its roots.
> Man's life is a day. What is he?
> What is he not?
> A shadow in a dream is man . . .

With luck, thought Pindar, there was a sporting chance of a summery hereafter where one might wrestle or race chariots, or play the lute under the incense trees. To the Greeks' intellectual 'why?', Pindar replies, 'Why not?' If we live long enough we shall certainly be 'walking with a sick body, yet so it was fated to be'. But whether we live long or briefly, we shall die, so to lose youth is not necessarily to lose out or lose all, for what we think of as the reality could be the dream. 'Why not?'

Hesiod calls the three ages of man sweat, thought and prayer, none of which will 'stay the plague of death, or keep old age away' but which will certainly fashion and shape the life-span. For him the 'sweat' was not of work but again of play – the running-track and the stadium. He is saying that there are other forms of strenuousness and other goals in life than the physical. We have to win intellectually in middle age and contemplatively in old age. There should be no let up, no part of our living when there is nothing to strive for. At whatever stage, there exists a goal. Distress comes when we continue to aim at earlier goals. The poet Tyrtaeus, who loved and romanticized war, went so far as to include this among the games in which old men should never participate. He finds it hard to say which is the most indecent, a young man hanging around in the company of old men rather than being in the thick of battle, or finding an old man's body on the battlefield. The old man's courage is admitted but it does not excuse a basic tastelessness in an action which brings about the contamination of the young heroes with his ancient heroics:

> O foul reproach, when fallen with the foremost
> lies an elder, hindermost the young –
> A man whose head is white, whose beard is hoary,
> breathing out his strong soul in the dust,
> In nakedness his blood-wet members clutching –
> foul reproach, a sight no gods condone!
> Naked he lies where youth were better lying –
> sweet flow'rd youth, that nothing misbecomes.

Except that it is youth and middle age which define what is unbecoming conduct in the old, not the old who feel it. Their acceptance of standards of seemliness in areas where, privately and deeply personally, no unseemliness is felt, is one of the major concessions which the aged have to make to society. The Greeks, in common with all civilizations, demand, of course, that the old are never embarrassing about sex. Mimnermus hopes that he will die before he becomes 'an old man hateful to maiden and boy, and fashioned by the gods for their annoy'. When one is young it is impossible to imagine that something so acutely overwhelming as sexual desire can be repressed, or to associate an emotion which appears to be the prerogative of youthfulness with senescence. Yet we know, inconvenient though it may be to society, that many old people retain a strong sexuality. When, as it usually is, this is accompanied by experience, technique and that releasing of the libido which occurs at this time, the longings it creates can be as troubling in their way as those of adolescence. But should there be any manifestation of an old person not being in full repressive control of these urges he or she is seen as either dangerous or pathetic, though nastily so in both instances. The old often live half lives because they know that they would arouse disgust and fear if they attempted to live whole lives. All passion is not necessarily spent at seventy and eighty but it pays the old to behave as though it is. Teenagers incline to be more amused than disgusted (as young and middle-aged people are) by geriatric sexuality, and they will often listen to the courtship reminiscences of sixty or more years ago with a similar kind of raciness to that of the speaker. Elderly people who are prim with their middle-aged children are frequently sexually open in their talk with grandchildren.

The will to live in the old was an even more aberrant notion to the Greeks than that the old should make love, and few of their writers described it. But Anacreon, who lived to be eighty-four, when his teeth were 'a ragged row', still did not want to die. He was deep in years but not so hopelessly deeply out of the world as the dead, who were beyond any chance of 'scaling the upward track and winning their journey back'. Where there was life there was hope. Whilst the conventional view of his countrymen towards the life he spoke of was that it was bitter and revolting, Anacreon asked to be allowed more time to taste it with joy. To want more time is the one thing which is quite beyond the teenager's comprehension. Here the longings and demands of the old become mysterious to him.

Many old people, however, appear to reach a point and then make a declaration. 'This is as far as I will go,' or, 'This is as far as I will let it take me.' Like Oedipus, who reminds a friend that

> to the gods alone
> belongs immunity from death and age:
> All else doth all-controlling time confound.

Earth's strength decays, the body's strength decays,
Faith dies, and faithlessness bursts into flower . . .

they remind God that they have reached a dangerous situation
and that they are not going to face up to it. Sophocles, who
lived to be ninety, made those who outlive their day 'redouble
all sorrows under the sun' and totter along in a 'ruining over-
flow'. Intellectual vigour preserved him from this fate and
made him attractive to young friends to the last.

> How blessed Sophocles, who, dying old,
> Was old in happiness and skill of hand.
> Beautiful were his Tragedies, and many;
> And beautiful his end, who lived untroubled

wrote one of them. It is among the few positive views of old
age to be found in Greek literature. There is a current notion
that this active serenity belongs to the wishful thinking of the
young, and not to the experience of the elderly, but it is less
rare than is commonly thought. It usually derives from
benefits, balances and assurances which go far back into an
individual's past, and is not just an eightieth birthday present.
Euripides, who reached his seventies, put up a fight against
age, which he called woebegone and murderous, by continuing to work. Call this work his swan-song, if you like, but
it will be a sound which will help his contemporaries to
'destroy the beasts of their fear', as he said. He is daring: 'Old
as I am, a swan melodious from the grey down of cheeks to
sing.' But this bravado does not last and, looking around, he
has to admit that the old men he knows are nothing but noise
and shape, and no more than the mimicries of dreams. The
poet Palladas, who died aged seventy, rejected the accumu-
lation of wisdom principle and saw each day as a birth and a
death. Many old people – and almost no young person –
accept this.

> From day to day we are born, as each night wanes,
> And nothing of our former life remains.

The alien course of yesterday is run;
What life we have this morning is begun.
Say not, old man, that you are rich in age:
Of years gone by you keep no heritage.

The young do not see the old struggling along in day-to-day births and night-to-night deaths, and organizing themselves to cope alternatively with the light and dark hours. However fragile they are, they regard them as monoliths, hard and enduring from all that has happened to them. In the past a young man looked at an old man and said, 'It is myself,' and shuddered. In the present a young man will look at an old man and say, 'He is my brother,' and help. Self-detachment allows him to participate in things which would be unendurable to the self-identifying. This helping of the brother who can in no way be oneself has become a cult. It may bring an old man some comfort but it also makes him uneasy.

The old man recollected his childhood demand of 'tell me a story' and then realized that he had lived past the point where it would be possible to 'live happily ever after'. If they lived happily ever after, 'they grew old, no doubt, and how did they manage then?' But he admitted that old age need not necessarily kill all the happiness that youth hopes for. To have known happiness is to know it, though to a shrunken degree, most likely, until the end. And he was supported by those great sights of his own past which nurse and dutiful visitors could never see, pleasures and successes which had actually happened to him and him alone. He said that they gave him poise. In fairy-tales it was the virtuous actions of youth which guaranteed the happy-ever-after.

His grandparents apart, a child's first confrontation with either the powerfulness or the powerlessness of the aged is via the nursery-rhyme and the fairy-tale. Here is age as an anything than burnt-out condition. Benign or wicked, it is a positive force which the young have to contend with. The negative realities of the old woman –

And nothing she had,
And so this old woman
was said to be mad.
She'd nothing to eat,
She'd nothing to wear,
She'd nothing to lose,
She'd nothing to fear,
She'd nothing to ask,
She'd nothing to give.
And when she did die,
She'd nothing to leave

– are rare. The Grimm brothers in the ferocious stories they collected present age as an enemy. It is vampirish. Its only use for youth is as a source of nourishment to its own strength. In 'Hansel and Gretel' old parents twice expose their children to death because there isn't enough food for themselves and their offspring, and when another old person finds them she intends to sustain herself by devouring their young flesh. In 'Faithful John' an old king arranges things so as to control the free will of his son from the tomb. The young man defies this over-protection, kindly meant though it is, and after many risks and perils he finds his own fulfilment and joy. In 'Snow-White' an ageing beauty wants to murder the loveliness of youth. In the cruelly anti-semitic 'Jew Among Thorns', the old and the rich try to cheat the young and the poor. In 'The Six Servants' an old woman works out a system to stop a young woman marrying. Most of these evil old people are bested by youth, and in the most hideous manner. Youth stamps them into the ground in its revulsion, as it might an infected old rat. Youth's pay-off for the old in Grimm is pitiless.

Hans Andersen, on the other hand, introduces some of the most subtle and kindly studies of old age in fiction. In his stories the old and the young link hands in acts of common preservation, or the old act as guardians to youth, and as

magicians when all else fails. The old help the young in order
to awaken feeling and responsibility in them. They are pushing
them towards emotional maturity. They strike bargains. Love
us and we will protect you. The amount of childish involvement in old age in his work is remarkable. The old retain the
reins, comically if necessary, as in 'The Garden of Paradise',
when the wildest of all young men, the Four Winds, though
blowing free in every other respect, never get out of the control of their earthy old mother. In a strange tale about bachelor-
hood as a chronic condition, it is the ancient widower who
weds the pretty girl rejected by his adult sons. In 'The
Naughty Boy', an old poet gives a beautiful lad shelter for the
night – and receives Cupid's arrow in his heart for his pains.
In 'Holger Danske' a great-grandfather is recognized as the
repository of patriotism, and venerated. 'The Elder-Tree
Mother' is one of the greatest allegories of old age – 'Some
call me Elder-Tree Mother, and some Dryad, but my real name
is Memory.' In 'The Buckwheat' a widow weeps at the hubris
of youth and in 'The Old House' a small boy sees an old man
and wonders if anyone gives him kisses. He is told, 'Nothing
will ever be given to him again except his funeral; he is *old*.'
The little Match Girl, dying from cold, strikes her last matches,
not to warm herself but because her beloved grandmother's
face appears briefly in the flame. 'The Old Street Lamp' and
'The Fir Tree' both deal with discardment.

In Andersen it isn't age itself which receives the respect of
the young but decent, dignified age. Wise age. Selfless age.
When an old china mandarin attempts to break up what he
considers to be an unsuitable passion between a china shep-
herdess and a china chimney-sweep, he goes too far and is
smashed to smithereens. And occasionally the young will
destroy the old even when they have been good to them, like
the soldier who kills an old woman who has smothered him in
gifts because he has to possess the very means by which she
can be so generous – her tinder-box. He wants her authority
and not just what she can give him by exercising it. In 'Ole

Luk Oie' Andersen presents the comforter of the old and the dream-provider to the young. The Dustman polarizes oblivion. The young sleep to dream, the old to forget. 'It is incredible how many elderly people there are always wanting to have me with them, especially those who have done something bad . . . "Come and drive our thoughts away," they say.' How far Andersen has influenced children's literature it is hard to say, but he remains the leader of those storytellers who see a special relationship between the newcomers to the world and those about to leave it. His advice to the elderly is, 'Learn to be forgotten and yet to live.'

Emile Cammaerts, a Belgian poet and patriot who lived in England and who was intrigued by the character of its inhabitants, was struck by the Englishman's refusal to grow old and grave. His high seriousness seemed reserved for sport, not for the seniority of his years. 'I remember hearing a schoolmaster shouting to his boys during a football match, "Don't *play* with it," meaning the ball – and wondering what such an exclamation could mean. I did not know then that it is only on the Continent that games are *played*; in England they are *performed*, like a stage drama or some kind of religious rite.' He also found that the English writers' craving for poetry was another consequence of the race's 'childlike spirit'. The supremely authoritative gestures were not made by whiteheads on benches but by middling-good players on golf courses and cricket pitches. He might have added in the pew at the average eleven o'clock Matins. Americans too are said to find the old Englishman disconcertingly young and *not* playing the game where years are concerned.

One of the most influential of children's authors, Kenneth Grahame, lived the full span with little mental or physical sign of ageing at all. He was one of those people who,when they die, do so as an old boy, rather than an old man. At fifty, a friend said, the creator of the immensely influential *The Wind in the Willows* and *The Golden Age*, remained 'almost beatifically young, with the clear and roseate complexion of a healthy child'. Although he was an astute businessman holding an important position in the Bank of England, Grahame retained the wide-eyed, untouched air of an innocent lad who was still under nursery law. This innocence, his biographer Peter Green states, began initially as a deliberate act:

> When, many years later, Kenneth Grahame came to create the idealized picture of his childhood, his main object was to preserve something essentially transient from oblivion, a talisman against time and change. [Sir Walter Scott's *The Talisman* lay by Grahame's side the night he died.] Each successive blow at his sense of permanence and stability drove him further in upon himself. In *The Golden Age* and *Dream Days* he set down the vision he had had before, like Traherne, he was 'corrupted by the dirty devices of this world'; they are his bulwark, the fragments he has stored against his ruins. The quality he values above all is timelessness. Time destroys legends, puts children beyond the reach of fantasy, gives no warning of coming bereavement. 'Time Tryeth Trothe', runs the inscription on the sundial in *The Golden Age* . . .

Kenneth Grahame's ruins were as real as any man's. He was in the world for seventy-three years and they carried plenty enough effluent to contaminate the pure waters of the River Bank – his association with the fairly grown-up *Yellow Book*, the threat of proletarian politics – 'I divide the whole population of Europe into English people and Blacks' – and the decapitated body of his only son on the railway line at Oxford – yet he contrived a way of preventing them from doing so. And his genius for propagating a delicious English myth comprising 'the Cockayne of boating, food and rural seclusion', as his biographer describes it, prevented these limpid currents from becoming murky in the lives of his countless readers too. As he aged, Grahame spent increasingly long stretches of his life simply idling. If it were possible, he became more and more unmarked by what was happening to him, his eyes clearer and his large white moustache more dazzling. Shortly before he died A. A. Milne scripted *The Wind in the Willows* for the stage, and there was consternation! Milne had, they said, made the error (blasphemy, they meant) of setting out to please children only, from a book which, although it had begun as a bedtime story told to 'Mouse' (Grahame's son), was now a manifesto for thousands of Grahame's contemporaries on how to stop the clock.

His last months were very strange. Although he suffered from high blood pressure, arteriosclerosis and fatty degeneration of the heart, he talked and walked like a man half his age. He plagued his stingy, nanny-like wife for tuck and was always slipping out of the house to buy ice-creams. He spent the last afternoon of his life by the river that had inspired a masterpiece which, he said, 'was clean of the clash of sex', and he died early the next morning of a cerebral haemorrhage. His gravestone at Oxford says that 'he passed the River on 6th July, 1932'. It was on the double drift of the Fowey and the Thames, not Lethe or Jordan, that he floated away, two English streams which had sailed him past the points where the perils of maturity lurked.

Had he deliberately set out to retain his first responses to life, which he did not, for it appears that staying-put in his boyhood was his way of emotional progression, Grahame could have cited some imposing authorities for his decision. He could also have claimed that, unlike most men, in his old age he was not regressive, for not having moved on from the realms of infancy, idealistically speaking, he did not have to return to them. The child, says Simone de Beauvoir, surpasses the adult by the wealth of its possibilities, the vast range of its acquisitions and its emotional freshness. The child, says Wordsworth, is a free agent because it has not yet entered the prison-house of adulthood. So, is it an advancement or a decline when our infinite possibilities shrivel to a pittance of achievements? Here the imaginative writers and the scientific writers are often at odds, although the literature of both eloquently agrees on the superiority of our first sixteen or so years on the earth. It also agrees that we each have something like fifty years' peak-like ascent which gives us growing perspectives and broadening views before we start the shorter descent, and have to put up with a gradually restricted scene and, consequently, a diminishing interest in it. One school suggests that greenness is not rawness but a state of primal vitality which returns as a kind of recollective strength to nourish us in sere old age. The other that ripeness is all. None of us can so plan our lives that they do not mature because this would require a very un-child-like decision. And so when we very occasionally meet with adults who are 'innocent' we know that this is not the innocence of inexperience, or of an applied morality, but a rare endemic quality. Such people know little about either ripeness or greenness. They are grown-up in wisdom when a child, and a child when mature. In old age their bodies seem to have had very little to do with chronological time and, because their intelligence is still busily and unexhaustedly accepting possibilities, their fantasies are not retrospective. But just as a few of us do not grow *down*, in Wordsworthian terms, neither does everybody like the notion of maturation. Albert Schweitzer found the word 'ripe' applied to a human being depressing. He wrote:

What we are usually invited to contemplate as 'ripeness' in a man is the resignation of ourselves to an almost exclusive use of reason. One acquires it by copying others and getting rid, one by one, of the thoughts and convictions which were dear to us in the days of one's youth. We believed once in the victory of truth; but we do not now. We believed in our fellow-men; but we do not now. We believed in goodness; we do not now. We trusted in the power of kindness and peaceableness; we do not now. We were capable of enthusiasm; but we are not so now. To get through the shoals and storms of life more easily we have lightened our craft. Our craft is now easier to manage, but we ourselves are in a decline.

When we are very old and there are whole continents of spent time in our wake and to re-walk in memory, the general tendency is for us to avoid the heart-lands which absorbed such a massive proportion of our adult energies and to return over and over again to where we were before we became anyone or anything. To where we were still all in the making. Some old people even manage to recover that delectable serial dreaming in which they indulged, half-awake, half-asleep, in the years approaching puberty, and to slip back into the role which satisfied them then and gave each day its rich inner life. They are constant visitors to a vanished geography, whether of village or town, and are at home in gardens under the concrete bus-park and in fields and meadows beneath runways, or in traffic-less lanes, or in streets with strong identities and familiar passing faces below the office blocks. The twentieth-century dead are still within the gift of living recollection. Neither World War Two bombing nor post-war gutting of so many of Britain's beautiful city centres will have absolutely destroyed them for as long as there are old people left to regress to them. And while there is pleasure in this compulsive backward viewing, there is also a comforting sort of misery very similar to that which children experience when they hug their own secrets to themselves when they feel the adult world's selfishness and injustice. The old are also not so much nostalgic or contemplative travellers into past time as moths being dragged back over and over again to what has come to mean their real incandescence. Age is a great all-over dulling of body and spirit, and men and women find escape routes from the cumbersome greyness to the days when they leapt and shone. But often the intensity of non-stop remembrance is not refreshing. It exhausts, and one old lady longed for a visitor to 'stop my thoughts of my life going around and around, and wearing me out'. She liked, too, to sit on a public seat and 'stare at the pretty children – they do me good. I forget "me" when I'm seeing them. You get very sick of "me" when you're my age. I daresay that that's the worst of being old, having all this "me" in your head!'

One of the fearful developments in the consciousness of many old people is that, in the eyes of society, they have become another species. Ironically, an intensive caring and concern for their welfare is frequently more likely to suggest this relegation than indifference and neglect. The growing bureaucracy, amateur and professional, voluntary and state, for dealing with geriatrics, makes some old folk feel that they no longer *quite* belong to the human race any more. They want those who really knew them as fully operative human beings to speak up for them. To tell these efficient planners who appear to be corralling them off from the other generations who they really are. Then they recall that the teacher, the employer, the priest, the neighbour, the lover, and 'Mr So-and-so with whom I dealt for forty-two years', are all dead, and that *nobody* knows them as they were. Children are frankly pitying, frankly amused or frankly affectionate where old age is concerned. Or frankly horrified. Nor, like Charles Dickens, can they see any evidence of a second childhood in senility. 'It is a poor, hollow simulacrum of it, as death is a simulacrum of sleep,' wrote Dickens. 'Where in the eyes of a senile man is the light and vivacity that laugh in the eyes of a child? . . . blush at that emptiness which libels the happy beginning of our life by giving its name to this horrible and convulsive limitation.'

In Dickens the old are extremely alarming figures and the young are rewarded if they don't fly from them or avoid them, or aren't rude to them. Dickens obliges his boys and girls to stand fast before the gorgon-head of influential geriatrics. He never asks them to understand old age, only to let it meddle, usually in some labyrinthine manner, in their future lives. His old people are sentimental grotesques with a wide-ranging power still, and a faint unease runs through even the most benign of his old person–infant relationships. All his old people, good and bad alike, flaunt their incorrigibility before the young. 'There is no *un*becoming what we have become', is their message. The young today see a mainly powerless old person and hear, via the ceaseless debate on the subject, about the economic consequences of this powerlessness. An old man is full of warnings, not promise, and would like to tell his grandson about Life, but he finds that he can never get very far without getting stuck in his own life, which is not what he meant. Always, always, it pipes to him from afar and his present quarter-alive self goes to meet it with all the imaginative strength it can muster. This long-ago childhood at first appears to him as amazingly accurate in all its detail. It is only when he begins to relate it to the boy who, so curiously, is wearing his expression and whose eyes and hair are his own made new again, that the accuracy crumbles, and stories emerge which, although truthful, are at the same time a travesty of his experience.

The old are only marginally interested in the talk of the young. The effort to listen to future-orientated ideas is enormous. Grandparental indulgence, politeness or a need to be wanted will produce an attentive ear for a short while. Then comes the exhaustion and a tedium built upon knowing that one had possessed, once, all that creativity – and where had it got one? Eighty doesn't want to listen to eighteen, it wants to tell it things. 'We want,' wrote John Cowper Powys,

> of course in a general way to make a favourable impression and to be admired and liked; but in the heat and excitement of the moment the universal craving to be listened to, just simply to be heard, while we complain and explain, confess and accuse, narrate and recall, soon sweeps away – at least *till afterwards* – all worrying speculation as to the impression produced by our monologue on the other person. Only to be heard! Only to fill the *whole* stage for one blessed interval!

It could be that the young, who are great cravers, have a special sympathy with a final craving to have one's say. And that this is the bond.

In the Sixth Form

'We are going to talk about old age,' says Robin. 'Nothing personal, you understand, as we are seventeen! I suppose that thirty could seem old to us at our age.'

'Some people *are* old at thirty,' says Tim. 'They are so bigoted. You aren't young any more when you aren't flexible. Seventy wouldn't be at all old for others; they aren't stiff in the head. They have stayed young inside and you can see it.'

'How old is old?' says Robin.

'What a question!' says Charlie.

'I have to ask it,' says Robin.

'My great-grandmother was old,' says Edward. 'Really old. She has just died. She was in her late eighties. She had five generations living behind her. She was head of five generations because she lived. She lived with my grandad's brother but she used to get very lonely because he kept going out to drive ambulances. We used to visit her whenever we went up north. She was a long way away. She got so lonely that it was almost a blessing when she did die. Families split up, they get further and further apart until they aren't families at all. Just relations. My great-grandmother was the head of five generations who hardly knew her. It was because she stayed up north.'

'It isn't quite the same with me,' says Frederic, 'because two of my grandparents have stayed in the East. They live far off in Poland, as a matter of fact. I visit them about once every two years and I'm the only grandchild they have got. It is wonderful to see their happiness every time I come to their house. As they get older and I get older, the happiness grows. I can't speak Polish and they can't speak English, so there isn't much to say. My grandad always tries to say he loves me in words but he really needn't bother. It is quite enough just to be there with him for two weeks. We just sit and look at each other until we have to grin. It satisfies them to have me there. I can tell that it does. They kiss me and smile. They possess me and it feels good. So it isn't quite the same with me.'

'It seems that it is *you* who possesses *them*,' says Robin.

'My grandfather always gives me a very clear picture of what it was like when he was young. Very clear. It's amazing the things he used to get up to. He's always telling me stories,' says Charlie. 'Old people like to compare their days with our days, don't they? For instance, outside church one day, when I was getting on my bike, the vicar said that he had to work hard for his first bicycle. Months and months in a factory, he said, before he could get a Standard bicycle. But nowadays you just get one for Christmas. My grandfather's stories are full of prices.'

'Talking of church,' says Linda, 'we had terrible arguments about it, grandfather and granddaughter rows. I told him flat what I felt. I said, I'm not going any more because I just don't believe it. You should have seen him, he was absolutely furious. I felt sorry for him because none of it really touched me – none of his furiousness. He was all worked up and I couldn't feel a thing. He believed so much. He'd agree that the earth wasn't made in seven days, but that's about all. But all the modern scientific things he called "theories". When he came up against something he hated he'd shout, "It's only a theory! It's only a theory!" Except for his defence of the Bible, though, I have to say that he was really quite modern. He didn't get on with me but he got on ever so well with my friends, who loved to see him. But they didn't have to live with him. Old age isn't very nice when you've got three generations in one small house. He was decaying. He was a very active man but then he went downhill very quickly. He just slid downhill very fast. Towards the end we just used to row continually and I'm sure I hated him. I didn't love him until he died, then I forgot about the hate and I just remembered all the nice things we'd done together. It was quite strange, really, quite strange.'

'There are a lot of old grandfathers who would be better off in a home,' says Terry, 'but they hesitate to take the plunge because they know in a way that it's degrading. Oh, it's degrading all right! They must feel like cattle, old cattle, when that happens to them. Yes, whatever you like to say about it, it is degrading. You've come down to something when that happens to you! They gradually stop being who they are in those places. For the family it's the final solution, isn't it?'

'When you read about old people in the papers or see programmes about them on television, they are always shown as sad and ill or lonely,' says Robin. 'There they are, the people who worked for a little wage and who are being dumped. But my grandparents keep going. They live with my aunty and they keep going. When I was in Italy I was, well, shocked, to see how much old men are still the head of the family. But here the family owns a lot of little separate houses instead of two or three crowded family homes, and so the old members have had to be put to the side. They have to visit the little separate houses in turn and their children say, "It's your turn to have them – No, it's not, we had them last year!" It's degrading when the head of the family is what we call a "responsibility", isn't it? Oh, they know all right that they're a responsibility – don't you worry! They know! We're a responsibility, but we shall grow out of it. They won't. They can't.'

'So I'm a responsibility?' says Charlie.

'You won't laugh later,' says Robin.

'I might. How do you know what I will do later?' says Charlie. 'How does anybody?'

'It certainly is very hard to imagine now what any of us will do later,' says Pat. 'I remember asking my grandfather about this just before he died and he said that you never think of yourself as old. He thought of himself as being a young boy of about twenty-two when he was in his *seventies*. His seventies! I thought it was horrible. I thought I would never let myself do that when I am old, old, old. I thought it was wrong. Horrible.'

'What I will hate will be the changed appearance,' says Linda. 'Everybody will see it and think, "That is an old person." I wouldn't want to be classed as an old person. You'll know what you felt about old people when you were our age, so you'll know what teenagers are thinking about you. Which isn't very nice.'

'Rubbish!' says Sarah. 'Going back to my gran –'

'We haven't left your gran yet, so we can't go back to her,' says Charlie.

'Well, my gran,' says Sarah. 'She's been pretty old for ages and the last thing she'd worry about is what any of you lot thought of her. She's interesting. She says she knows exactly when she's going to die. So my dad says, "Eighty-seven, eighty-eight, eighty-nine? A hundred then? What about a hundred, mum?" But she won't answer. "Hullo, mum," he says, "when are you going?" "Young imp," she says. "I know, but I'm not going to tell you!" She really has this set idea when she's going and she says she wants everything to be ready and organized. She says she wants to be cremated at Cambridge so people will say that she's the granny who went to Cambridge! She's not at all morbid about it. She talks about her death and she's even got mum to wash out her shroud.'

'Sarah!'

'She says that we'd better be thinking about something else to laugh about for when she's gone,' says Sarah. 'And that's true. I suppose you could call her a responsibility but we wouldn't. She's just gran.'

'I can't help it,' says Mary, 'but I'm always wondering what old people looked like when they were young. And somehow it just makes me sad. Because it has all gone and you think, how cruel!'

'I agree,' says Martin. 'It is cruel. You can be as kind or funny as you like, but to be old is cruel. Shakespeare – everybody – has said that it is cruel, and so it is. But we can't think of ourselves in that state. It is impossible. Nor can we think of the old as being like us. I suppose that if you really concentrated you might be able to imagine the old folk you know as our age, but ordinarily you never conceive such a thing. They are old, *they are old* – that is what you see and what you think. They are ill and ugly and their life is over.'

'I see them merely as people,' says Robin. 'I would need to be very imaginative to see them as Martin sees them. Just people, is what I say, if I say anything. What we are all saying now wouldn't normally cross my mind. Sometimes I can't even think of myself as being *five* years older than I am. I can remember in the primary that I'd look at the fourteens going to the grammar and think, "My God, they're big! What will I be like then?" But I couldn't imagine it.'

'I don't think the old want to be us,' says Colin. 'I don't think so. Society changes and they don't envy our society any more than we envy theirs. A lot don't mind long hair on us but they wouldn't have it on themselves, even if they could. Old people seem to want what they have had, not what the young have got. I don't know what they were told about hair but they're certainly very confused about it. But I'm confused now, so I'll stop.'

'Old people like medals,' says Graham. 'They know what they have achieved but they think we don't unless they have proof.'

'Do we talk naturally to the old?' says Robin.

'I talk naturally,' says Graham. 'My grandparents like to know what I am doing, where I'm going, etc., whereas my parents are more interested in how I'm getting on. So long as I'm not getting into trouble, my parents don't want to know much more. But with my grandparents it is different. They want to know much more! All the details. What did you have to eat? Were you sitting next to a girl? They're looking back and thinking, "Once I was like that." '

'I'm like Graham,' says Sarah, 'I never adapt my conversation. I know I keep pressing my gran, but she's the best example I have. Well, when I talk to her it's more likely that it is she who changes the conversation. When I go to see her with my boyfriend she tells us about all her boyfriends. She goes on and on about these young men she used to know. All about grandad, and what they did on their honeymoon. Michael doesn't know where to look but I can't help laughing. She never talks like this when I go to see her with my parents and they're amazed when I tell them what she said.'

'About sex?' says Robin. 'Is that what you are saying?'

'About everything,' says Sarah.

'My grandmother is very naïve about sex,' says Martin. 'Very naïve and innocent and young about it. Very romantic, I suppose you'd call it.'

'I think that newspapers have made a lot of the generation gap,' says Meriol. 'I blame them for doing so much to separate us. But we're getting back, we're getting back.'

'Our vicar – he's sixty – preaches about the generation gap all the time,' says Linda. 'You never heard such prejudice! The young are wrong, the old are right. On and on. I sit there with the smoke pouring out of my ears. We never do any work, we'd broken the apron-strings – which was terrible – and we were permissive – whatever that means. All the clichés. He's very hung-up about it. But I'm not sorry for him, I think he ought to know better.'

'Oh, they can be boring,' says Victor. 'Let's not pretend that they can't. Let's not pretend that they can't be awful and that it's often their own fault when they are pushed off somewhere. But they can't always help it. I sometimes feel sorry because they're not always thinking to the subject and because they're not aware of their surroundings. My grandma, she was brought up in Southern Ireland and she doesn't really know about the rest of the world, so she talks a fairly plain conversation. It's a bit annoying sometimes. Added to which she can't hear you properly and she says, "Pardon . . . pardon." '

'When does a person stop keeping-up?' says Edward. 'Pretty soon, if you ask me. Long before old age gives them an excuse to. My grandma thinks of Indians and Africans as sort of animals. When she saw a man in a turban in Ipswich she said, "If they are going to live in England they ought to be made to wear civilized clothes." She is very aware of foreigners. She doesn't like foreigners. She talks about the Homeland and the Commonwealth. The people of the Homeland are of a much higher degree than the people of the Commonwealth – black or white! Both my grandparents have malice and fear about the Germans. "Be wary of the Germans," my grandfather says. They worship the monarchy; Prince Charles's investiture on television and Princess Anne getting married, the Queen's Jubilee – all that. They are very careful and tidy. Once they didn't have anything, not a penny. None of the things we have. They are very careful with their television "because it isn't ours". They hire it. They treat it as something very valuable. All the same, they have saved up quite a lot of money by being careful and the house is full of furniture which grandpa made himself.

'He always refers to the past, never to the present, and particularly to the wars. He doesn't like to think about the future and keeps off it. He listens to the news on the radio, every news, and then he seems to cover it all up with remarks about the past.

'They both laugh quite a lot. They talk about being "silly" when they were young. They were "silly" with some boy or girl. "He could be silly when he liked!" she will say about him, and then they'll both laugh. They had nothing at all at the beginning of their lives. Money was rare then, you know.'

'Our grandparents certainly seem to have enjoyed the Second World War,' says Victor. 'They always cheer up when it is mentioned. They are very proud about how they endured its hardships. I've always felt that the war was the turning-point in their lives. It sort of trapped them somewhere between the old ways and the new. Our ways. They have only slightly turned our way, they can't quite face it, I think. So they're mainly looking back.'

'Our education is carrying us further away from them, perhaps,' says Tim. 'My grandparents are proud that I have got to this school, for instance, but I don't know that it is causing any separation. My grandfather is a miner but I know he sees himself in me. So what is happening to me is happening to him. That's how he sees it, I think. He has a huge understanding of things and of acceptance. I think what separates us from him is our freedom. He worked as a little boy. At fourteen he was a full-time worker. How can I understand what any of that means? A lot of old people call the young unprincipled just because we can't understand their working childhoods. My grandparents don't give a dam what I think. They'll stare at me physically, they'll watch how much I eat or listen to the way I talk, and nod to each other. I can see that I am very interesting to them and that I amuse them, but I don't mind amusing them. I know they think that boys are rather a joke. I sometimes have to pretend that I don't know what they are getting at! They are very strange, really, both a long way off – and too close for comfort! But I don't mind, I tell myself I don't mind.'

'I think that old people like young people around,' says Graham. 'They seem, well, to *love* young people. It's easier to talk to my grandparents than it is to my parents. They understand what I am talking about. The older they are, the more use they are. That is my experience. But they are healthy and clean. An unhealthy old person soon loses contact. Not so many people are going to come to see what you are doing when your health goes or when you get dirty. Your own friends keep dying every year, every month. You're dead lonely. Everything works to depress you. You don't know what is going on. Nobody asks you anything. You are perplexed by people not bothering you. It is a bad sign when nobody bothers you. Then you are old and ill, and you know it. But still you don't seem to realize that you are going to die soon, that it's all over.'

'My aunt died a couple of years ago,' says Tim. 'It was

cancer. She was old. They hummed and haa-ed whether they should tell her she was going to die and eventually they did tell her. Afterwards, she never mentioned it. She never said a word but carried on just as normal. So we had to stay silent and normal too but it was much harder for us. She went on shopping and gardening and having her hair done.'

'Death is more understandable to us than old age,' says Robin. 'We have more right to discuss it.'

'My grandmother is blind and she can't hear, and her life is absolute misery,' says Gillian. 'I would advocate euthanasia for her situation, as cruel as it may seem. It is worse to let her live. She has said she wants to die and in her situation she should die.'

'I agree,' says Linda. 'There are so many old people now. Everybody is staying alive too long. It sounds cruel, especially when you think of your own relatives, but I think that after about the age of seventy there should be euthanasia. It is a shame that so many old people are kept alive. They waste the tax-payer's money and fill up the geriatric wards and everything.'

'Linda,' says Pat, 'you don't really believe that?'

'Yes,' says Linda, 'I do. I do, I do, I do!'

'At *seventy*? One of my aunties is seventy and she's just incredible. The way she goes on she could be about twenty. Lots of relations on my father's side have been pensioned-off but they're certainly no burden at all.'

'My gran is seventy-five and she still goes dancing twice a week,' says Colin. 'She's gone dancing twice a week since the war. She's one of those nineteen-forties ladies, you know.'

'Dancing when you're old,' says Linda, 'how *could* she. . .'

'The old are jokes,' says Pat. 'Colin has proved it.'

'You can't look at them as a separate entity,' says Robin. 'They are human beings and have as much right to pleasure and food and friends as we have. Pushing out the old is savage. Thousands are being denied the full experience of birth because of abortion and now you are saying that thousands more are to be denied the full experience of dying because of the economic situation.'

'In the normal way people wouldn't live very long, would they?' says Linda. 'They'd die. It's in the Bible, isn't it – three score years and ten? Well that's *enough*. That's enough for anybody. I wouldn't want to live more than seventy. The majority of old people *are* burdens, and not just money-wise. They live on medicine. If you stopped their tablets most of them would be dead within a month, and a good thing too.'

'How frightened you are of the old,' says Peter. 'I haven't spoken before because I couldn't think what to say. Old age has never crossed my mind.'

'We don't get *naturally* involved, do we?' says Graham. 'We get involved out of charity. We aren't in their scene – even if it is a human one, we just make visits to it out of duty. Why pretend? How can we be in the old scene? It isn't very nice, when you come to think about it. It isn't very normal – for us. I don't want to live so long that I am rejected. You may think about getting old when you are seventeen, but only academically. The thought doesn't influence you at all. You are blind to the future unless you have an old grandfather who has your face, then you might begin to see into all the time which lies ahead. But it would also be natural to turn away from this wrinkled view of yourself. I've looked at my grandfather when he's dozing and it's me all right. Me in sixty years' time. I manage to push this idea away as soon as it occurs to me. I look at grandfather as at things which have finished, as at things which will never happen again. I'm near the end of my schooldays and already I'm beginning to know what it is like to come to the end of things.'

'When you watch an old person sleeping, especially if they're very old, you think, will they wake up again?' says Michael. 'It is like a play. You see the end events foreshadowed in the first act. You see things leading to what must happen later. One day soon they will never wake up. It is a kind of little death, this sleep of old men. It is the first act of a sleep drama which will end with them sleeping forever.

'When I watch my grandfather sleeping, I often think that I am seeing him dead. But catching anybody when they are asleep is strange. You look at them long and openly. You take your fill of them. You want to say that you are sorry for their being so much in your power and yet, at the same time, you notice that part of them seems to be beyond anybody's power. On this earth, I mean. When I see my grandfather asleep I feel less apologetic about staring at him when he is oblivious than I would if I was looking at my brother, say, because in grandfather's case there doesn't seem to be much of him left to be in anybody's power. Also, I've only seen my brother asleep in bed and undressed but grandfather sleeps downstairs in a chair with all his things on and in a room where everybody else is wide awake. So it is not the same. It is strange but it isn't intimate. When grandfather sleeps he seems to have no life at all. Then he wakes very suddenly, stands up, eats his tea. One second he is sleeping lifeless and the next he is switching on the radio for some news. "Have I missed the News?"

'I've heard somebody say that a man has the little death just after he has had sex but I think that sleep is more deathly than sex. You would think old men would be scared of sleep because I think it brings a kind of little death so close to their big death. Yet grandfather drops off at all hours and doesn't worry, and never ever tries to keep awake. He makes no effort at all. He sleeps and sleeps, and never says he's sorry. He says that he's a bad sleeper – it's funny. Perhaps he is in bed. He sleeps so neatly. He hardly moves or makes a sound. He just sleeps.'

'There is a good thing going between childhood and old age,' says Edward. 'I never think of old age getting nearer death because I am so aware of death all the time. It's old age when you start lamenting, and it's senility when you don't – or can't care any more. My family has always been in farming and the old farm-workers tell me of all the things that have gone on in the past. I listen because their talk is good, not because they are old and need an ear. I know a lady of about ninety who lives down the road all on her own. Lovely furniture, she's got. Pounds' worth of furniture. She is always in contact with young people, I mean *naturally*. She still runs the Red Cross in the village. She still gets her own water from the well. We all talk to her and we all like her. Everybody in the village has become her family, although her own family rather ignores her. Anyway, she is old, we are young, and we are friends. So what!'

'I suppose you always have an idea of yourself, even at ninety,' says Gillian.

'When I visit the old I have to reach out,' says Robert. 'They are so far away. I am extra polite and kind. I am extra polite because our generation is supposed to have the worst manners, and theirs the best. Is this true? But I don't think "are they fitting in?" and things like that. I say that everybody who is alive fits in. I don't talk to the old about the past because it is condescending. I talk about the present because if you are alive you are in the present. Don't forget the old often enjoy being taken out of their past.'

'I see it all very differently,' says Mary. 'Since the eight of us have been visiting the county council home for the old we have been bound to see everything in a different light. A hundred old people in a building are not the same as grand-parents. We started going last year. We go to one of their lounges on Thursday afternoons and play dominoes. They call us the Domino Girls. We play games and records. We aren't real friends, just the Domino Girls. About twenty of the old people play with us, the rest just sit there and criticize. The old women love to sing and recite. They know poetry by the yard and lots of songs and hymns. And even big chunks of prose from Shakespeare or the Bible. Their education seems to have been all learning things by heart. They like playing cards too. When we gave a party some of them wouldn't come.

"Why?" they said. They thought little of themselves and couldn't see why girls should want to give them a party. Most of them were deformed in some way because of their old age. They sort of crouched, eyes closed. The staff breezed by and treated them like children. It was a strange thing to see one of the nurses come with a huge rubber ball, throwing it to people and ordering them to throw it back. A few of the brighter ones refused this game. We felt furious for them. There was one old lady of over a hundred with only one leg, and they used to make her go to the toilet in front of the others. They used to bring the chair in and put her on it, and it was so *awful*. The other old women used to roar with laughter. It was like Bedlam in the eighteenth century. A great many old women together in a home – ugh! "Here they come!" they cry, "the Domino Girls!"'

'I don't really feel anything about the subject,' says Peter. 'I know I should after all that's been said, but I don't. It's because I can't.'

3 · The Old People's Home

All are limitory, but each has her own
nuance of damage. The élite can dress and decent themselves,
  are ambulant with a single stick, adroit
to read a book all through, or play the slow movements of
  easy sonatas. (Yet, perhaps their very
carnal freedom is their spirit's bane: intelligent
  of what has happened and why, they are obnoxious
to a glum beyond tears.) Then come those on wheels, the average
  majority, who endure TV and, led by
lenient therapists, do community-singing, then
  the loners, muttering in Limbo, and last
the terminally incompetent, as improvident,
  unspeakable, impeccable as the plants
they parody. (Plants may sweat profusely but never
  sully themselves.) One tie, though, unites them: all
appeared when the world, though much was awry there, was more
  spacious, more comely to look at, its Old Ones
with an audience and secular station. Then a child,
  in dismay with Mamma, could refuge with Gran
to be revalued and told a story. As of now,
  we all know what to expect, but their generation
is the first to fade like this, not at home but assigned
  to a numbered frequent ward, stowed out of conscience
as unpopular luggage.
                        As I ride the subway
  to spend half-an-hour with one, I revisage
who she was in the pomp and sumpture of her hey-day,
  when week-end visits were a presumptive joy,
not a good work. Am I cold to wish for a speedy
  painless dormition, pray, as I know she prays,
that God or Nature will abrupt her earthly function?

W. H. Auden, 'Old People's Home'

Farewell house, and farewell home!
Richard Crashaw

Mrs Robins,
Matron of the County Council Home,
aged fifty

A man who dies at forty will usually show one cause of death, wrote Alex Comfort, a man who dies at eighty will probably show nine or ten, so that had we cured the one that in fact killed him, he would have died soon after of something else. Behind this bleak truth lies the reason why so many of the aged leave home for homes. They are deteriorating. Their mortality which has been kept in check or which has been concealed for so long is now unhideable from themselves and from their families and neighbours. The effect of these last diseases, their breaking-down of the organism, is called 'not being able to manage'. The pressures, from inside and outside, then begin, and just at a moment when the smallest decision requires a mighty effort one is asked to make, what is for most people, a tremendous choice – to go on managing, and knowing that you can't, or to be managed. To pack a case and leave the rest. Travel light has always been the advice given to pilgrims and the old people's home repeats it, though for its own convenience, not the new resident's. However difficult it may be to cope with old treasures as well as old bodies, some realization of the similarity of their plight when they are asked to give up their possessions to that final stripping-away of all things in 'We brought nothing into this world, and it is certain that we can carry nothing out' might be borne in mind by today's professional managers of the aged.

As we are fast recognizing, it is not the fault of the majority of those into whose paid hands we place the old that fundamental aspects of their institutions (including many private establishments) are reminiscent of nineteenth-century schools, barracks and workhouses, but because we still hold back from any realistic look at the needs of today's aged. When future generations study how we dealt with these first and second generations of the lifespan full-timers, they will be shocked. The present position cannot change until we drop our detachment. It is *we* who are helplessly involved in the gerontological situation and who, subsequently, will be wanting geriatric assistance, not 'them'. Until society can say 'we are them' things will remain much as they are. The old do not want out-reach, they want association. Even the best old people's home is marked by disassociation, and the old know it. What they come to terms with when they enter these doors is this mark of disassociation. It is not always an unhappy thing to have written-off one's independence; often it is a relief. But it is profoundly disturbing that by doing so one has severed links which held one to the centre, however precariously. We have to admit that our own potential agedness grows within us as a first step towards destroying the isolation of these convenient fastnesses. The rest is simply a matter of money and imagination, both of which have been in notoriously short supply.

There are now vast numbers of old people's homes. The variation in their standards makes any generalized criticism worthless. All that one can say is that many of the larger sort which are run by the local health authorities are too reminiscent of the institutional systems of half a century or more ago for comfort, and that many private homes are dreary and extortionate. But some of each category are administered by truly remarkable individuals who have a vocation which few envy, that of being unable to differentiate, so far as human contact is concerned, between the interest to be found in the personality of an octogenarian and in that of a man of any age. Very often the dweller in the old people's home stays tenuously connected to the ordinary sociability of the outside world, and still has his earlier taken-for-granted feelings of belonging to it, because a stranger in the shape of matron, nurse or assistant takes on herself the multiple roles of the deserting relative, friend, neighbour, etc.

What is clearly wrong is that when we grow old we should

be extracted from home to *the* home. That this should occur is not entirely the fault of society. The old have their own self-indulgence and part of it is to give up too easily. One of the ways to avoid the old people's home is to learn how to stay in our own homes. Knowing that we are pretty certain to reach seventy and eighty, we should plan long before these decades hit us how we should protect ourselves from the old age managers when they do. Anyone visiting a big old people's home will see there dozens of residents who could still be in their own houses – and not even in those of their children. And there is, indeed, a movement to return residents to their homes when a spell away has restored their health and confidence.

The best kind of old people's home is the little, discreetly controlled unit such as an Abbeyfield house with its half-dozen residents and supervisor, where one has a latchkey and a roomful of one's own furniture. Some of the worst kind are the geriatric barracks which are still being built with their picture-windows (which the old hate) and their 'cheerful' lounges, their numbered doors and their impersonal brightness; a functionalism in which the aesthetics and sensitivities peculiar to old age, though perfectly well known, are considered not at all. It should be a must, for example, that every home, large or small, should contain a sitting-room other than that which contains the television-set. The old suffer cruelly from enforced television and muzak in institutions. Also from a foolish way of being spoken to by a certain type of attendant, and from the greatly increased noise in a public building, the crashing of things in huge kitchens, telephones, electric polishers, central heating, car-doors, etc. The Fabian Society's *New Deal for the Elderly* calls for a halt in the building of such old people's homes and for the launching of a properly costed (£100m) programme to pay for what they really need. So far, says the Society, successive Governments have concentrated on things such as subsidized rail travel and the relaxation of the earnings rule and have spent little thought or money on how old people, particularly very old people, *should* live. Certainly they should not live six to a bedroom and forty to a lounge.

'The ideal way to age would be to grow slowly invisible, gradually disappearing, without causing worry or discomfort to the young,' wrote Sharon Curtin, staring with contempt at American attitudes towards the aged. The old, of course, do not grow slowly invisible; on the contrary, they become quite uncompromisingly conspicuous, which is why we, although we would never confess it, are grateful for the old people's home as a concealment. Among much else. Mrs Robins neither defends nor execrates the policy which has produced her old people's home. She has fifty-one old men and women to look after and she does her best with what she has. Pre-eminently, she has a heart and plenty of common sense. She rather enjoys the muddly grandeur of the Victorian country-house which shelters all these remnants from the local terraces and bungalows, the allotments and pubs, and has no sense of being 'other' than them. She is thoughtful and contained, and at the same time very warm. Her understanding of senescence is quick, kind and without theory.

*

It is like practically anything else one can mention, isn't it? It works, it is possible – when there is acceptance. Not total acceptance necessarily, or a kind of complete giving in or giving up, I don't mean that, but about the same amount of acceptance which you have needed to live your life at all. You accept that you can't put the clock back; that is acceptance number one. You accept that life is coming to an end and that it is natural. Not to accept this is unnatural. It certainly isn't 'brave'. Although now and again you do have someone who braves it out, as it were, in the very face of her senescence (it is usually a her) and it looks gallant and sad and pitiful all at once.

We had such a person here. She would not talk about age, would not, would not. Her real one was on her birth certificate but she'd had the one she preferred for so long that to her it was her true age. She would not join in any of the activities here, the fun, the community singing, the laughter, but kept well outside. She genuinely thought of everybody else as old and herself as middle-aged. Her predicament was extreme, and could have been quite awful, yet somehow she coped with it. Out of practice, I suppose. But she *was* a very old woman and I felt sorry for her. Her appearance was mysterious and was somewhere between a very old fifty and a very young eighty. Her entire femininity seemed to depend on age-concealment and being forced into an old people's home was indescribably confusing and dreadful to her. I must say, I half admired her bravado! It reminded me of Dylan Thomas's 'Old age should burn and rave at close of day'. Yet not quite like that. This woman was, well, snobbish about age. She looked down on it and on those that had it. She didn't join in because she knew that she was younger, and thus better, than the rest of us. But she *was* mysterious – I give her that! She had managed to muddle the whole business about time and herself, and that cannot be denied. She had done it. I liked her.

Out of the fifty-one people we have here, I should think that ninety-nine per cent are contented. And I don't mean that they have all given in or given up. I mean that in the course of their long, long lives they have all had to accept a whole mass of things which made the slow acceptance of being old, and then coming here, rather normal. They have nearly all been very ill, or bereaved, or in two wars, or broke, or disfigured, or forsaken, or disappointed. I mean that big, bad things have happened to them, as they happen to us all, and yet one survives, as they say. Coming here is for most of them a bit more of the surviving which by now they have got used to. They are not simply resigned, no, I wouldn't put it that way. Many of them are actually happy. I hear them sometimes talking about their youth in a laughing way, and with no real longing to have it back. Coming here is acceptance in its last setting, that is how I think of it.

An elderly person requires respect. I cannot say this too strongly. In a place like this respectful attitudes towards the old are the key factor to the success of the work. It isn't ideal here but we all live with each other as well as we can. We are in community, I tell them. It's a bit late in the day to be in community, isn't it? But there you are! We haven't got everything we could do with, but amenities aren't the be-all and end-all of happiness. These old people are from the times when nobody had much. You hear of old women in rich hotel rooms or in bright high flats, and aren't they tragic? Of course, often most tragic.

How often I have asked an old man in his tidy little house who weeps, 'Is it the pension – isn't it enough? Are you uncomfortable? Is it the food?' 'No, no,' he says. It is because he is surrounded by neighbours who aren't neighbourly and sometimes by relations who don't talk. He has discovered that he is lonely. 'I am lonely, very lonely,' he says, and it is the first time he has said it. He hears what he is saying and it is a shock to him. It could be the same for the young, too, of course. You don't have to be old to suffer like this, though you usually are. Well, in this big old house there is always somebody to talk to and plenty of corners to tuck yourself away in if you don't want to talk. To be able to have a long talk whenever you feel like it is quite a luxury when you're old. Part of my respect towards the old is not to speak to them all the time. One of the worst things about being eighty is the constant foolish chat, the patronizing little sayings which keep on coming your way. The value of a place like this is that you can get plenty of the talk which you used to have before you got very old. There is none of that 'concern', none of that hovering over them which sends old folk up the wall. It is different on visitors' day, I can tell you! Then we get the specially hushed voices-for-the-evening-of-life and it makes you sick. And the guilt! So much guilt with some visitors that you have to shut your eyes and cars. Families are agony. They breed injury. And sometimes, before they came here, the old person has made a son or daughter ill with their old age, as many old parents do, and then they can't say much at all. They sit face to face trying not to think.

The aged often find it very, very difficult to give up their independence and come here. Some don't survive the ordeal; they simply die. Very soon after the transfer they die. When I see some people I know from the start that it is pointless and wrong to persuade them to come here. We had someone recently who had lived for years and years with the bachelor son of a very close friend of hers. As she got old, he found it increasingly difficult to help her. Then she broke her hip and she came here. And she *could not* settle down. Could not, could not. Then she took to her bed. She gave up. She'd sooner give up than settle down. She felt she had the choice. Her friend's son saw the choice, took compassion on her and took her back with him again. And immediately all her old energies revived. She is now ninety-seven and still very well and moving about. *And* quite easy to live with! She'd learnt her lesson. It shows that people of strong character are right not to give up their homes and that they should also use some of their strength to cope with their special needs and fads if they are living with a younger person.

But it isn't easy, oh, it isn't easy for the person who will eventually make a go of it here in the old people's home to make the decision to give up all they possess, pack their clothes and be brought in the taxi to a place like this. Stop the milk, give the cat away, change the address on the pension-book, shut the front door . . . Oh, just imagine that day! Usually it is the doctor, the relatives and myself who decide what would be the best way to tell her. To break it to her. That she should go into a home for her own good. I go to see a prospective candidate personally before they come here, and particularly when they find it hard to make the decision. They don't understand that if they linger the waiting-list will get so long. In any case, old people don't think about administration or what you might call general convenience; they think about

themselves. They are self-centred like children. There is only
one problem on their world, and that is themselves. But still,
if a stranger calls on you and says that tomorrow or maybe in
a fortnight's time you should be taken to live the rest of your
life in a place which you have never seen, then you can't but
think of yourself. Just when you can't bear the smallest change
you are to be given total change. It is huge and terrible to hear.
I say it over a cup of tea. I take them on a visit to the home and,
with a bit of luck, they see somebody they know. Or knew.
And then it could be, 'You'll be all right – look at me! You'll
have plenty to do and they feed you well. And no more
worries!' The anxiety will begin to fall away then. But usually
they sit there, heavy with quiet, and you know that they are
telling themselves, 'So it has come to *this*. It has happened –
at last! I'm in a home, I'm in a home. I'm old and I'm in a
home. It has happened to *me*. Oh, my God, oh, my dear Lord!'
Well, try and imagine it for yourself. No, you can't imagine it
for yourself. You never do.

It is not the same for someone who has made what I call the
half-way break. That is, a man or woman who has come to
the point where they have to leave their son's or daughter's
family setting, where there are grandchildren, and where
there has been a growing recognition that it is not their home
and that they aren't entirely wanted. Some little house where
they can feel the squeeze. This is very common. The old
person feels intrusive and a nuisance. The young people are
tolerant but not loving. They wouldn't hurt him but they don't
want him. He isn't father any more, he is their old-age problem. They read articles and watch television programmes
about it happening to other families. They get advice. They
don't want him dead – what a horrible idea! – but they don't
want him for another fifteen years. And he has sold his house
and given them a lump of money for their mortgage – 'It will
all be yours when I've gone, anyway.' The strange thing about
such a common situation, of course, is that dad often *is* happier
in the old people's home than the children who have put him

there, but he can't say so because it sounds ungrateful. And they have guilt, poor things. And so I find that I have to comfort them, rather than my new resident! Families are agonizing things and I sometimes feel that there are old folks who aren't all that upset to be shot of them! But truth is whispered.

If an old person comes straight from his own house or flat it is quite another story. They'll think about it and talk about it all the time. For a bit. 'My home.' And when they say this they'll often cry. They cannot bear the thought that it has gone – 'my home'. Their address. Their road, their village. It all happens so quickly, often after an illness or a mishap. The doctor tells the social worker and the social worker tells us, and the days of looking after oneself are over. The reactions are mixed. Anything from downright relief to fright and shock. Some old people come straight from hospital after a relative has been here to make the arrangements and this can be a good thing because it will seem like an extension of the hospital treatment – a convalescence. And then, after a month or two, home recedes. Home begins to go away of its own accord. The day of arrival straight from hospital is most important and all the staff are geared to it. The new resident always gets special treatment and he is never left alone. Everybody works to prevent them worrying and showing them where things go.

'What would you like to bring here from your home?' I ask. 'A favourite chair, perhaps? Your little coffee-table?' Nothing much but something. Small pictures and ornaments. Sentimental things. I always ask them, 'Is there something special you would like to bring?' But nothing much.

This is a council home and there must be about fifty like it in this area. Some are purpose-built and very clinical. Door after door with numbers and not much character. Such buildings are a bit hard on an old person who has spent her life in a cosy little house. I don't like them. This home was a family mansion for a hundred years and it might not be very convenient but it is domestic. You don't feel as if you were entering an institution when you come in through the front door. The first snag we came across was the huge private bedrooms. In order to accommodate our fifty-one old people in eighteen Victorian bedrooms we have had to make one six-bedded room, two five-bedded rooms, three two-bedded rooms and just two single rooms. Our residents are all individuals and they include our loners. They aren't anti-social, they are just loners. I always do what I can for the natural loner. There are those who just cannot share a room, who just can't join in, though lack of money and space force you to do things which you hate. I hated to ask a person only yesterday to share a room with five others, one of whom suffers from asthma and another who gets confused. It was a bad experience. But this new lady was very good. She said she was glad to have got into the home and would put up with its difficulties, but it wasn't a nice start.

I was a nurse for ten years before I became the matron here and I had worked with old people for another ten years. Yet I never accept the bad things. I am constantly asking myself, should this be so? Should that be allowed? Is this right? Is that decent? I am not hardened by my work and experience, but softened by it. An old people's home has got its disadvantages as well as its advantages – like life. So the main disadvantage here is that too many residents are sleeping in really close quarters. The advantages are that, being so many, the old person can avoid those he has nothing in common with and can have a good chance of finding a person he likes. It's all a bit crowded, a bit shabby but it does have variety and choice. We provide what privacy we can. And the old are far more adaptable than you might imagine. Many of the residents are full of practical common sense and they've had to spend most of their lives making the best of things. After all, most of them have been through the mill, particularly when they were young, and what seems like something dreadful to the young of today, or something to condemn by the investigator, is often not so much as noticed by some of these old folk. However, I do my utmost to give them what is necessary for their comfort. For instance, when Age Concern asked me why don't you put curtains round each bed, I said, certainly, why not? But when I asked the residents if this is what they wanted there was a majority vote against them. Though the few who did want curtains wanted them very much. So I made a greater use of screens. Administration and medicine apart, I see my true role here as someone who has to maintain homeliness as much as maintain a home. I don't pretend that we are just a big family because I can never get it out of my head that we are the poor odds and ends of a great many families. But we are a community, I'll say that much.

You hear people say – you are for ever hearing it – 'Oh, God, I pray that the time will never come when *I* have to enter a place like that!' Though when the time comes it is quite different because *you* are different. Being old makes you different, whatever they say, just as being young makes you different. And there are men and women here who have been old for just as many years as they have been young – really young. After you have become old, you get older! You don't stay still even if you have moved into a state where there is little movement and reduced thought. You are fading and finishing as you go forward. Strangely enough, it is quite a positive experience.

Many of my residents have been preparing themselves for coming to a place like this years before they actually arrive, although they probably weren't conscious of doing so. They have been shedding responsibility bit by bit ever since they retired, or their partner died. By the time we meet them there often isn't all that much to give up. Their house, for example, may not have been five rooms and a long garden for the last ten years; it has become one room with a bed and the telly and the teapot in it. They haven't used all the rest for ages. Even the fact that it was the family home seems to get less important. The change between the children who slept in its bedrooms and played in its garden, and the fifty- or even sixty-year-old sons and daughters who wander in and out, wondering what to do, gets too great to have any connection. Sentimentally, I mean. But there are those who clutch and cling to everything they've had and known, of course, though my experience is of visiting an old person and of expecting to have to gently ease her out of her little property-dominated world – only to find that she has stopped holding on to it long ago! A lot of old folk will trade in their independence for a bit of company and 'not having to manage on my own'. They haven't reached this stage suddenly. Often the old person comes to the home not from a home any more, but from a lonely, neglected, dirty, dreary situation and after a while she says to herself, 'Life hasn't come to an end after all!'

The very first thing I tell a new resident is that he is not going to be regimented and made to live to a strict schedule. In other words I say, 'We can't help that you have all ended up under one roof, but we will let you live as individually as you can in the circumstances.' Everybody is called 'Mr' or 'Mrs' unless they insist on a Christian name. When you are old you are on your dignity. We try and give full respect. Visitors will say of a lot of old people together that they have had their individuality taken from them, that their faces are expressionless, and that it is all sad, wrong and awful. But what *I* hear them saying is, 'I too will be old and I won't be myself, and my face will be a blank, and it will be awful, awful.'

You can hardly expect anyone who isn't a resident or who doesn't work here day by day to admit that our home has its own genuine life, its own genuine vitality. Of course we have our wars and rows and depressions but mostly we have plenty of plain ordinary give and take. After a time we forget that everybody is 'old'. They are just people. Visitors are always saying, 'Oh, you do wonderful work' – as if we were in contact with lepers. In some eyes we are, I suppose. It is high time that everybody remembered that however old you get, you stay human. An extraordinary thing happens to the very old, they sometimes get back into full living for a bit. There are some ninety-year-olds here and they can do anything. We had Mrs Bowers who, at a hundred-and-two, made something for an embroidery exhibition with the finest stitches you could imagine, then thought that it wasn't perfect so she unpicked it and did it all again! She died at a hundred-and-four and was a delightful companion and conversationalist to the end. No one could say that time had diminished Mrs Bowers.

You can't run a place like this, which is all about endings, and ignore the religious thing, whatever you think personally. Generally speaking, most of our residents belong to religions which have strict disciplines which they have never observed. That puts it in a nutshell. They are particular about being registered 'Baptist', 'Roman Catholic', 'Jewish', 'C. of E.' etc., but that is about all. Or 'Moslem' – we have them now. The minority who observe the disciplines do have a different kind of old age. At the same time – and I have always marvelled about this – because I have always thought that these practising religious people would be anxious to have a minister or a priest with them when they knew they were dying, I am surprised when, somehow, nobody ever asks. I say this who sees death as all part of the day's work. *Nobody* has ever said to me on their deathbed, 'Send for a priest or minister' – not even the Catholics. I do it. I do it myself. A word, a prayer, a look, a touch. What the old person seems to be asking to be done I always do. Whatever it is. I have learnt all this through my work in hospitals as well as with the aged. In hospital we would say, 'Would you like to see So-and-so?' And they would say yes or no – usually no. No, thank you. Thank you, thank you, the dying say. It means, 'Don't say any more, don't ask me anything more, I'm sorry I'm bothering you, don't question me, let me be now.' Something like that. 'Thank you, dear.' Very old real Christians get beyond ministry. Whatever it is they've got to have at the end, it is waiting to be found inside them. Just before they die the old seem to understand that they are 'beyond all this'. They are lying there, breathing

and listening, and sometimes talking, but only out of a kind
of politeness, you feel! Just being as mortal as possible until
the end, so as not to upset anyone, but quite uninterested in it.

It is such a slow process to grow really old. When you get
to it, last year and the year before all join up and become part
of the present moment. A month is just another day. Friday
may as well be Tuesday. But day and night, they stay import-
antly different. Most of the old people I have helped have got
used to being old. It is ordinary to them and they hardly ever
discuss it. You don't often find anyone demoralized by his
collapsed body, or anything like that. You must give the old
credit for understanding the facts of their kind of life. They are
acceptors in the main. You accept being near death and having
no strength, and your face all funny. You accept because you
have no other option, and that's all there is to it! So there is
really not much point in dwelling on these things. You have
got several diseases because you are wearing out and coming
to a stop. You cope with them according to the person you
were long ago. If you have been a brave or clever or interesting
person, you will reflect these assets until you are finished. I
often hear residents say, 'Five years ago I was still at home, I
was still doing everything,' but in the same breath they will
add, 'Oh, well,' and smile. The one thing you aren't is surprised. Regretful, maybe, bitter occasionally, but not surprised.
Your one big dread is mental illness. Senile dementia. Residents will say, 'You will tell me if you see me go a bit funny,
won't you?' They think that they will be able to pull themselves together. Sometimes they will become white and silent
when the others tell them about something irrational which
they have done. Or said.

You could compare old age with having worked hard all
day and, by the time evening comes, finding that if you can
manage to work just another hour you will have done all you
could. The light isn't good enough to do any more, so you
have to pack up. Finish. Sitting back and saying, 'I have
finished' is the general outlook of an elderly person. It's just

as well, isn't it, because no one wants them to go on, even when they can. Many of the residents here have been deserted. Some are stranded. That is what those of us who aren't old cannot imagine.

Keeping an Eye and an Ear: the Home-Help, aged forty-five

I'm a registered home-help at the head office in Ipswich. I have a time-sheet each week and they pay me once a fortnight. I get a good car allowance. I'm also a nursing orderly in a geriatric ward, so I see one old person who is still at home and a lot of old people who have lost their homes. Each day. I do my best for all. It was the Social Service who came round to ask me to look after the old lady in the village and I said yes because I like old people. Always have. When you've done something for them they always seem so pleased. I say to myself, at least I've made somebody happy today. Though not always. Sometimes you think to yourself, now what have I done wrong? But you learn to take this bad mood of the old people. The old can be very bad – wicked!

I use my judgement, I take it careful. I give my old lady at home about an hour a day. It would cost the authorities £30.40 a week to keep her in hospital and it costs them 84p an hour seven days a week for me to see to her. I try to keep the hour regular, always the same one early of a morning. Old people like a routine and they get very confused if you make an hour change. It's a bit difficult for me because I do this nursing shift work so there are days when I call on my old lady in the afternoons. It makes her that confused. No use explaining!

All sorts of things muddle her. The new money still gets her very muddled. She'll get a handful of change and I'll have to pick it out and count it for her. She hasn't gone shopping on her own for ages. She's most particular and very, very fussy. I've never met anyone like her – never. The whole reason is that she worked for a lady in good service and she can't forget it. She'll always have the best if she can. She can now afford little extras and she'll see she gets them too. She won't be palmed-off with anything less. When I've got her a bit of shopping, she'll look at the meat and say, 'That's not right. That's not what I ordered. That's not what I said!' Scolding like her mistress. I would eat the cheaper cuts myself, but not her! Only the very best. I did slip up once. I went to a cheaper butcher when she told me to go to the expensive one and she saw the name on the bag. Oh dear, I heard about it all right! She shops where the old master and mistress shopped, and nowhere else.

She's got two or three little bits of silver and dozens of little bits of brass, and she polishes the lot two or three times a week. Everything around her shines. She'll take the curtains down and say they look a bit grubby, when they aren't. She'll always have a little duster in her hand and always be doing a mite of polishing. She's being a good housemaid the livelong day. The other morning she said, 'I've got my sink right clean, come and have a look, see what you think.' It was that bright. I said, 'What did you do with it?' 'Dirt,' she says. She just got a handful of dirt. She's got a blackberry stain on her white sink and that wholly worries her, you see. A bit of bleach would have got it off but 'I won't have that,' she said, 'that I won't!' Old method, you see. A tea stain on a cup and it's out into her garden for a bit of dirt. Old method.

It's the same with other things. She got an electric cooker but she won't use it because she said it's still hot when you turn it off and so it wastes the electric. She's been used to cooking with the old bread ovens and now she loves her little old oil stove. I'm a bit worried about her and the paraffin. She's got no flush toilet, just her privy down the garden and she'll never let me empty her toilet-pail. She does it all herself. She baths with a saucepan of hot water and the sink. The Social

Service said they'd help her put in a flush toilet and a bath-
room but she wouldn't hear of such a thing. She stays as clean
as clean. She'll have her hair done in Woodbridge and order
the best setting-lotion. She gets up very early and even after
she'd had her hysterectomy – and she was turned eighty-five –
she was soon up making the tea. She's healthy but lonely.
That's her state. Probably I shouldn't say it, but it's her joy
to have me there. I tire of her talk as it goes over and over. She
repeats, she repeats. It's all the same talk over and over. But
it's her little bit of joy and I put up with it. That's why it's
bad when I change the visiting hour. She's all waiting and
ready, and getting herself in a tizzy, and then I don't come. It's
the world coming at an end.

My old lady is very fearful – full of fear. 'Don't you fear,' I
tell her, 'never fear.' But she does. She's only got to go to her
shed and she'll be locking the house. She's very, very wary and
goes around locking and unlocking all day. It's bad for her in
the winter months. She's been contented with her life. She
boasts she's had to work hard. She's a countrywoman like me
and she'll accept more than a townwoman would. She never
criticizes her lot nor wishes that it had been any different. And
she's open-handed. Not like old Mr Allott who just sits in his
chair with his fingers clenched and grousing. Miserable old
man. He watches television and thinks what a terrible place
the world is. People have got greedy, he says. But he's greedy.
He's been after money all his life and now he's nigh ninety
he's still the same, saving where he can, scratching it away.
He thinks I'm a servant and not a home-help. 'Get on with
your work,' he says if I happen to stop to say something.
Makes me smile. My old lady likes to hear about him and all
the village news. They all know things about each other that'd
make your hair curl.

She's always asking to go out in the car with me, but she
doesn't realize the cost of travelling. She'd go out every day
if she could. I think that being in my car is her favourite
thing, although most old people like a visitor best of all. The

rector visits her – the 'parson', as she calls him. But she don't go to church. Not into it. Her husband's buried at the church but she don't fare as if she want to go in, she'll just stay outside with his grave. She loves flowers. She's been used to seeing cut flowers in a house. She arranges them like flowers where she worked in the big houses. She used to wash for the big houses and all this linen was brought to her cottage in a wheelbarrow. How she used to manage all this washing in her cottage without the use of anything, I don't know, but she did. She had an old brick copper. She said she'd stand up till two in the morning ironing with a box iron. Sixpence an hour she was paid. Her husband was away in the army and she washed. When he came home he was our postman.

She doesn't read. I have taken her newspapers but she doesn't look at them. She's lost the sight of one eye with cataract. She got television but only after her husband died. How she wished he could have seen that, she says. But she prefers her wireless. She's always got that on. Filling forms worries her, of course. If a bill comes in she has to pay it the very next day, or she can't rest. She hates to think she owes money. She went into service when she was twelve and up to London. She married a soldier there and came back to Suffolk with him. 'I managed to see a little bit of the world,' she says.

But she does clack a lot, as the saying is. She does talk and talk. She'll clack about her death. She's got to be put alongside of her husband and her grave *must* be lined with flowers. She kept a lovely nightdress and that was going to be her shroud, she said, but then her poor old neighbour went and she sent it along and told them to put *her* in it. So now she goes through her things and asks me 'Will this do?' What do I think? When I take her shopping in Woodbridge, she'll be having her eye on nightdresses, wondering if they'll do for her laying-out. She's going to be with her Dick – she's certain of that. So there's got to be this here nightdress and these flowers. She was that upset when I once said something about cremation. I soon got off that tack. She says she must go to where Dick is.

I think myself that's why she keeps herself so nice, for her Dick. She's over eighty and fresh as a daisy.

Now it's another tale on my ward. I deal with lots of old people there and most of them are from the villages. Few come to visit them until they're on their deathbed, and then you'll hear all the whispered talk about their little house and their few sticks, and their things, and who is to have what. If there's money and a bit of property they'll all be there then, the relatives. My ward is full of the over-seventies to the nineties. The families don't come because they say it's no good, they won't know us. But the staff all say, come and see them and give them a chance. Just take this poor old soul out for a little walk. They all get up every day, all thirty-four of them, and you can have very sensible conversations with the majority of them. Yesterday seven of them went to Felixstowe and you should have just seen their faces when they got back! But it wasn't one of their relations who took them. Usually they just sit in their chairs. Physiotherapy ladies come up and show them how to do things but they go on just sitting. They don't walk in the garden because there's nobody to walk with them – we're all too busy on the wards. Some's minds have gone and they think that they're sitting with their sisters or their old friends from long ago. They'll make close friendships which don't last, and then they'll cry. One minute they'll know you and the next minute they won't. In the villages where they come from, their neighbours will say, 'Oh she's gone away, or he's gone away.' They're as good as dead to them. You'll get those who'll give an old person any mortal thing bar a bit of company.

None of my old ladies on the ward uses make-up. None of them have photos of themselves as girls. If they want lipstick or to have their hair done, they've only got to ask, but they don't ask. They give up. I'll take them to the toilet and the minute I've got them back they'll do it in the bed or on the chair. Yesterday I changed one of them three times. Three dresses and three sets of underclothes. If you pad them they get sores so the only thing to do is to wash them over and over again. Change and wash all day long. If it was a child you'd know she'd grow out of it. But you don't grow out of much when you're eighty.

I hope my old lady dies in her sleep and doesn't fear. 'When I die, dear,' she says, 'I want the scrubbing-brush put in with me. And the duster.' I can't imagine her on my ward. She'd have a fit to see what went on there.

I read their case notes. Their house was dirty and full of mice, so away they go. So that's the way it is then, some manage, some don't, some stay at home and some are off! 'Where's old Mr So-and-so?' you'll hear it said. 'Gone away,' they'll say. And they won't do much about it because to them it's just like being dead.

The Old Leading the Old:
the Retired Engineer, aged seventy-seven

The most important thing with the old is visiting. There is an art in visiting. You don't just go and knock on somebody's door and say, 'I am the official from Age Concern, what can I do to help you?' The person who opens the door might be perfectly happy, although eighty, and there is nothing to do. No, you look, you watch, you think, as you move about in your village. You think towards agedness and then you see a very different neighbourhood. You see what the old see when they look out of their doors and windows. You look out for those who have long ago forgotten what it was like to be looked at and thought about. If there is obviously some sort of emergency (the milk is still on the step in the evening), you knock on the door and say – But what do you say? You say hello. You see consternation because nobody has said hello lately. Not for donkey's years sometimes. You call again. And again and again. You are doing your Age Concern work but the old person being visited knows that he is simply being visited. He knows that he is in receipt of a charitable act and that there is no true relationship. He knows that you and he have nothing in the world in common except old age. The old person knows this all too well, ah, too well! He doesn't talk sometimes but you know he is saying, 'What's all this about, eh? Who are you, Old Man from Age Concern? My friend? How can you be?'

But you can bring a bit of luck. I found an old man who lived on his own and visited him when I heard that he was called mad. He wasn't, needless to say, but he was crazy about genealogy. And so am I. So we welcomed each other's craziness and became real friends at once. He was seventy-seven, a retired doctor, and what you might call a stickler. He is very outspoken and insists on being addressed in the correct form, with all his degrees properly set out, etc. Eccentric. Many old men become sticklers. They fight against modern casualness and because they believe that they are personally preventing the destruction of civilized standards, they don't care what the world says about them. My stickler was such a lonely old man but he'd sooner be lonely than not addressed correctly, or put up with people who had thrown away his standards. I talked to him about genealogy and this opened a whole field of interests. Now he pops in here and there is a constant to-ing and fro-ing.

I'm a little bit of a stickler myself and in the past I've been through my own lonely time. It was after my business failed and I was living away from the family in a little room in London and working all hours in order to 'get back'. Getting back once you've lost your footing is so hard, though eventually I did. Oh, but it was hard and I knew what it was to have people around who could afford to be careless with all the things which made up what you believed in, and which kept you together, as it were. And it's a bit like this when you're getting on. It is so hard and you need to have the support of decent manners, you do really. The young have no idea what it is like to be made to look a fool just because one finds it easier to go on doing the right thing.

I myself got interested in old people just before my retirement. I was going to join them so I thought I would take a look at them. I was searching around for something to do because I knew it was important for me to have some sort of object in view in my new life. How strange – my new life is my old age! I'd had all sorts of experience in running things – the parish, the British Legion, etc. – and so I met the organizer for the welfare of the elderly in the county, a lady. She was employed by the Rural Community Council, and she it was who introduced me to my new life of old age. And so I came to Age Concern. And, as I said, one of the most important things we had in our branch was the visiting. I couldn't visit everybody but I worked very closely with the health visitors. I did all this for quite a while but then Age Concern in Gower Street became rather political. They appointed a director. They attended trade-union conferences and got political, and welfare for the elderly became a political issue. They said that they'd vote for this or that party according to what it would do for pensions – which spoilt the image of the people who were doing a first-class backing job. We gathered information and they pushed ministries but we didn't go on wireless and television at the first opportunity, which is what the present people do. It isn't quite the same as before. When one gets older one doesn't change. But whether it is a good thing or not, I'm not sure. The truth of the matter is that I'm too old to be doing Age Concern.

But I go on keeping an eye on the old. I went down to see an old girl near here a couple of years ago. They said, go in there because she is blind. See what can be done. See what has happened. And so I went in there. She had a little fire. The window was broken and there was a howling draught. She had got her own coal in. It was a very ancient cottage with no modern things in it, none whatever. I sat there and chatted to her. The rent collector hadn't been round for six months and she had about eighty pounds in her bag waiting for him. He never came. Nobody came. And because nobody came her life in the little house folded-up, her being blind and all. The county council's special organization for the blind eventually took over. It was a strange case where an old person had been literally stranded although it was common knowledge that she was there. It was her situation, her house without any modern fitments and her just sitting there, month in and month out, by her fire, which just weren't recognizable to those living round about. Poor old girl, she couldn't make it out. It was uncanny for her. Old age *is* uncanny – it's weird.

4 · The Beloved Holocaust

I tried to peg out soldierly, – no use!
One dies of war like any old disease.
This bandage feels like pennies on my eyes.
I have my medals? – Discs to make eyes close.
My glorious ribbons? – Ripped from my own back
In scarlet shreds. (That's for your poetry book.)

A short life and a merry one, my buck!
We used to say we'd hate to live dead-old, –
Yet now ... I'd willingly be puffy, bald,
And patriotic. Buffers catch from boys
At least the jokes hurled at them.

Wilfred Owen, 'À Terre'

'Modern society, far from providing the aged man with an appeal against his biological fate, tosses him into an outdated past, and it does so while he is still living,' says Simone de Beauvoir. Though frequently men, when they are still very young, have so immersed themselves in some powerful current of emotion that there is little possibility of their extricating themselves all that much later on, when history proves, notwithstanding their bravery, that the notions to which they were so early committed were either naïve or downright unexamined evil. Rationalizing or even managing to forget the worst, they continue throughout long lives to glorify the best. Some, like Blunden, will admit that 'this is not what we were formerly told', to illustrate the special innocence of their generation, though not to repudiate its misdeeds. In any case, the awfulness has always been so obvious as to need no comment; what needs their loyal support for as long as breath lasts is the good. The Great War's 'good' began to be summarized in various philosophical and even liturgical forms while the battles were still raging, and converts to it have had unique aids for practising it in a most moving language and in a multiplicity of shrines.

It is strange to think that we are now very near the day when everyone who fought on the Western Front will be dead. For this extensive company has so long been interwoven in European and American, Indian and Commonwealth, as well as British twentieth-century growth as to seem permanent. Now 'we that are left' are octogenarian, the stragglers of a host which has marched out of earshot. To the veteran who has lived by the faith of the 1914–18 brotherhood, it is as poignant a moment as any since the Armistice, this drying-up of witness.

One of the best imaginative attempts to capture and project the better nature of the Great War was Toc-H. Originally, it was an inventive part of a mainly Anglican mystique by which the orthodox church of the period tried to accommodate itself to an unprecedented moral disaster. It was the other side of the medal displaying the ubiquitous drum-banging parson whose special knowledge of, and influence in, the old town and rural parishes made it easy for him to press men into taking the King's shilling. 'One of the greatest aids to recruiting was the Church,' wrote Major-General Sir Ernest Swinton, 'which from pulpits of all denominations preached the military cause with a fervour that made a deep impression on those who heard the stirring Christian call.'

Toc-H began as a memorial to a young lieutenant, Gilbert Talbot, who was killed on 31 July 1915 on the final day of the trio of battles known as Second Ypres in which over 100,000 men were destroyed. It originally took the form of a rest centre in Poperinghe, a little Belgian town on the edge of the Ypres salient, a corner of the Flanders plain. Flanders itself had long since established itself as Europe's modern brawling ground and Passchendaele, Messines and First, Second and Third Ypres were all fought a few miles from Waterloo.

'We didn't call it Flanders ourselves,' said Robert Graves in a broadcast. 'We called it going up the line. Nobody talked about Flanders. Talked about France usually, or Belgium. I don't remember Flanders ever being used except by the newspapers.'

But however named, the area itself had been caught up with British interests and ideas for centuries. Ypres is actually named after a Briton named Hyperborus and it was its destruction by Richard II which drove its craftsmen to emigrate to East Anglia and there create the wool trade which financed a brilliant medieval architecture. Chaucer, in *Sir Topas*, calls it 'Flandres, al biyonde the see' and knew 'Popering, in the place'.

Talbot House, Toc-H for short, stands a few yards from Poperinghe's *place* and was opened in December 1915 by the Bishop of Winchester, father of Gilbert Talbot, as a refuge for those having a respite from the line and for those about to fight. Run by a priest named Philip Clayton on classless rules, it became one of the prime influences and creators of the brotherhood cult which ex-World War One soldiers shared in a very particular sense. Toc-H originally thought of itself as a kind of spiritual club for men between eighteen and thirty. In 1922 it received its charter to 'remain young when the youngest of us here grows old', as the Prince of Wales put it. The Prince, or 'our young man', in his Toc-H blazer and flannels, small and with a film-idol face, was lighting the Lamp of Maintenance and, 'for a moment Guildhall was a vast dug-out, a grotesque exaggeration of that one in Battery Valley on the Somme front, where a whole company had to live for a week at a time, emerging only at night for the relief of the outposts'. Toc-H societies all over Britain 'took light' from the Prince's lamp.

'We have built a house that is not for Time's throwing,
We have gained a peace unshaken by pain for ever,'

they declaimed. Those who resent the youth-myth of the

seventies should study the youth-myth of the twenties in which survivors from the trenches were bathed in a transcendental rhetoric which derived from public-school Hellenism and a mixture of Tractarian and social Christianity. Whilst the dead received every imaginative attention possible, Cenotaph, Unknown Warrior, the War Graves Commission and the Menin Gate, etc., the living believed that their own terrible and wonderful experiences gave them powers which would influence the world for generations to come. Now old men, they find themselves talking of something still sacred to themselves – but almost impossible to convey to their grandchildren. Not the war as such, but its formalized mystery.

'When I went round the battlefields this year,' said William, 'I said to myself, O.K. that's my last time. I had a young man with me, the dietitian of a big London hospital, and *he just didn't know*. And how could he? I only know because I read it. I just missed it. I was a kid then, eight or nine when the war began. My father knew it but I didn't know it, not personally. But I was *near* it and I've listened to the old-timers and, although I wasn't actually there, I do know it. In a sense. The old men remember the good times. When you listen, it is to the good times. It's so far away now. Imagine, sixty years ago! It is a long time. Time enough for the misery to drop out.'

William is nearing seventy and his long friendship with Frederick, George and the Major has grown out of his initial fascination with their war experience. 'There's a certain feeling about these old men,' he says. 'They've got what nobody else has got. It is their sense of fellowship which I love. You don't find it among the chaps from the last war, you know – it's not there.' He has accompanied them on many trips to the battlefields in France and Belgium. For those whose morbidity has never travelled in this direction, it may come as a surprise to know that, within the context of sacred sites, places such as the Pool of Peace at Spanbroeckmolen, which originally was a crater made by a vast explosion of ammonal in 1917, the cemeteries at Tyne Cot, Messines, Hooge, Voormezeele, etc., and architecture such as the Menin Gate are part of the geography of one of the twentieth century's main pilgrimage centres. Similar memorials to the dead of the Second War have not attracted nearly the same interest. Veterans began to re-visit the trenches and the scenes of the great formal military massacres immediately the war was over and many thousands, like William, Frederick, the Major and George, have travelled there and 'kept faith' ever since.

In his novel *It was the Nightingale*, Henry Williamson describes the first return:

> The wreckage of Bourion Wood was covered by green scrub. Far away on the horizon lay the old Somme battlefield, like a distant sea fretted by waves of wild grass and poles of dead trees. He [Philip Maddison, Williamson's autobiographical hero] longed to be once again in the desolation of that vast area, so silent, so empty, so – forsaken. Somewhere in the misty distance were the failed objectives of July the First, that dream-like day of terror and great heat; and below the horizon of fear was Albert and the Golden Virgin . . . As the night wore on and he could not sleep, he began to believe that the entire valley was permeated with the spirits of the dead, and the ghostly part of himself was being called to join them.
>
> Did one lose a part of oneself, in spirit, as one shed part of the body in normal growth? If not, where was his lost part? Was it still lurking in the marsh, an essence of old emotion? Surely that would only be natural? Memory rules life, or most of it. For years the lost part of himself had lurked in the marsh, seeing wraiths of men in Khaki, laden and toiling, wraiths of depressed mules sick with fatigue and mud-rash, walking in long files up to the field-gun batteries, past wraiths of howitzers flashing away with stupendous corkscrewing hisses upwards, wraiths of pallid flares making the night haggard, while bullets whined and fell with short hard splashes in the gleaming swamps of Ancre.

. . . Was there a demoniacal influence in the marsh . . .?
The perpetual and restless spirits of old wrong and imposed
cruelty and hate and despair wandering among the reedy
shell-holes, among broken wheels of guns, and the rusty wire
in the long grasses? The young green had grown again,
hiding old bitternesses, but the desolation was still there.
The young danced at their Jazz-Balle; the cunning made
profit; the money-markets ruled the world as before; the
war was still continuing within the crystallized mentalities
of human beings; the war had brought no purification to
the world, only to those who did not matter any more, the
sensitive survivors of a decimated generation.

'You get on the boat any time between twelve and one for
Ostend or Calais,' said William. 'There would be fifteen or
twenty of us, half of which would have fought in the war.
But we get less, of course, we get less. By virtue of age, you
know. Well, we land at Calais, say, and Toc-H meet you at the
dockside with a coach and then you go to Pop – Poperinghe –
which is about fifty miles. Then you spend the evening in the
Old House. Upstairs there is a library and bedrooms and the
top floor, which was originally a hop loft, is the chapel. You
can still see the hooks from which the hops were slung. You
can see the joky notices from the war. On the wall near the
door, "Pessimists Way Out" and on the stairs, "No Amy
Robsart Stunts", and on the door of Tubby's room, "All rank
abandon ye who enter here". In the chapel is the carpenter's
bench which they found in a shed in the garden. Goodness
knows how many poor devils said their last prayers in front of
it – it is the altar, you see.

'Toc-H isn't sectarian. It doesn't matter who or what you
are. Its motto is "Think fairly, love widely, feel bravely and
do humbly." That is all it asks you to do and if you've done
that you've done the lot.

'When we're on the short run, that is Friday to Sunday, we
have a tour of the Ypres Salient. Ypres was never captured by

the Jerries. It was blasted to hell but they never actually got into it. There must have been hundreds of thousands of men lost there. It was when the German army was about a couple of miles from the trenches round Ypres itself that Sir Douglas Haig issued his order of the day, "With our backs to the wall; each one of us must fight to the end." That was in 1918. We walk round Hill 60 and Passchendaele, and think. Some of us take our wives, some of us walk on our own. The Old Comrades' and Old Contemptibles' Associations have been taking parties to the battlefields for years. They started going soon after the Armistice. It was a holiday, you see. There was a Ypres League and they used to publish a journal. People from these societies kept on returning to the Salient to see where old Tom went down and where old John caught it. I won't say sentimentality, but sentiment grew. It had to. Then the commercial tours began to take over. People love to see a battlefield.

'Time has covered most of it up and you don't see much. I go over it with maps so that I can visualize it then. My knowledge, I am told by the old-timers, is comparatively true and I give the impression that I know what I am talking about. The old-timers value these trips, never mind what they might have thought of the war when it was happening. I don't think one of them would have missed it. They value their experience in as much as they know that it is only they who have got it. Exclusive, you see. Over the years it becomes more and more valuable. It is *very* valuable now. I don't know whether Jerry feels the same.

'I haven't ever met Germans walking around the Salient. They didn't do as we did, and establish a War Graves Commission. There are a few German cemeteries but they are nothing like ours. Very dull and Germanic. They used to bury different from us too. They'd have fifty men under one granite stone. All our cemeteries have been given to us for ever by the Belgian Government.'

In *It was the Nightingale*, Henry Williamson's ex-soldier

hero displays shock when he sees his first German cemetery near Vimy Ridge. The naked white sub-soil of the area had been turned uppermost, so that nothing could grow there, and

> scores of thousands of tall black crosses, acre after acre of blackness under the summer sky, were lined up on the barren chalk which could not support one poppy or charlock. 'What ferocious mind had ordered such a revenge upon the living?' asks the visitor. 'It could not have been the idea of any man whose body had been used against its will as part of the businessman's war . . . here was the frustration of love that was the Great War.'

A certain amount of nostalgia grew, William concedes. 'But time has passed and you wouldn't know Passchendaele now. It's just like Wickham Market. Everything has been re-done – although they never stop finding bits of this and bits of that. In the field, while ploughing, things will turn up. They're still horse-ploughing the fields of Passchendaele. And, say what you like, at Tyne Cot and up at Zonnebeke there is a hushness. It hits you, or at least it hits me! Such a quietness over the countryside and you hardly see any birds. You don't get birds over there. Maybe the bombardments murdered the birds – I don't know. And at every cemetery gate, always on the right, you'll find a book with the names of everybody there. I just missed it all, didn't I?'

Holding the Ypres Salient for almost the entire length of the war produced, as well as its particular mysticism, its particular mockery in its defenders. The Salient itself had achieved its unique reputation for invincibility after the Germans, thwarted on the Marne in October 1914, had tried to reach the Channel ports that same autumn and had been checked by the small British Expeditionary Force which came to be known as 'The Old Contemptibles'. From then until the collapse of the German armies in 1918 both sides contested every foot of mud, day in and year out, with, eventually, a crazy indifference to the cost in terms of wounds and death. Thrice, the endless attritional shellings and forays blew up into the immense battles known as First, Second and Third Ypres, in efforts to break the impasse, but, apart from the frightful slaughter, nothing was solved until the 'Big Push' in the summer of 1918. All this fighting took place on a dull strip of Belgian farmland fifteen miles in diameter. Of the 200,000 British and Commonwealth soldiers killed there, 90,000 were actually lost in the mud itself and have no known graves, and the price of defending Ypres added up to a fifth of our total casualties of the war – and about two-thirds of total losses in the Second World War. Those who endured it raged at its imbecilities at the time, became very angry with the way it was popularly misrepresented in the newspapers by some of the worst yellow journalists ever invented, and sardonic and satirical regarding life generally. Their trench newspaper called *The Wipers Times or Salient News*, which covered the entire period of the Ypres battles and which was nostalgically reprinted in 1930, reflects attitudes which would have shocked the platitudinous and patriotic home-front. It is one of the conditions of old age not to feel the old anger. The decades water down the just vehemence. Feeling and righteous doubt are wiped out by something referred to as 'perspective', and unlike irreverent pain, irreverent humour is nipped in the bud. It belongs to being young and not knowing any better. Sometimes when one is listening to old soldiers, one has a vision of dumb, brave victims clutching poppies in bleeding hands. Reading between the lines of publications such as *The Wipers Times* one catches little glimpses of those aspects of the personality which age, and not the war itself, has suppressed.

The first issues were printed right next to the medieval Cloth Hall in Ypres under shell-fire and, under the thin veneer of 'fun', a sort of amused happiness which seems to have become defunct, *The Wipers Times* produced the kind of criticism of the war which would have disturbed Bottomley and Northcliffe then, and which means little to its veterans now. When the Menin Gate has come to symbolize a khaki

Via dolorosa, it is uncomfortable to be invited to 'The Menin Gate Cin'ma' to see a programme consisting of, 'Soldiers at Play', 'Inferno' (with 50,000 artists), 'Piggles goes a-Sniping', 'All is not Dead that's Dirty' and 'The Road to Ruin'. Or to sing, 'The Trenches ain't the Proper Place for Kilts' and 'Star Shells Softly Falling'.

Or, in the ads column, to be invited to 'Build that house on Hill 60' and to buy 'Our new consignment of highly decorated cars . . . handsomely appointed throughout and easily known by the Red Cross painted on the side'. Kirschner pin-ups were preferable to the ubiquitous society beauty. 'You poor little dears,' wrote Lancelot in his letters to Lonely Ladies, 'how we pity you, how we sob for you, and how often we think of you with great big tender thoughts . . . Tell me, do you *really* all wear those short skirts and things we see such pretty pictures of in the illustrated papers from home?'

In the Letters column Flamsey MacBonald wrote, 'As I was going over the top last week I distinctly heard the call of the cuckoo,' and Choir Boy wrote, 'I feel constrained to draw your attention to the terrible state of the church tower of Neuve Église.'

'*The Wipers Times*?' say the old men, 'oh yes, that was fun.' But now their recollected emotion is shaped by writers the majority of them knew nothing about at the time, Remarque, Binyon, Owen, Sassoon and Blunden.

George, the Walking Wounded, aged seventy-nine

What of us who, flung on the shrieking pyre,
Walk, our usual thoughts untouched,
Our lucky limbs as on ichor fed,
Immortal seeming ever?
Perhaps when the flames beat loud on us,
A fear may choke in our veins
And the startled blood may stop.

   Isaac Rosenberg, 'Dead Man's Dump'

George, in his late seventies, has lived and will die, he says, by 'the spirit of nineteen-eighteen'. That was when he was eighteen and when a bullet crippled him for life. He has lived with pain and disfigurement ever since. One leg is bowed out and shortened so that his movements are gripped in a vigorous rolling motion. In spite of such a handicap, he looks well and strong, has had a successful business career and is celebrating his golden wedding. The war remains the moral pivot of all his experience, attitudes and dreams, and the older he gets, the more the trenches call. He is aware of belonging to a group which was for a long time fairly average and ordinary, but which is now dwindling into exclusiveness. He is part of the diminishing brotherhood and of the remnant that was actually present to pull, as Rosenberg put it, 'the parapet's poppy'.

> Poppies whose roots are in man's veins
> Drop, and are ever dropping;
> But mine in my ear is safe,
> Just a little white with the dust.

George could righteously annex another line from the poem – 'It seems you inwardly grin as you pass strong eyes, fine limbs . . .', for this is what he has actually done ever since, though not sardonically. Now old, he has no doubt whatever that his bad wounds were a good price to pay for what the war eventually gave him and it is hard to detect a scrap of regret. For him, its idiocies and injustice are as legitimate a part of its terrible splendour as its celebrated camaraderie. Omit nothing, nothing extenuate, is how he sees it, ghastliness and loveliness devouring each other as, due to the special social realities and myths of the period, they would never do again. 'You would think that after all these years you'd forget 1918 but it's in your bones and you can't, it's in your blood and you can't.' In the grotesque bones with which it left him and in the blood which drained out of him for six hours on a summer's morning in a field near St Quentin.

'You see, I have never looked upon it as a disability,' he insists. And he is right. Seeing this sudden wrecking of his body within the spread of nearly sixty years is to see that it has been creative. 'When I came back I walked about on crutches and why my wife ever *thought* of marrying me, I'll never know. Fancy marrying a *cripple*! I was so young when it happened and it was so long ago that I can hardly remember being straight. Sixteen days on the Western Front made me like this – and made me, as I am now. That's all there is to it. There's no good letting your troubles get you down when they can set you up, if you know what I mean. Before 1918 I played tennis. After 1918 I had this bike with a fixed wheel and a pedal cut off, and I rode it about with one leg. I was too young to be changed by what happened. The changes all came after it had happened.'

Like so many old soldiers, George's beliefs are centred upon a form of Anglican nationalism, masculine and kindly, which found expression in symbolic reunions, summer camps, rallies and social welfare during the twenties and thirties. Now even to its most loyal adherents, most of them very old, it is plain that the whole thing is worn out. It is activated by the sentiment of their own involvement and must disappear when those who were actually implicated in the guilt, as well as in the heroics, of the war, themselves disappear. Like those who sum up traditional good manners with references to giving up one's seat to a woman, George grouses about contemporary irreverence towards the national anthem and hymns sung at football matches – 'It doesn't mean a thing to them any more.' But this 'it' intends to convey something far more complicated and profound than standing to attention for 'God save the King', of course. George is voicing the familiar bewilderment of so many old people when their ethics and customs have passed through the phases of being popularly shared, popularly challenged and popularly ignored.

'I don't know whether I should say it,' says George's old friend, 'but I'm beginning to wonder if Toc-H hasn't fulfilled its function. Toc-H to me and the other old-timers isn't anywhere near what it was once. It was a movement for certain. But we can't get anyone young in – it means nothing to them. It means no more than the Crimean War means to us. So I think that Toc-H has fulfilled its function. And as I've been a member for over fifty years it sounds as if I've fulfilled my function too! That's what getting old means. The things you belong to wear out and yet you feel you have to go on making do with them. You feel loyal, you see, because you had them when they could do you a bit of good.'

George says, 'I met Tubby Clayton with the Prince of Wales in 1929 when I accepted the Lamp of Maintenance for our Branch. It was in the Albert Hall. I was wearing the old round, real silver badge – "For King and Empire Services Rendered" – and the Prince started talking to me. In those days it was an honour to wear the badge and the Prince of Wales said to me, "You've got an honourable badge there," and I said, "Thank you, sir," and he passed to Tubby and he said, "He's got an honourable badge there," and he passed on to the next man and he said, "You've got . . ." I'm one hundred per cent behind the Royal Family, indeed I am.'

George gets up from his chair and says, 'Feel there. Go on, feel there.' Fingers surprisingly plunge into a tunnel near his hip. He extracts a bullet from a drawer; cause and effect.

Also his diary for 1918 in which the Church calendar and personal entries neatly share the little space. The Epiphany and 'Barbers. All hair off. Lecture on Gas. Bayonet fighting and Organized games.' The beheading of St John the Baptist and 'Over the top'. A double rubric.

*

I was eighteen when I joined the Eighteenth London Irish Rifles in January 1918. I remember after I'd been wounded only eight months later, getting a letter from home saying how pleased they were that Parliament had ruled that nobody under nineteen would be in the front line. In fact, the trenches were full of boys as well as men. We'd all got to the stage when we'd only got boys left – and children-sized boys, some of them.

Anyway, here I was, training at Chiseldon until that July. I was very Christian and even when there wasn't a church parade I'd always go to the six-thirty service on Sunday nights. Or I'd listen to the Wiltshire bells tolling when I was on the parade-ground and wonder if I would be saved to go back to the old church at Hillingdon and hear the tolling there. Silly little things. I'd had a bit of a shock already and it had made me serious. When I was fifteen and a server at our church, my mother got brain cancer. One evening she called me to her bed and said, quite calmly, 'George, will you read me the Twenty-third Psalm?' I found it and started. When I couldn't go on, my mother said, 'Never mind, never mind.' The doctor then came in with his bag. He got out a syringe and a bottle, dipped the syringe, held it up to the gaslight, deliberately – so that I could see him doing it – dipped it again, and then injected her, saying, 'I can't really do anything about it, you understand?' We waited a minute or two. 'Mother's asleep,' he said. She didn't wake and I was eternally grateful.

So now here I was, already experienced with death, and learning to march 120 paces to the minute – the London Scottish always struck up the bagpipes when we passed their

H.Q. to annoy our officers – and painting the coal stocks white. We really did. And then on 8 July we landed in Havre, where I promptly got into trouble for turning out the guard when the C.O.'s car passed. It was flying his flag but he wasn't in it. You know, it was the mad stupidity of the army as much as the fighting and hardship which made us such friends. On 12 August we had to parade and were told that the sixth battalion of the London Regiment had been wiped out. We were given new numbers, transferred to this unit and ordered to the front line. On the way we camped at Round Wood and it was there that I experienced the worst bullshit of my soldiering. Haig was coming to inspect us before we fought and for days we spat-and-polished in the pouring rain, even being made to drag the gun-limber chains through the gritty mud to make them glitter. On the great day he passed on horseback at about 400 yards' distance.

Two weeks later we reached a line the Germans had just vacated and on the next morning, after being made to drink a lot of rum, I went over the top for the first time. Everybody has written about it and nobody can describe it. Not really. The legs and the arms of the dead stretched out, the ripped bellies of the horses steaming and stinking. And the dead faces of mates looking up at you out of the filth. Filth. Men made into filth before your very eyes. 'He's finished,' you'd say to yourself, and, in a way, you were glad he was! Because there was this agony about having to go over the top. It was useless agony because you'd *got to go*. How I prayed then! 'Over the top!' it was, and there you were, running and falling. After the first time I fell asleep in a trench filling with water and was nearly drowned. We were on the Somme. It was solid carnage, noise and death. There was so much death then that it doesn't matter to me now. Or should I say, it doesn't worry me now. Now that I'm getting on for eighty and when there's not a morning when I don't thank God for it. Day come, day go.

On 25 August, about four in the morning, the whole front

opened up with a barrage which I shall never forget. This was
the day I committed murder for the only time. I threw a Mills
bomb down a German dug-out which was sniping at us. Two
days later we went over the top at 4.20 a.m. and advanced
three whole miles! The next day I wasn't so fortunate. After
being filled with rum again I went over the top at 5.15 a.m.
I caught my packet. I lay there unattended till nearly noon
when they sent some German prisoners out to fetch me in.
Eighteen months and five major operations later, I started
my present life. It was only natural for those of us who shared
that sort of thing to have enough in common to keep us going
later on. Anyway, you couldn't share what the war gave you
with men who weren't in it. How could they understand?

Now it will soon be 'over the top' for all of us again! Yet I
don't think that you really consider life coming to an end
even when you are old. You don't dwell on it, you know! And
you're sorrier than ever when you lose a friend. When you're
a young soldier you can lose friends but when you're old you
never quite get over losing anyone or anything. I think you
know real loss when you're old. And silly things strike you;
when they put me in my coffin will they be sure to see that I
am dead. Nonsense. But it occurs to you. Old age is very
much what you make it and I try to make it busy and interesting. I'm President of the Toc-H branch and Chairman of the
League of Friends of our hospital. I keep at it, and, what is
more, I do all this big garden.

Douglas Haig's Batman, aged eighty-five

The blinds slipping lower and lower upon an area of the past
which has provided meaning and drama in one's life is a particularly bewildering aspect of senescence. Not to be able to
recall is in some instances not to be. Time has plucked from
the brain not only its 'rooted sorrow' but also the great codifi-
cation of one's essential experiences. The hardest facts give

under the pressure of recollection, they cave in, and no amount of trying can recover their true shape. 'You remember, don't you?' insists the kindly voice of family or friend, as it repeats the tales once told to them, priming the pump, trying to re-start the old flow. But the old man does not remember. He cannot. He is alive and healthy-looking and eating his dinner, and will later ride off on his bike, but he'll no longer know what befell him here and there, then and, almost, now, than would a stranger. The years have not only 'razed out the written troubles of the brain' but much else beside. 'You remember, don't you?' prods the would-be helpful and oh, so patient voice, but still you do not. How can you? Trying to fit these things which one is being told back in one's skull is like attempt-ing to do a mathematics in which the symbols themselves have become inexplicable.

The slide into brain disease is often so gradual and so pro-tracted that the eventual eclipse of one's brightness is scarcely noticed. Though not so with Thomas. For him it is like being outside himself. The centre of his personality with all its dates and faces and happenings has disappeared, or practically so, and not even all these well-meant suggestions of what it con-tained can do much to bring it back. Every now and then something recognizable floats into his mind and then, surely, the rest must follow? But never. Thomas was nearly eighty before he began to forget on such a landslide scale. It hasn't left him foolish, simply remote – and remote to himself as much as to others. What often occurs, as Simone de Beauvoir says, is that 'every individual does begin to go downhill after a certain point' and that what we like to think of as either an admirable or tolerable old age really means 'that the elderly person has found a physical and mental balance, and not that his physical being, his memory and his possibilities of psycho-motor adaptation are those of a young man'. And yet, as with Thomas, a senescent imbalance comprising a physical vitality amounting to adventurousness and even a kind of beauty, plus a head whose treasures have already been seized by death, is also endurable. In fact the contrast between his easy, active physique at eighty-five and a brain which is not so much vacant as seemingly unmarked lends mystery to him.

He is a widower living alone in the country, in a little property which might have started out as one of those chicken-smallholdings which could be acquired for about £140 during the late thirties. Margaret from the next bungalow, a young woman with husband and children, not so much 'does' for him but extends her life and family so that they include him. She comes in and out but disturbs nothing, makes his bed, brings food, cuts his hair, fills the oil-stove and chatters comfortingly. He is always 'Mr'. He meets her warmth sometimes with eagerness, occasionally with bemusement. He loves her children.

Margaret: 'He loves children – any child. A child on the bus to him is a wonder. He is mesmerized completely by a child until it is out of his sight. A child is a miracle to him. He has got some wonderful books of engravings of children. You feel as if you are in them. They are great treasures of his because he is captured by the beauty of children.'

She is touched by the opposite directions in which this octogenarian boy and her thirteen-year-old Kevin are travelling, one towards being grown-up and the other towards a bed in her bungalow and the grave. She actually enters Thomas's house as she might enter an adolescent's room, seeing plenty which doesn't suit her but disciplining herself not to meddle. She doesn't say what she thinks when, one moment, she sees that his cup is sometimes no more than a white glow to his speedwell-blue eyes which have cataracts, and the next, he is away on his bicycle, jaunting through the village, a showy old jackanapes with hair and beard flying. Or when he weeds the garden and can't see groundsel from pinks, and makes holes and muddles like a baby. It is the liveliness of his agedness which pleases her. He has thickly-growing, strong hair like a youth and the lines are vanishing from his skin, which looks like varnished tissue.

The biggest thing in his life was the Great War. Margaret knows the story but he doesn't. Not any longer. He saw the war from a unique angle, being Douglas Haig's batman. With this fact in mind, he becomes tremendously interesting to both visitor and friend. Whilst the muddy line sagged, held, broke in its carnage a few miles back, Thomas was laying out razors and towels for the man who was in charge of it. At the end it was the Commander-in-Chief, not Passchendaele and the Somme, who left the indelible 1914–18 mark on Thomas's long life. So much so that he eventually changed his own name to Haig in tribute. 'I am very proud to think of the reason why you did this,' wrote the Field-Marshal's son to Thomas half a century later. 'I am interested to know that you served my father in the Montreuil, although that was a long time ago . . .'

'Lord Haig was your friend, wasn't he?' says Margaret, taking a chance and rushing the memory-door. Thomas smiles his 'big smile', as she calls it, but can add nothing, not even yes. The strange thing was that, after the Armistice, Haig's servant refused to collect his medals. He was twenty-seven in 1918. In 1975 he surprised Margaret by a great outburst:

' "I don't know, I wish I'd got my medals, I wish I'd seen them. I wish I'd got them – I do, I do! I wish I'd *seen* them. I should have seen them. I should have looked at my medals. I wish I'd got them just to look at . . . only just to look at, you know." He said all that!'

Thomas fetches a huge volume of engravings of an old Royal Academy exhibition and remarks, 'There was a picture I was going to tell you about and it has completely gone. It's in here but it has gone.' He adds, 'If you've got anybody and you can call them a friend, that's important.'

The Suffolk Recruit, aged eighty-four

I expect I would have been eighteen, yes eighteen, when I
went. I went from Kettleburgh. I went to Ipswich, that's where
I had to go. You had to go where they pushed you, you know.
I was in France – that's where I was, in France. Yes, I was on
the Somme. It was terrible. I don't know that it was the worst
place but it was terrible enough. Terrible enough for some
men to catch something off certain women for the purpose so
they couldn't be returned to the trenches. Some men missed
months of the war like that. I stuck it, of course. But it was
terrible, no doubt about that.

I lay out between the German lines and ours. I was in no-
man's-land. There were several with me, all nowhere. On
machine-guns in no-man's-land. We was in shell-holes. There
was a shell-hole here and a shell-hole there, and we cut
communion-trenches to each other. I was the relief for the
gun but I wasn't a gunner. Good gracious – me a gunner!
But they didn't trouble then whether you was a gunner or not.
You see, when a regiment got cut-up it was anybody for anything. Anybody! And that was me. That was the trouble of it
in them days. So we was out there, and it was a lovely sunny
morning, though during the night it had been raining. I was
layin' on one side of the shell-hole and my mates were layin'
around me, and the sun was a-shinin', and it was morning,
and I thought, 'That'll dry me a bit like,' as I lay there.

Then, all at once, there was a little ol' plane up above and it
was goin' round and round and round and round, and I
thought myself, 'That's a signal!' Oh, but they was now
shellin' like anything. There was hundreds of shells now
comin' over, one and another, and I thought myself, 'Well, I
don't know . . .' So I got and stood up. The chap that laid the
other side moved and I went where he had been. I got my
trenchin'-tool out. A lot of the shells was comin' from over
that side, the German side, so I started pickin'-down the bank.
Because a shell-hole is like a pond, y'know, and I thought that

if I made a den in the side, I could get in there, y'see, and be covered. I was pickin' and pickin' away and these shells were still a-comin' over, and it was a marvellous thing that was to hear them as they come. Then I could hear one a-comin' and my mates all hollered, '*Look out!*' We were blown-up.

It was 1916. When I come round, my mates what were left weren't many. Two had come off the gun and they were all right. They'd done the wounds up for the others. But of course, they couldn't do them all. There were wounds that were beyond them, wounds beyond all reason. Well, I won't go on about it. I never heard nor felt them doin' anything to me though somethin' had been done. That shell had hit me from the hind, y'see, as I was scrabbin' the bank to make a shelter. A good job I worn't facin' the centre, do I'd have been blinded. So there it was. I come-round hearing this sergeant a-sayin', 'Oh, I don't know what I'm a-goin' to do, oh, I don't know what I'm a-goin' to do. What *am* I goin' to do?' He say, 'They ain't come back and they won't come back, so what am I goin' to do?' And on and on like that. He was a-worryin' about somethin' y'see. He sent two men over the top to inform the captain that he was out of action because our wires were cut. But the men hadn't come back and he knew narthen'. On and on, he went. He was in a pickle.

And I thought, 'I don't know . . . ? If Jerry come over here, what will he do – shoot us? Probably. Most like.' And my blood was runnin' away and I kep' goin' off and comin' round, gainin' my senses and losin' 'em, and hearin' this sad sergeant. Next time my senses came back I said, 'Sergeant, I'll volunteer to go over and give a report.'

He said, 'What *you*?'

He thought I was mortally wounded-like so he didn't say no more to me. But he said to a chap that was with him, 'Will you go too?' There was no more to be said. The chap simply got up and I got up, and we struck-off, and all I thought was, 'This chap will know where to go.' You see, my blood was runnin' away and if I didn't get back to the main trenches for treatment I would have perished anyway. And I could also let the captain know where the sergeant was. That was my thought.

We got a little way. We were low on our bellies because of snipers. The boy was in front, wormin' through the mud. We'd got to crawl, I reckon, a hundred yards, but who can say? There was shell-holes to go round. 'Keep a-hold of my foot,' the boy said, 'that'll drag y'. Keep a-hold of my foot.' So I held to his boot with both hands and he dragged me with him. Eventually we got there and this chap jumped into the trench and hauled me over in a hurry. The captain took a look at me and said, 'Fall-in two men and take him to the dressin'-station.' And away I went. It was brave, they said, but what else could I do? If I'd stayed in the shell-hole I should have bled to death. So I was dragged away from death by this boy's foot. Brave, they said, but no more than common sense really.

So these two men got a-hold of me and we started to go down the trench. When we'd got half-way down this here communion-trench we met some chaps comin' up with some tea. Do you know, that cup of tea, that did revive me! Revive me! I've never forgot it. How that returned the life to me! Then the ambulance came up and took me away, and that's how I got away. My conscious faded on and off. I know I was layin' down and that there was this padre, and he said to me, 'Give me your address.' As soon as ever I told that I flopped. He thought I'd gone and he wrote home to Suffolk to say I'd *died*. Imagine. Anybody would, seein' me out like that, but imagine the home with the news in it. Singin' woke me up. I come round in a lorry full of men that were singin' for all they was worth. I lay listenin' between faintings. Then on and on, but now in a barge. A barge! Then a ship. Then England. At the hospital they found my hands clenched and when the nurse pulled them open, 'Ugh! Stink!' she said. My palms war full of clay from the battlefield where I'd scrabbed. They had been like that all the time. I hadn't opened my hands. 'Oh, stink!' shouted this nurse as she scraped them. She squeezed my arse for all she was worth and I heard one – two – bullets drop into the bowl. She was rough but, poor gal, she was doin' her best. They found I had caught it in both cheeks of my arse. The nurse tore my bandages off three times a day regular from now on but, poor gal, what else could she do? How she hurt, but I don't blame her. Some did worse, didn't they? You can read their names up on the church wall.

The Artilleryman, aged eighty-four

I have no friends left from that war. I had one at Woodbridge until a few years ago but he's gone. He was in the same battery as I was. We went to France together but he's gone. I've got no friends left from that war.

It is over fifty year, isn't it, that war? It don't seem that long ago, that it don't! Over fifty year – well I never! It's funny what stick in your mind, like, about it – that war. The fust time I come on leave, a woman I knowed very well, *very well*, she say to me, 'You ain't bin wounded yet, bor?' I said, 'What *are* you talkin' about, what *are* you sayin'?' Stupid woman! She thought all of us should be wounded or killed. And she worn't the only one!

There were about eight from this village killed. I knew 'em all. They went to school with me. I was fortunate in gittin' through as I did. I went to school till I was fourteen with these boys. Then I started wuk on the farm an' so did they. Of course, my father he had the forge and he thought he'd like me in it, but I was the little 'un of the family. I'm not a man of big stature, see. I recollect goin' to a door to repair a pump and a parson opened it and he said, 'Ha! A blacksmith! I was expectin' a big, strong and mighty man!' I say to him, 'It's like this here, the blacksmiths *were* men who were strong in the arm and weak in the head! But now they're strong in the head and weak in the arm.'

But I'm not tellin' the tale. We all went to the war, me and the other boys. There were bigger families then and lots of boys about here. And so we all went to war. And by then, although I weren't a man of big stature, I *was* a blacksmith – my father seed to that.

I listed directly arter the war bruk out, the first of September 1914, and went into the Hoss Artillery. I went over to France early fifteen and was out there until the end of eighteen. I went through the lot, you might say. Me and Harry – several on us there were from round here. You wouldn't credit what happened to us, you wouldn't really! Mind you, I wouldn't have missed it – not now. Not now as things are. But that was a rum ol' job all right! I remember all the details of the war most distinctly. I was up in the front-line trenches. I was in charge of ammunition for the guns. I was cheerful – we all were. We called it the 1914 spirit. Everybody wanted a goo in that war. They all fared to want to join in, like. Us 1914/15 boys volunteered. I am glad I went; I'm proud of it, and no mistake. We use to sing a song that went somethin' like this, 'How will you fare in the old man's chair' if you don't have a go? It means, how will you feel when you're old if you didn't do your duty? I'm glad I went. Glad? – I'll say I am! I was in the Fourth Suffolks. They got cut-up a good bit. I got cut-up a good bit too, but I wouldn't ha' missed it, that I wouldn't! As God's my Maker, I wouldn't ha' missed it, cut-up an' all.

I shall always remember that it was the first day of spring 1918. I'd bin hom on leave and I'd jist got back to my battery and my major, he said, 'Goo up to the front with ammunition.' I'd only got fifty more yards to goo when I was bowled over. I was ridin' me hoss at the time, and that's all I knew. About the hoss I never did know. It was at Cambrai. It was when the ol' Germans properly bruk through. I came-to in the orspital in Albert. Here I am on a stretcher and here are two nurses that raised me up. One had got a mirror and she was holdin' the thing in front of me. I wondered what that was for and so I asked, and they was surprised to hear my voice. That was plain. 'Ho,' she says, 'I thought as how you might like to see yourself.' I couldn't see that it was me. I was that black in the face and I'd got this big T stamped on my forrid – in indelible ink, you know – to say that I was enjected. I was twenty-five then and was in orspital sixteen weeks over that. That turned out I'd got badly wounded in the shoulder and along the arm and in the back. I was marked for Blighty but soon we were put on a railway that branched off to Trouville and we didn't git hom to England. There were German submarines about, that was why, they said. I was marked B3. In July I had to proceed to the Indian Remount Depot.

We didn't know where it was but we knew we'd have to goo to Paris first. When we got to Paris we found we had to goo to Marseilles, so the sergeant he say, 'How about havin' a little look round at Paris now as we're here, like?' So we did. We stayed three whol' days and we should ha' gone straight through. The sergeant tuk us to museums and sech-like places, and we found lodgings all night in the Marine Barracks there. Eventually we went to the Gare de Lyons to git to Marseilles. 'Say nothin',' said the sarge, and we didn't. Not the usual sort he worn't, as you could've guessed. He'd ha' gone now, I expect, do he'd ha' bin ninety.

Eventually we got to the Indian Remount Depot – on trams. I hadn't contacted Indians before. There were about forty British troops with them and they had no end of horses. The farriers belonged to the Army Service Corps. I couldn't make out why I, an artilleryman, had been sent there. I remember being an orderly sergeant for a day. I went into this here mess-room where all these fellers were, gave a thump on the table, and hollered out, 'Orderly officer! Sid down. Any complaints?' Well, these fellers, they were complainin' due to dry bread. The bread was dry. For breakfast, dinner and tea, dry bread. I shouted, 'Probably you're wonderin' why I've bin sent down here, an artilleryman?' (They had bin there all the whol' war and hadn't heard so much as a shot fired.) I said, 'Do you know what is gooin' to happen? They're about to send all cavalrymen back down here and send you buggers up the line.

And when you git up the line,' I said, 'you'll have biscuits and bully, and bully and biscuits *stewed*! So come you togither now and stop your yawlin'!'

That was the kind of sergeant *I* was!

I was one of the starters of the Soldiers and Sailors Association in the village before the British Legion was begun. It was a big thing, a big thing, but it's narthen' now they tell me. Believe me, I wouldn't ha' missed it, cut-up an' all!

Frederick the Francophile, aged eighty-one

Quiet night-time over Rouen, and the station full of soldiers,
All the youth and pride of England from the ends of all the earth;
And the rifles piled together, and the creaking of the sword-belts,
And the faces bent above them, and the gay, heart-breaking mirth.

. . . When the world slips slow to darkness, when the office fire
* burns lower,*
My heart goes out to Rouen, Rouen all the world away;
When other men remember I remember our Adventure
And the trains that go from Rouen at the ending of the day.

    May Wedderburn Cannan, 'Rouen 26 April–25 May 1915'

Frederick is a handsome, urbane London bachelor for whom France has been a heaven on earth. Perfectly groomed and meticulously turned out – he is the type of man once associated with the best quality shoe-trees, studs, hair-brushes and linen – he could be taken for sixty. As a railwayman, he has been able to use his special travel passes to return to France many times since the First World War and to acquire a sparkling extension to what would otherwise have been a very modest existence. Like many Parisians, his public elegance gives no clue to his private means. He has the easy manners of the loner who is accustomed to making good conversation with strangers in cafés, pubs and trains. Because he is so un-aged and seems scarcely to have so far been touched by the usual deterioration, he is not reconciled to being an old man. While the gentlemanly patterns upon which he has modelled himself make it imposs-ible for him to be vain and self-concerned, he retains the poise derived from the advantages of his early good looks and charm. Still living on his own, used to easy, detached relation-ships and quite unused to having anything done for him, he is beginning to wonder 'what next?' While the post-First World War rites which meant so much to him, the old com-rades' associations, the Cenotaph and Armistice Day 'have faded out', Frederick himself – again without pride or hubris – does not feel that *he* has faded. Inside, he is the dashing young Londoner in Rouen; outside, there is pressing advice about getting into an old people's home. It is for his own good, they say. Anyway, he should think about it. *Think* about it? How unnatural for him to think like that! How odd that others should do so. It is not as though he has been a bother or ever asked a soul to do anything for him.

*

I was nineteen and a half when I went to the war. It was an impressionable age. If I make allowance for the years, I can see myself at the war and I see the same person as I am now. I put myself back into my youth. I often do. I visualize certain places and certain characters, and I can see myself, and I know it is me. But I don't think that this applies to everybody. There were soldiers who, once they came away, never wanted to see anything of it ever again – the majority, I'd say. That was the end. The curtain came down. But if I find anybody interested I like to talk about it and tell them things they don't know, for nobody can ever *imagine* what the conditions were like. I'm surprised that I'm as fit as I am. The war means something special in my life. I think of the life and the attitude we had then. Now it is an entirely different world so I feel a great gratitude that I passed through all that. I really do. I'm always pleased when I remember.

I would say that it was the most important thing in my life to have fought in the First War. There was no comparison between the First and Second Wars. I was forty-five in the Second War and soldiering with recruits of twenty-two, but I didn't feel the gap. I just became a recruit again myself and didn't resent the youngsters at all. But it was not – definitely not – the same thing, and I've heard others my age say this. There wasn't the same comradeship. The conditions were so bad in 1916 that it was a vital thing if you could be a friend. You got huddled-up sometimes in a dug-out, or you would cuddle-up somewhere else in the deep mess to try and dodge shells, and you became emotionally warm towards the man you were with – very. I think of one fellow in particular named Bishop who came from the East End of London and he was always laughing and joking. A fellow with a ruddy complexion who was the picture of strength and happiness, and he shared everything with me, and I know he loved me. Soon killed, of course, this fellow, this comrade.

I knew I would get it some time or other. I'm not frightfully brave in any shape or form and there were few in my battery who didn't get what we called 'the wind-up' during a bombardment. But I never got shaky, I don't know why. There were fellows, you know, who were really cringing and doubled-up – I was never like that. I just believed that if your number was on it, you'd get it. So I never got the wind-up. I think of death now though! I'm still not afraid of it. I tell people, 'Don't think I'm morbid, I've had a good life, I've done a lot, but I'm now of an age when I'm going to become a bit infirm so I hope I go out as I am now. I'm not an old man in my ways – yet.'

My most enjoyable times in the First War were in the saddle. When the weather was fine and you were riding along the road, you wouldn't have changed places with the King! We used to have reveille at two in the morning and then get on the road, ride all day and pull in at a big farm in the afternoon – glorious, it was. In a horse regiment the horses come first and we'd rub them down, water and feed them while the cooks were knocking-up some grub. Then the nearest village and *vin blanc*, and we would be the happiest of men.

You know, when the war broke out they couldn't cope with the spirit. I don't suppose anybody can appreciate it now but I would like to stress it, this amazing spirit. I was at Woolwich and all night fellows would crowd in, stepping over the sleeping men. They just couldn't cope. The way they came up ready to serve and all filled with the patriotic spirit. It was fantastic. I've lived long enough to know a little what it was all about. The Kaiser was the menace. The Kaiser had got certain ambitions and the war was the result. Oh yes, I know very well what it was all about.

There has been criticism, of course. The glaring example is Haig, who has been pilloried since the war. I've never read any of the books on Haig and I don't want to read them. During the war I never had much of an opinion of him. I had a certain feeling about people and Haig didn't inspire me with confidence. But that's not to say *he* wasn't confident. I don't think Haig was a man who played light with lives. He wasn't strictly religious but he was God-fearing and a man of integrity. He's been labelled as a man who easily sacrificed men, but what can *I* say about that? He makes me uneasy, so I don't read about him.

But I'm a bit old-fashioned, of course. You can't change some things. I'm cosmopolitan, though, at the bottom, very much British. It has been a very sad thing for me to see the Empire go. When I was a lad – I was the eldest of a family of nine – we lived cheek by jowl with the nobility, and I never heard my parents cast any disparaging remarks. They knew certain prominent people and they knew their own station and accepted it. There wasn't the acrimony. There was this acceptance of class which made life interesting. Mind you, when one analyses it, one realizes that it was not quite right for one section of the community to have all this and another section to have nothing much. You can't argue that that's right. And I do regret the poverty when I was a boy; terrible, terrible poverty which wouldn't be understood now. Like the First War, it was worse than anything which can be told about it. Therefore, I have to agree when some people argue against my times. Nevertheless, I regret the change in gracious living. I was very fortunate to be a fourteen-year-old boy in the West End of London.

I knew what prostitutes were and all that sort of thing just by looking at them. But I had no idea what it was like to be with one – anyway, I hadn't the money! But I was interested to see what went on. I can always remember the streets at night, about half past eight, with the cabs drawing up at the Café Royal and Oddenino's, and seeing such elegant gentlemen in evening dress and their ladies. And these would be the only kind of people you saw in that part of the West End. None of the hoi-polloi ever got down there. Now the world and his wife are carrying-on there – sordid. It wasn't in those days. You take the wonderful Empire in Leicester Square. In the promenade there, which was frequented by the first-class ladies of the town, there weren't vulgar persons or drunkards, or anything like that, there were beautiful women in beautiful clothes. It was termed the 'International Club'. Englishmen who had served in the colonies, governors, district commissioners and those kind of men, they always went to the Empire. That was *the* place, you see. It was all very beautiful, very nice. But what is it now? They were the days of class distinction, if you like, but things were done nicely then. Sometimes I half wonder how it is that I've lived all these years since. It is only natural that if you've lived to be eighty and you've been moving about, that you've seen the lot.

It was France that changed me. Not the war but France. You remember Haldane saying that Germany was his spiritual home? Well, Rouen is my spiritual home. It was the first big French town I'd ever been in and it was absolutely fantastic. I always gravitate there. I was demobilized in July 1919, and I was back in Rouen in September. I was Francophile absolutely. There were very, very few like me, just some fellows who met girls in France and married them. I didn't have what you might call an affinity with France but I *liked* it. The horses, the architecture, the carts, the shops – everything was different there and it suited me. I spoke French but I can't remember learning how to. If I'd been a bit more sensible I could have found myself a job in France in the Imperial War Graves Commission and never had to leave.

I went back to France several times a year but I didn't go where I fought. But on the fiftieth anniversary of the Battle of the Somme, in 1966, the British Legion organized a pilgrimage and I went with a very large number of other men, and I remember that I was absolutely amazed because they were all as old as me. I was seventy-one. We told each other, 'You're good for your age' – all the time. 'You're good for your age.' I was very moved when I saw where we had fought. But I couldn't get my bearings at all. A fellow from the Worcester Regiment said, 'Trees can grow in fifty years.'

I'd been to Ypres to see my brother's grave but when I returned to where I had been in action and where Lutyens' great memorial is, I was choked, I was absolutely choked. I'd never seen the memorial before and, as a design, it is absolutely hideous, but on it is written that it commemorates 72,000 men who have no known graves. It took me about a week to recover when I got home. This village in 1916 had at the most a couple of dozen houses but I remember it particularly because we had no dug-outs there and we were out in the open. No shelter at all. We stuck sticks in the ground and put our waterproof sheets on the top. And this was when tanks were first introduced. They first went into action at a place called Flers on the Somme, but we knew nothing about them at all.

I remember an officer came up and he said, 'Could you tell me where the O.C. tanks is?' 'Tank' was a code name, you see. I thought he meant water-tanks. About ten o'clock at night two or three of these other tanks came up and laid alongside of our battery, and then went over at about three in the morning. It was only then that I knew what a tank was.

I am not going to say that my generation was better than any other generation, but somehow it seems that we were a little bit up on the plus side! If only because so many of us kept so well in our later years. We were a pretty good breed! A good vintage. But now I feel I am in a stranger's world. It is a feeling which increases day by day. I'm a Conservative but I'm not a hide-bound Conservative. In fact, I once voted Labour, so I'm not a reactionary. But I feel a bit isolated now – very much so, in fact. I don't like what is going on all around me. One of the reasons why I wouldn't care if somebody told me, 'Well, you've only got a couple of years left,' is that I don't feel as though I belong here any more.

I left my job as a railway supervisor five years before full pensionable retirement age because I just could not function. Forty-six years with the railways and then not being able to function. Because of the mentality and tyranny of the trade unions. Everything got most unreasonable, so I left early. The spirit ran out, I suppose.

I always regret my age because there were so many things I could do and I can't do now. But if there's not much physical satisfaction, there's still a great mental satisfaction. Sometimes I get, well I shouldn't call it a superiority complex, but a pleasure because I can go back further than somebody else and say, 'I was there, I saw it.' They would know nothing whatever of things I actually saw and did. That does give me a bit of satisfaction. Nothing shocks you but they don't understand this. Unless you're a bloody idiot, if you've lived for eighty years you must know *something*! But for some reason you're not supposed to know what you know, or what the young know – not any more. But you do. That is why it is bitter to be old.

The Wounded Lieutenant,
aged eighty-four

I've had pain and inconvenience from the war for close on sixty years. I am deaf and my wounds still hurt so badly that I have to recite poetry to myself to get to sleep. I would never take a drug and I'm not the sort to make a prayer, so I say these poems in the dark when my leg hurts. This wretched knee of mine keeps me awake, year after year, and I recite hundreds and hundreds of lines of poetry to keep my mind off it. I usually start off with Gray's 'Elegy' – I find that very soothing, very pain-alleviating. I like that poem more and more. Then Dryden and Pope and Kipling – 'On the Road to Mandalay' – oh, a very mixed bag indeed! Shakespeare, of course. In hospital, just after the First World War, I was immobilized for many months. I couldn't do a thing for myself so I learnt long passages of Shakespeare by heart and said them to myself. That is how it started. It gave me an enormous amount of pleasure. I find that reciting poetry when you have pain and can't sleep is something between an anodyne and a prayer.

I'm no good at what they call the 'eternal'. Some old people say that they are approaching it or have a belief that they are coming to it, but I don't. I feel I should, but I don't. I feel I want to make my peace, but with what, with whom? I'm not a religious man. I was in upbringing but most of it has vanished. I go to church occasionally and observe the conventions, but I don't devote any thought to faith. It is not a big feature with me. My education apart, I am a villager – fatalistic, you know. It all comes out at the end. You know what you *don't* believe when you're in your eighties.

And I'm deaf. This ear went first because it was damaged when I was blown-up at the Front. The deafness increases slowly and inexorably. They tell me that when I am ninety I won't hear anything at all. Silence. But I haven't heard the

kind of talk you get at ordinary social gatherings for a long
time. You're apt to guess at what people say and it makes you
look a little senile. But I'm not senile. It is just that at parties
and things you've got no sense of direction. It makes it very
tricky. It has made me a fireside man now, undoubtedly a
fireside man now. I resent these disabilities – when I remember
them! But when a man's very old all kinds of abnormalities
become very normal, you know. You can't help being old.
You can't help being any age. Here I am, near eighty-five, and
I can't help that!

I don't regret the war in spite of hospital and all the rest of
it. When I joined up I was a diffident, bookish young man,
the worst possible mixer. The army brought me out and
eventually it gave me a tremendous amount of confidence. I
was proud that I'd managed to get an external honours degree
but I soon found that in the army there were all kinds of academically deprived men who were better people than I was.
And that many drunken officers were braver than I was when
it came to it. I was terrified of so many things and I met men
who were frightened of nothing. Of course, we all put on a bit
of a show to hide that we didn't need to put on a bit of a show!
If you get me.

I was a young hermit when I joined the army. For years I'd
worked all day and worked all night to get this external degree.
Education for a village boy like me was rare. I joined a roughish
Yorkshire battalion and as I was one of the few who could
read and write they put me in the office. I enjoyed two or three
miserable months with forms and things. Then they discovered that I had been a very keen member of a rifle-club and
soon I was transferred from this desk and made a sergeant-
instructor of musketry. And that began the big change in my
life, that was the moment which led to everything that happened afterwards.

I had quite a passion for the rifle. Soon I had a marksman's
crossed rifles on my cuff, and my new rank was thought the
best in the army. We had an excellent Mess and less fear and

less ritual. We sergeants could scrounge anything on earth! It was a very enviable position, even if the pay was ridiculous. It was a bob a day with an allocation of three shillings to my mother. I instructed a squad on Wimbledon Common but soon I got so tired of the whole business that I applied for a commission and they sent me to a very posh officer-cadet school at Bushey Hill. It was the Household Brigade Officer Cadet Battalion and usually they only looked at upper-class candidates for it, but as they couldn't find enough of these to fill its ranks they took men like me. It was a further accession of confidence. I loved the disciplined training. It was something I had always enjoyed, I really did. It was a disciplined world when I was young and it was possible to enjoy it. Discipline was engrained in life and you got a taste for it.

Well, as I say, I had a passion for the rifle. I would browse in every handbook to it. I loved my rifle. I went on a musketry course and got a 'D' – distinguished. I had a good time at this officer-cadet battalion. It made me very healthy and put weight on me. They worked me very hard indeed and by the time I left I was a very confident young man indeed. I was drafted to the First Royal Berkshires, which was packed with subalterns waiting to go to France. This was one of those old battalions run by port-encrusted regular officers who looked down on me as complete scum. This was the only army snobbery I met with. They made us walk about the town in parcels of three and we'd spend every morning in Fuller's teashop. This lasted for a month. In the evenings all the regimental plate was brought out. There were toasts to the King and the feeding was marvellous. I'd never known anything like it. Even at luncheon they had a side-table simply loaded with delicacies. They didn't deny themselves anything. And in the middle of the war, too!

Then – France. I went over the top some half a dozen times and it is the most terrifying of all experiences. I endured two gas attacks. The first one was mustard gas and it was just like that picture by John Nash. Half the company was laid out by gas and I was blinded for about five days. When you are blind you don't think that you will ever see again but it wasn't very painful. One morning I realized that I was seeing the medal ribbon on the nurse's chest and that my blindness was past. Later I was gassed with phosgene, which really was an alarming business. We walked up and down the trenches in our gasmasks looking at hundreds of gassed rats.

There were quiet days and bad days. The brigade commander was that fire-eater General Ironside. He was six foot four but when he walked the trenches he looked seven foot, easily. After two bad engagements in which we had suffered terrible casualties, and he ordered us out again, there were protests. But he took no notice. We went in behind one of the early tank attacks; it was a fiasco. They were supposed to lead us but it was so foggy that in the end we were leading them. Most of the tanks had burst their tracks. It was horrific and ruinous, too awful to talk about.

I must have had a strong country constitution because I found that I could get along under almost any conditions and that I was comfortable when I was only bedded-down in a dug-out with sandbags. My batman made tea. The war went on and on. I feel its drag still. Strange to say, I was often very, very happy. I was not a deep thinker then – more of an accepter. Things had to be pretty impossible or casualties really massive before you started questioning what was going on. But there was no question about comradeship. It was made all the more intense because of the fact that so much of it was brief. The whole atmosphere was strongly conducive to deep and intense friendships. And to mourning. Comradeship was a very powerful emotion in all sorts of ways.

Early one morning I was sent out to silence a Boche machine-gun on our side of the Canal du Nord. I had a trench knife in one hand and a pistol in the other, and I fancied myself. The Boche came round the corner and I shot at the first man and missed him. I think you sometimes missed because there were times when you couldn't bring yourself to kill. I may not have been a positive killer that morning. The German boy pitched his grenade and the next thing I knew was that I was bleeding all over the shop, and that the corporal who was with me was dead. I had come round in this muddy trench with my leg and hands smashed and spouting arterial blood. I tried to drag myself along the trench but it was too painful. So I thought that I would have to lie down and die. I was sure of my death and I was very, very hostile to the idea. I was very angry over the way things had gone. I was completely conscious and sensible, and was saying aloud, 'This *is* a messy way to die. Nobody near to give you a word. Nobody here and you are dying. Where will you lie to do it – die?' I wasn't furious because I was smashed and spoilt, but because I was left all alone to die.

A bit later I was being carted along in a waterproof sheet by some soldiers. I fainted. They took me to a casualty clearing and I remember a few things. I remember someone repeating, 'You should have gone down the other day, sir.' What did this mean? 'You should have gone down the other day.'

The staff were scandalously overworked at the hospital. There were about thirty seriously injured men like myself. I remember begging the sister to take all the letters away because they were tied tightly around my painful leg. And at another time I recall seeing a gigantic German helmet walking the wards. And then I began to pick up. And then, just when I should have been getting better, and just after a meal, there was this queer warm feeling drowning me. The wound in my arm had haemorrhaged. That set me back. I would have been in England if this hadn't happened. I was marked down for England. England was a long succession of hospitals, all of them in the height of luxury. Lady This and Lord That, and beds in the ballroom. For weeks I had my knee bent three times a day. When I saw the nurse approach, my teeth fairly started to chatter! It was the sort of pain I had never known before. Very bad. All sorts of treatment lasted a year all-told.

Then I knew that if I stayed in hospital a week longer I'd be fit for nothing at all.

So I applied for some teaching jobs – teachers were in very short supply – and I came down for an interview, got the post and went back to the hospital to tell them that I was leaving. They were very angry with me indeed but they couldn't legally stop me. I never minded the disfigurement, never once. But I minded about my new clumsiness. I was baffled by the difficulties in getting up and down. But what dominated my thinking was the pleasure in surviving. I had got through. This ruled everything. I had lain down to die all on my own and here I was, in this fine grammar school, sitting at the master's desk telling the boys about Shakespeare. You've no idea how pleasurable it is *not* to die when you are young! I was limping and dragging about, and I hurt most of the time, but what did that matter – I was in the world!

You hear old men say that their bodies have become a burden to them. My body became a burden to me when I was twenty-four but I wouldn't say that I found it a burden now. It is very far from being a burden. Because it hampered me so much when it should not have done – when I was young – I hardly think of it at all now. Of course, there are days when you find you can't do as much and you notice the stiffness or tiredness which is part of old age, and you can't help but see that certain disabilities are increasing, so that you feel annoyed, but someone like myself doesn't experience that awful 'break-up' feeling – because one was all broken-up sixty or more years ago, I suppose! Now I'm being philosophical. But I'm an old schoolmaster and I have a right to be. The Western Front proved many things for me – including the fact that I inherited a very good constitution! 'Blown to hell, sergeant-major,' I'd said when they found me and rolled me on to that waterproof sheet, 'blown to hell.' But it wasn't true, was it?

The war clings to me. The other day, while driving my car, with my leg bent up, I felt a small, hard, rough scrap of something between my knee and my trousers. Another bit of shrapnel had worked its way out.

The Legend Wears Thin:
the Major, aged eighty-one

At eighty-one the Major is lanky and elegant. For him old age is the time when you leave the world as you would expect to find it, in terms of one's private papers and possessions generally, all neat and tidy, and, as a place for a new society, with an example and some good advice. He has documented his own existence almost from the start and has never missed a day writing-up his diary since January 1908. A passion for literary moralizing, adage, aphoristic sayings, proverbs, mottoes, and the like has resulted in an almost equally long run of day-books. Whilst half a century of photography preserves many albums of illustrated autobiography. He is the kind of man who documents himself and who is yet not egotistical. He is highly intelligent and unguarded, discussing anything and everything with a striking directness. He is a widower and lives with his housekeeper in a cottage which still shows all the detail of its thirties' restoration. There is a very big garden and, distantly, a modern estate which the Major calls 'the executive-type slum'.

He admires the greater equality of the present time, but little else. He feels that he is dying as the West is dying, with all its hopes and standards made obsolete, and he is deeply sorry for those who have to cope with the immediate future. He prays for them. He thinks that something awful must soon happen and feels both guilty and grateful to have had the last of the good times. 'I think if I wasn't a Christian that I shouldn't think that life was worth living now ... I think we've got to start again *and try not to go forward*. We've got to go back to square one. We've forgotten square one.'

His whole life has been dominated by a long succession of popular sages. Currently, it is Schumacher. But there were many others and their ideas and attitudes signpost his talk. 'My heroes were Studderd Kennedy and William Temple. I'll now surprise you – Marie Stopes was one of the great women of the world – as great as Florence Nightingale and Marie Curie in her way. I was brought up on *Married Love* and she was important to me.' But on the whole the Major represents a once broad upper middle-class culture which was taught how to ask questions by twentieth-century Christian-Socialists.

He has absorbed himself in his old age just as he absorbed himself in every other period of his life. There is nothing that happens to him, his daily routine, his stamina – fifteen miles for a charity walk, continuing cold baths, his bicycle rides, etc. – his current reading, his worship, his sexuality – 'bottom-pinching, you know. You have to watch that when you get old, bottom-pinching' – his food, which doesn't totally interest him. He wants to die in this state and dreads the hospital.

His once strongly emotional feelings for the trenches have died down and he reviews them sceptically. He now thinks that it was his generation which began the collapse. 'We shall go through hell soon.'

*

I am surprised that so many of the younger generation are so much more interested in the First War than the Second one. Myself, I've had enough of war. I'm tired of it, really. It was not among my most enjoyable experiences. Why is there this interest? Edmund Blunden was a friend of mine. He was a year or two younger than me. We were in the same trenches at the same time. I read his book, *Undertones of War*, every three years and each time I say to myself, 'Thank God I haven't got to go through all that again!' Things like:

> Who that had been there for but a few hours could ever forget the strange spirit and mad lineaments of Cuinchy?

A mining sector, as this was, never wholly lost the sense
of hovering horror. The day I arrived in it the shimmering
arising heat blurred the scene, but a trouble was at once
discernible, if indescribable, also rising from the ground.
Over Coldstream Lane, the chief communication trench,
deep red poppies, blue and white cornflowers and darnel
thronged the way to destruction; the yellow cabbage-
flowers thickened here and there in sickening brilliance.
Giant thistles made a thicket beyond. Then the ground
became torn and vile, the poisonous breath of fresh
explosions skulked all about, and the mud which choked
the narrow passages stank as one pulled through it, and
through the twisted, disused wires running mysteriously
onward. Much lime was wanted at Cuinchy, and that had
its ill savour, and often its horrible meaning.

I can't think of anything more boring than trench warfare
and when I am asked to talk about it, I say, fifteen per cent
of it was absolute hell, fifteen per cent of it was damn good fun
and seventy per cent of it was sheer boredom. The best thing
about the Great War was its contrasts. Freya Stark said, 'The
great pleasure of life is the pleasure of contrasts,' and she is
right. The contrast of the trenches and leave, the contrast
between being out in the trench and inside the billet, the contrast between misery and comfort – these contrasts kept you
going and made you happy.

But you didn't expect to last long, quite frankly. And yet
you never thought of dying. I always got into trouble with my
wife – we were married during the war when I was twenty-one
– because I wouldn't talk about it. About death, she meant.
My nearness to it. It was near but I never felt it to be near.
Not then. It is near now and I do think about it. It doesn't
worry me in the least because of my having flirted with it in
the trenches and then as a mountaineer. I take a Christian
view of it and now I am busy tidying-up for my executors. I
am destroying the rubbish and keeping what I think will

interest my children and grandchildren. The war is now a
long time ago but, as I come towards the end, it seems quite
close, to be honest.

I've been back to the battlefields many, many times. I went
out twice with Edmund Blunden. I'm glad I went back. I
enjoyed myself immensely. I attended the Toc-H Jubilee
and also the opening of the Menin Gate, and I've driven
round the graves at the veterans' pilgrimages. Regimental
reunions and a bit of beer. The pull is the memory of comradeship in adversity – that's the pull. I took my two sergeants back
with me and one of them has lived on the experience ever since.
On the pull. We remembered the tragedy of it and the beauty
of it. The Commonwealth War Graves are very beautiful
indeed and inspiring. The more I see them, the more I have
the memory. And yet I was too busy after the war to feel what
they called the 'lost generation' thing. My children were being
born and I was starting up in the soap trade up at Stockton.
I've had such a busy life that I've not had time to reflect very
much up till now.

During the last twenty years I find I have thought increasingly about the war, thought sometimes strange thoughts. I
thought that if I was a farmer farming Flanders fields, and I
had a little walled cemetery in the middle of my land, that it
might be a blinking nuisance! Truth is, I can't believe that all
those fellows buried out there are any longer remembered.
They were a great inspiration to us who were alive with them
but they can't be expected to inspire those who weren't. Guilt
is the right word behind the beauty of these cemeteries but it
wouldn't be nice to mention it. People make comparisons now.
A young fellow who was with us, reading the thousands of
names on the Menin Gate who had no known graves in the
Ypres Salient, and talking of another 30,000 dead at Tyn Cot,
said, 'A mere handful compared with the Jews bumped-off
in the last war.' And yesterday, on the wireless, something
about Leningrad. But when I am at the Menin Gate, to me it
is Gethsemane and Calvary all over again. This was the first

war in which the French allowed their enemies to bury their dead. In old battles men were dug into the mud where they fell, so these war cemeteries were thought of as progress. But guilt is behind their beauty. Give them their due, they are worth seeing. It is worth going. They are worth my going now to see their stress on death.

I've lived for eighty years. I've been wounded twice and I've had bad accidents. In a credo which I wrote during the Blitz, I quoted Browning's 'This world's no blot for us, nor blank. It means intensely, and means good; to find its meaning is my meat and drink.' I've tried.

I think I work and play harder in my retirement than ever I did with my firm. I earned my living by sitting on my bum with a telephone trying to buy raw materials to make soap and margarine. Doing nothing, for the most part, as I waited for the market to drop. Climbing was then my main spare-time interest. I remember going up to the roof of Unilever House, getting through the railings, standing on the edge and looking down on the Embankment. When I found that it didn't make me sick, I started climbing in the Lakes. That was forty-one years ago when I got bitten and ever since I've lifted up my 'eyes unto the hills', climbing all over the place. When I retired I ran the Citizens' Advice Bureau here and I still spend a great deal of time visiting the multiple-sclerosis and geriatric wards in the local hospital, listening mostly. When you are old and ill you need listeners. I'm a listener.

I live with a housekeeper and a fellow comes and does the garden once a week, a dago – a bit lazy. I get up at twenty to seven and have a cold bath. I was brought up on cold baths. We were four boys together and there was always a scramble to get in last because at that time the water was getting quite warm. Father would be kneeling down quite near us, and leaning over his shoulder to say, 'Don't make so much damn row, boys, I'm trying to say my prayers.' That's the only way to teach children what prayer really is – a natural activity, plus silence. On Sundays I go to early service to say my prayers and to matins to see my friends. But I always have a sleep before I go so I don't nod off while I'm there. My wife used to say, 'I never worry about Tom getting into mischief. I know he'll fall asleep at the dangerous moment.'

I'm known locally as 'The old bugger on a bike'. I'm on my bicycle all day and every day, and it's becoming very dicy indeed. Anything may happen at any time. Never mind. We're all living too long now. I am frightened of losing my memory and ending up on a geriatric ward. I've *seen* a geriatric ward! When I was young, the old, with few exceptions, were looked after by their own sons and daughters, but they aren't now – more's the pity. I was born the same year as Rudolf Hess and Harold Macmillan, a wealthy baby in a Christian home. I was very lucky. And now I'm dying in the twilight of a spent civilization. My young friends will have to be at their best to survive. I think we deserve all we are going to get. The cruelty of people now is worse than the cruelty of the war.

5 · The Valley

When we played on the tip it was jet-black, proud and
growing. The engine-house at its top, which
played out the hauling cable, was full of wheels that sang
wonderful velvet, grassy songs. In those days we did
not notice the tip's colour, its blasphemous lack of green.
The young are great accepters and the tip, like the
pit, was the centre of our world. But grass of a sort grows
over it now, a dim, grudging grass over the dramatic
undulations, like a landscape on the moon. The old tracks of
the tramlines down its flank are a contracting,
sardonic furrow. The engine-house is now an empty shell
upon its eminence. The winds blow through it and
the ferns creep back into their old kingdom.

Gwyn Thomas, *A Welsh Eye*

The Longest Marriage in the Valley

They are now in their nineties and have been married for
seventy-three years. They were born about the same time as
Walter Coffin, the first man to sink pit-shafts in the lovely
Rhondda, died. It was Coffin who not only dug Rhondda coal
but who blazoned its superiority to the world, attracting all
kinds of speculators to the scene. The Roberts were involved
in the emotional mixture of slavery and rich Christian-
political culture, music and isolation which dominated their
Valley community right up until the day when they were old.
They have been old for a quarter of a century and they have
lived to see their kind of Socialism regarded as a kind of holy
fairy-tale, idealistic, impractical. The earthly paradise they
preached and prayed for in the huge singing chapels, Hermon,
Calvary, Adeiladwyn, Bethania, Bethel, some of which were
having their grandiose foundation stones laid when they were

children paddling in the fawr, is actually here, but nobody seems to notice. Or, if they do, to cheer. The matter-of-fact acceptance by the young of what to them are still the prizes of Utopia staggers them. They are a bit flattered by the young, who treat them as talking history books, but they are genuinely intrigued by the sheer casualness with which everybody under sixty accepts abundance. The worst conditions to be found in the Valley now would have been considered luxurious conditions when they were twenty-one.

Megan, getting on for a century, belongs to the *Gwyr y Gloran*, the indigenous people of the area, but has not stayed detached from the pits. Ever since a girl she has been passionately involved in their politics, and she still retains the poise and authority of someone whom no committee would dare to ignore. She smiles a lot. In her day both antagonist and colleague must sometimes have wondered quite where they stood with her. She was the town activist and wise woman married to the local charmer. The legend of both their good looks and intrepidity gains rapid substance in their presence. They tell you something and watch how you take it. Owen, at ninety-three, larks about as though he is keeping faith with himself at nineteen. They say he goes into the butcher's and says to old ladies, 'Let's have a dance!' and that they look stern but pleased. They are both old hands at being equivocal and daring. The reforms they worked for have long become a legislation which itself needs reforming. As for the moral climate which sustained them then and sustains them still, this has become incomprehensible to the majority. Their home has the slightly battered look of 'open house' about it. Owen built it himself before the First World War and ever since the Valley has put the world to rights in it over constant tea.

The town descends steeply from their doorstep. Little of it existed before they were born. Now it reaches along the banks of the Ogwr River in stiff grey terraces of colliers' homes from which, at the mine end, further rows herring-bone off up the hillside. The plash and murmur of the river is constant, and can be heard incessantly. It rises some 1,300 feet above the Valley on Mynedd Pwlly-hebog to rush past the pits and ironworks on its way to Kenfig Sands and Swansea Bay. A few miles away the two swift Rhondda rivers Fawr and Fach descend the mountains to become one at Porth and flow through Pontypridd to empty into the Taff. All the old people of the Valleys associate these rivers, so often polluted and inky as they passed by their windows, with images of freedom. A century's grit and industrial garbage is now being extracted from their surrounds, and enormous parcels of granite chips, held together in elegant oblongs by wire-mesh, are being stacked, one upon another, along their banks to make crisp clean walls. The mountains tower on every side. In the recent past they made it psychologically difficult to think away from the Valley as well as making it physically tough to leave it. Beyond the most splendid mountain, Mynydd Margam, lies the Vale of Neath. Like the river, Margam has a symbolic force in the memories of the old. *Margam*, they say, and it has the sacred noise of Sinai.

The town, they said, was 'chapel, pub, chapel, pub, chapel, pub' all the way along. Not now. A certain desuetude in its shopping streets weighs in favour of the old for post-war typical High Street progress has missed the place. The many small shops have a cosy twenties look and the little town itself an arrested quality which must make it easier to be old in than most places, with their supermarkets, heel-bars, discos, boutiques and the like. Shabby welfare halls and workmen's institutes, the Constitutional Club and pretty Edwardian fretwork *pissoirs*, hooked on the hillside for the use of the miners, remain unaltered. The dead lie in a steep bank above the allotments under a cumbersome hanging garden of stone-masonry and majestic texts in Welsh and English.

For the old able to manage the descent from their stepped terraces to the main street or to walk the considerable distances created by the linear sprawl of a Valley town, post-war

developers have added little to its familiar outlines. The
station has gone, the cinema is a vast crumbling hollow. Each
were important sources of release in the lives of the old and
are stuffed with recollections. But what the old miss most is
the turbulence of the past, its crowds and oratory as the population swelled to make the area, by the twenties, a dense mass
of individuals being welded by hardship, rage and hope into
a special society. There were people and things they had cause
to hate with all their hearts, and their eyes light up at the
memory of them. They fed and thrived on bitterness, and
have nothing to recant. An old miner told the writer Trevor
Fishlock, 'The community spirit then was something that
glowed and kept you warm like a fire. All that has gone now,
of course. We used to know pretty well every person in Maerdy
and now we know hardly anybody. The old community spirit
has disappeared and, if you ask me, Maerdy has gone to the
dogs.'

But it is a form of romance to trace too close a parallel
between a long lifetime and events belonging to local and
national history. Most people exist with only the occasional
peripheral thought that they, personally, are part of an age or
an epoch. Neither does their own overlap with figures from
a remoter past hold much significance for them. Queen
Victoria, yes – most of the people in this book are penultimate Victorians – but not Brahms, say, or Tennyson, Tolstoy,
Thomas Huxley, Cézanne, Bismark, Gladstone, etc., who
were all alive when they were children. But in certain situations, and if the span of man's life may include the talk of
his parents and their generation, there is a special significance.
Where a single lifetime encompasses the creation of a particular
society, for example. Such is the significance of being very old
in the Rhondda and Ogwr Valleys of East Glamorgan. For
anybody over seventy-five in that originally beautiful and then
incomparably soiled landscape can claim to have witnessed it
all, the moulding of a new society by a ruthless industrial hand.

Before the subjugation of the area by nineteenth-century

coal-owners it was a wild, lonely, pastoral countryside with sparsely populated parishes celebrated for the longevity of their inhabitants. In 1697 Edward Lluyd the historian wrote, 'Most of the inhabitants of this district are very healthy, there being divers of above a hundred years old,' and E. D. Lewis, checking the Register of Burials for the Rhondda parishes after the last war, confirmed that this continued to be so until intensive mining blackened the neighbourhood. Then what a change. People today can recall grandparents who were 'old, old people at forty-one'. Neither the indigenous element nor the emigrants from western England and north Wales, tempted by even such toil because of poverty at home, could expect to exist for long. A few of the Glamorgan agriculturalists, the *Gwyr y Gloran*, retained their independence and kept themselves apart from what was happening in the valleys and now the grandsons of farmer and miner alike join to heal the scars.

The heavy rainfall, an average of seventy inches per year, polishes the miles of slate roofing and softly drenches the pennant sandstone walls. It brings the river to the boil and pours across the high forests. 'When Irene Morgan returned from Australia to see where she used to live,' said Mrs Evans, 'the only thing she had forgotten was the rain. "Oh, the rain!" she kept on saying. She had forgotten how to understand it you see and she left because of it. I don't feel it myself.'

Perhaps the most startling visual transformation of the townlet for the old has been caused by the vivid use of plastic paint on the identical decorative detail of a thousand Victorian cottages. A feature of the terraces is the fancy-brick or sandstone framing of doors and windows. These frames are frequently picked-out in Bermuda Blue, Geranium, Tango, Mimosa, Blue Grass, etc. matt and emulsion vinyl paints – using the palette language of the manufacturers – creating something of the folk-art effect of barge-painting or fairground gaiety. A long street so treated is gaudily attractive. Very early in the morning young miners canter through the town on ponies, and a reminder that industrialism can melt into farming in a matter of a mile is the careful shutting of garden gates and shop doors against the mountain sheep. The old miners often talk like farm-workers and the years spent below ground have produced a craving appreciation of all that grows above it. They also experience a permanence other than that decreed by time because they represent the stay-at-home element of many thousands of families who fled industrial Wales during the great depression. Many of them are less culturally and consciously Welsh than their grandchildren because of the long English domination of their toiling and political lives. Their fervour is awakened by memories of the common plight, strength and identity created by ecstatic chapel services and noble early-twentieth-century radicalism, and less by the language question. Concepts of Welsh nationhood mean less to them than the passionate oneness born of the days when they were a fragment of a savaged and exploited human work-machine. So firmly and fiercely were they welded by the ruthless pressures of their early lives that even such large questions as those that nationalism poses are less meaningful to them than recollections of the spirited cultural defence which they, as a community, put up in the black days of the coalmasters. Thus even with the 1977 unemployment figures for the area creeping towards the 5,000 mark and a new unease abroad in the Ogwr, the old people of the district remain stamped in heroic terms by the tragic and transcendent happenings of their youth. Whatever the present recession may bring, it cannot bring this misery and strength back again. To have seen and felt both makes it hard or impossible for the old to be concerned overmuch with modern factory redundancy or the Welsh Language Society. Also, as Owen and Megan proved, the old have a way of turning their backs on the community, however much they once worked for its good, and, in Hazlitt's phrase, living unto themselves.

The reason for their introversion after decades of outward-going effort for the neighbours, is their long, long marriage which has been for some years the wonder of the Valley and is now a wonder to themselves. Seventy-three years. Contemplating it causes them to dwell on its beginnings, which in turn causes them to think of themselves as lovers. Ghosts of themselves as teenagers appear in facial expression and gesture as they tell a tale which rouses their own incredulity. Thinking of themselves when young, they intermittently are young, showing off and exchanging banter. A certain pathos breaks into the performance every now and then as they recognize that there is a touch of foolishness in their situation, and that people have a similar amused interest in them to that which they might covertly show towards unusually youthful newly weds. Time has put them on show. It has also caused them to observe the phenomenon of each other. They are both near to being a century old.

OWEN: How did we meet? We met by appointment. She was a student teacher when I first saw her – and what do you think I fancied about her first? Her legs. We went for a walk and we've walked hand-in-hand ever since.

MEGAN: I ought to have a medal for living with him. I think sometimes it's very wonderful to have had him all these years and not to get tired of him. It's wonderful, it is really. It is seventy-three years. And longer than that even because we actually met eight years before we courted. He came to this Valley to work for a fortnight.

OWEN: I stayed. I built this house.

MEGAN: When people see that photograph of him they say, 'We can understand why you married him!' He is eighteen there.

OWEN: I was twenty-three when I got married. Now I'll soon be ninety-four. Twenty-three, ninety-four, but it's getting like a dream to me, being with my wife all that time. We've had our life but I wouldn't mind being young and having it again. The tragedy about human life is that it is so short. However long you live it is short in the end. There isn't a *long* human life. When you are old it is short. I'll tell you a story about the old man and woman that lived to be a hundred. The reporter went into the editor and the editor told him, 'Go down to such-and-such a street and there's a couple there and they're both a hundred years old.' The reporter said, 'Oh, I've got something better than that . . .' The editor said, 'You go down there. He's a funny old man.' So the reporter went and the daughter answered the door, and the reporter said, 'I've come to interview your father.' 'Well, he's a funny old man,' she said, 'but come in.' So the reporter said to the old man, 'To what do you attribute your long life and happiness?' And the old man glared at him and said, 'Who the hell has been telling you that I was happy?' So that's what we'll say – no we won't. No, we won't say that. As a rule the old get crotchety, but we haven't. They all pay us that tribute.

MEGAN: We are the oldest people in the Valley now. The young come regularly every week with their cars. All the visitors are young. Some come Sunday morning and another comes Sunday night, or else I wouldn't go to chapel at all. My chapel is everything. It is the best part of my life.

OWEN: We were church people until we came to the Valley, tremendous church family. It is only an accident that we happen to be chapel now.

MEGAN: It is all the same. It doesn't matter. I don't mind a bit. It is the same goal for all of us.

OWEN: I've never done anything in public life but my wife has. All her life. She was the first woman to go on the local council. She was a soapbox speaker and all. All through the depression. We were with the Labour Party when it first started but I'm disgusted now with the Labour Party. We were Socialists. The old days were sincere. We were all so sincere. George Lansbury came to the Valley and there was a big meeting in the Workmen's Hall on a Sunday night, and you'd think you was in a prayer-meeting. He would come down from London and pay his own fare and put a sovereign in the collection. The Labour leaders of today wouldn't give you tuppence. There was Keir Hardie, we had him here too. We went preaching Socialism across the valleys but today they are all twisters. Now they say we're moving into a new depression.

MEGAN: I taught them Socialism.

OWEN: Those were happy, awful days, awful, awful, happy days! People were very, very poor then. Everybody was on the poverty line. People worked to survive. Just survive. It amazes the young just to hear it. They are our friends but they are terrible. They want everything straight onto their plate. Even the miners don't work as they used to. Two miners would meet by that seat on the mountain-side between four and five in the morning, walk to work on the other side of the mountain, at a little wet colliery there and arrive back at the seat about eight o'clock at night. And the last words they'd say would be, 'See you in the morning about half past four.' At the end of the week there would be 25s. Those men were broken at fifty. But how they worked!

MEGAN: I taught them Socialism.

OWEN: And then, take the main street on a Friday or Saturday night – it was so full you could walk on people's heads. And now you hardly see anybody. Only motor-cars taking people away. For a mining valley it is still very good but it is altogether different.

My wife is suffering from arthritis but I've never had no illness. We're not big eaters. We have our niceties and what we fancy but we're not big meat eaters. My wife can't do much these days so I do the work in the house and then I garden. I spend my days in the greenhouse. If you get stuck in your chair you're waiting for your funeral. We both sleep splendidly. Sleep is very good. We sleep and sleep. Sleep is so good. Being in health makes all the difference but I'm not the same man I was when I met her, say.

206 · *The View in Winter*

Greedy for Daylight:
the Miner's Mother, aged eighty-two

There is a sonnet by George Barker in which he describes his
aged mother as 'a procession no one can follow after but be
like a dog following a brass band' and, at eighty-two, Mrs Parry
possesses a kind of monumental maturity which has its own
special rhythm. She sits out her last days in the classic maternal
pose, heavy-armed, large-lapped, almost worshipful, her face
lit by the light thrown by her white hair. She lives in her
marriage house, which is part of a short grey terrace in a
precipitous road above the coal-washery. Its back garden is
canted into a high wall which seems to be preventing the
mountain from sliding into the kitchen. In front, a new estate
has blocked the huge view which she loved. She sits in a
print pinafore by the roasting coal fire watching gulls wheeling
and parading on the back wall. Her thin wedding-ring and
the different-sized safety-pins fixed to her breast glitter. Her
legs are bandaged under the grey woollen stockings and look
like the stuffed legs of a dumpy toy. Her hands are fat, gentle
and comforting.

In the front-room two married daughters in their forties
are papering the walls as fast as they can in order to drive back
home and cook their husbands' teas. 'It was their idea,' she
says, meaning that it and other demonstrations of their duty
towards her have to be accepted. Her eyes pursue the gull's
flight as she talks, like somebody watching tennis, and her ears
catch at the cries of children playing in the road. The birds
and the quarrelling games provide her with a daylight pattern
of abstract movement and sound. When night comes she
switches to television. She has retained one child from her
big family, Robert who is middle-aged and single, and who
works in the coal-washery. Somehow, walking badly, as she
does, and half in an ancient dream, as she is, she still manages
to do everything for him, just as she did when he was a boy.

There is a strange contradiction between her arresting stillness and the business involved with the daily round.

She is exceedingly sorry to be old and delighted to be alive. Although stiffening and drifting, she loves each day and is unreconciled to mortality like that expressed by hymn-writers such as William Williams of Pantycelyn when he said, 'I am dust, from dust I came, the worm is my brother, the earth my mother.' Like so many of her generation, the last years of her life have been in such economic contrast to the first half of it, every bit of which is burned upon her memory in vivid detail, that she is eager for more. More time, more time, is her prayer during her eighties.

*

It's not impolite to talk about being old because we all get old. Those whose privilege it is to be old, that is. Some haven't had that privilege. Some go out of the world when they are young and I feel awful sorry for those. Life is so very sweet, isn't it? So very sweet, I think. I still find it sweet. If you make it miserable and dull, then it is you and not life that is to blame. I don't resent being old at all – except it would be nice to be forty again! I would then have so much life left to come. You know new things when you are old and you say to yourself, 'I wish I had this much brains when I was younger.' Wisdom, you know. You think a lot and see things in a different light. I see a light which is not what I saw back in the twenties.

I was here when I married. I never moved out. I would never change houses. I didn't want to go into other people's dirt. I'm a bit fussy, like. I try and keep the wheel turning even now. I'm gone eighty-two but they see me doing my own washing and scrubbing the doorstep the same as I've always done since I've been living here. I've been living here for fifty-seven years. All my family has been born and brought up in this house, so it means more than a house, you might say. It's just a bit high coming up here from the main road, though I'm used to it, aren't I! The majority of people who were living here when I came are nearly all gone. Just a few straggles of their children are left. I haven't been much to associate – just on my own always.

My husband always worked in the pits. He was sixteen when he went into the pit. After we were married we stayed here. It was very poor down there so we stayed up here. It used to be hard. Hard! There wasn't much money, you see. It was very poor then, from 1921, and from 1919 when the food was so short. Do you know that our generation worked for next to nothing? The children have more pocket money now than what I brought my children up on. My husband had to retire early because he wasn't well. He started to lose his health and so he left. He was about sixty. He started working in the water when he was sixteen and his health went at fifty. The water shortened his life. Pick and shovel, pick and shovel, just pick and shovel. All the years. Lots of them like him too. The grandchildren all want to hear stories of the old days – they all love to hear stories. Things were so different then – you wouldn't believe. On one Saturday fortnight out, like, we walked all the way to Bridgend just to walk in the park! That was the only convenience we had.

I liked the old people when I was young so I hope the young like me. Where I worked the young lady would say, 'Rhiannon, you do so-and-so today,' and the old lady would say, as soon as her daughter's back was turned, 'Oh, Rhiannon, you skip it.' We didn't have holidays. We never used to think about them hardly. We used to spend our spare time along the river. If I took you to where we walked for picnics, you'd be weary I'd say. Walk, walk, is what we did. If you walked right across to mountain-end and right across the far valley, I'd say, 'That's where *I* walked for picnics.' Oh, but it's beautiful there! Oh, it is beautiful when you have walked to it. The spring was there for making tea and we'd carry our teapots and kettles and things. The boys would fish and paddle and swim, and we would go on with our bit of knitting. We had to have something to do, like. I met people there from the other valley and they'd be knitting and sewing. They loved it better – our mountain. They said they'd rather be coming over there than be at the seaside. *Much* nicer. It was so lovely to walk through the country then, through the woods, you know. It is difficult country to walk in when you are old. We have to walk to the seats and watch the traffic on the roads, not walk to the spring in the mountains.

If I can scramble out to church I don't mind. It is nice to be able to *go* out, see. When I was having the children I used to sit on the boundary wall and watch them going to church. All so many. Now, lorries and cars, and no people. What I miss is our view. They have built all those houses in front of us, see. It was all empty and I used to sit at the table and watch the birds fly along the side of the mountain, and now they've taken this sight away. The people who live in the new houses are young girls with families. They'll do anything for me. Their children have all got to live and they've all got to play, and I'm glad to hear their sounds. My own children were loving to me. They always went to put a ha'penny on the card to buy me a Christmas present. They saved up the whole year. I've still got the presents even now. They paid their ha'pennies for months, you see.

When I look back at that time and remember – well, today they'd never believe you! They would say you were exaggerating. No money, no money. You were lucky to find a penny for the gas, if not – the candle! But we gave no trouble. It was lucky, I suppose, that we gave no trouble. We had allotments, and they helped.

It surprises me to be so old. I always wish I was about forty. There are so many things now. I've got so much to live for now I'm getting uphill, or downhill, whichever it is. I'm getting old too quick! The time goes so fast. It flies away. It's Thursday so soon and I don't know what I've been doing all the week. We didn't have any chances at all when we were young. We worked too young and too small. But there, we have got through. The young today don't have to do what we had to do, but I don't mind. Times have changed and the world is changing, and the money has leaped up.

I sometimes think about death. I think about it to myself. I don't say anything. And then I tell myself I mustn't go far in this thinking because God knows best. But it is natural when, you know, you're getting on. My old neighbour was sent away the other week and she died. Like me, she'd seen hard times. I used to tell her, we'd had more downs than ups! And now she's died. So I just try and not think of my own death too much and just stay true to my religion, as I know it, and trust that it will help me with death. Religion is difficult, you know, and I like to keep it on the right path. This exorcism thing about taking the devil out of that poor man has worried me – frightened me, really. It really gets you, see – something like that. It makes you wonder whether 'tis true or not. Whether it's truth or imagination. That poor man wanted a doctor more than he wanted anything. We'll all eventually meet on the same train, won't we? We're all journeying to where God is, aren't we?

I don't sleep well but I don't mind. I like a little read, I like a little story.

Running Out of Words: the Repairer's Widow, aged eighty-six

Just before Christmas, suddenly and without warning, and after a busy, ordinary day working in her home, she was thrust to the brink of the grave. The widow of an underground repairer, living alone, her five daughters married and with their own families to look after, she had no hint of what was to happen towards the end of this typical day of dinner, tea and housework. For weeks she swung between life and death, knowing nothing. It was 'her girls' she thinks who dragged her back to earthly consciousness. 'I was never without one of them. Never. They were work and worth to me. They were replacing each other all the time. Well, there you are, I'm thankful to have come back as well as I have. I had excellent daughters.'

It is plain that everything by which they understood and recognized her has not returned, and that without these familiar aspects their mother has acquired an unknown quality. She rather enjoys the drama and the resultant consternation. She is very ill and still, and dying, but now able to take a fully intelligent interest in the process. She has big amused eyes in a smooth oval face and a defiant voice. As well as the fragility left in the wake of bronchial pneumonia, she is crippled with arthritis. She doesn't lie abed but is attractively dressed, carried downstairs and placed on the sofa in the front room. It was the room in which she was famous for 'doing the alto' in such songs as 'We Walked in the Garden' and where she now likes to play Scrabble. She kills time with Scrabble while waiting for death.

Her father was killed in a pit accident when he was forty-eight. Her husband lived to be eighty-five. A great singer, he had founded the Valley children's choir and accumulated a mass of musical scores, although he couldn't play a note. When he died she cleared them out of the house. 'All his sacred books, *Delilah* and *Saul*, *Messiah*, and *David the Shepherd Boy*,' said her daughter, 'she threw away. I had to go and collect them out of the dustbin and give them to someone who was interested. It was like throwing his life away, I thought.'

*

I was born on the top of the road near the florist's shop. I should be dead. Two months of my life disappeared. Well, I'm a marvel woman, see. We don't know what's in front of us, do we? So give me the old days every time. There wasn't a lot of money about but life was about. Life. I don't think I would change what I had if I could. I wish I was a couple of years younger, mind. Oh, but I don't know . . . It's terrible

today, isn't it? Money, money, money, all the time. [Amnesia.]
That's what happens to me now. I go on as normal, then my
head will go like that and I'm lost. I used to try to stop it but
we make a laugh of it now. I used to grumble about it but now
I see it as a bit of a rest. I say to myself, now today, so and so.
Then later I say, I won't worry about that today – I'll do it
tomorrow! And I get away with it! I've got beyond that state
of caring too much. Same with looking. Even though a thing
can be close to me I can't always tell you what it is. I like
children talking. I like looking at them. I know what a thing is
but I can't tell you what it is. Words, I mean. They have to
come to me. I can't find them when I'm looking for them,
they're not there.

There's more here than when I was little. There wasn't
anything then, just the river running through. The church
wasn't there, John Street wasn't there. Nothing, it was all
fields. I can remember just the river and a little footbridge
going across. As a family we used to go and see my husband's
grandmother in a brake. That's all we did. Oh, and one day a
year to Porthcawl for the Sunday School outing – about
twelve miles in the train. That's all we did. I can remember
the big strike. It went dark. It was like night mid-day. Soup
kitchens, you know. Strike after strike. And they were the best
days in spite of everything. People were much more sociable
and kind. Dadda used to go round with a lovely little singing
party to collect money for the distressed areas, and I would
collect for wreaths from door to door. But give me that life
before today's life. We were more together then. It is not my
nature to be miserable. I enjoy life and I enjoyed that life.

Those days are gone. We had five of ours working in the
colliery. I had to change the water for each one, see. The boiler
on the coal fire. Had to wash all their backs. They didn't wash
a lot of backs then because they thought it was weakening.
Some would never have their backs washed. My husband
had a skin like a beautiful woman's. A beautiful skin – lovely.
And beautiful hair. The pit didn't hurt his skin but it gave

him emphysema. He would walk up to his hands and knees in water in the drift. We heard the men going to work early in the mornings with their hobnail boots on. Then, singing on top of the hills. Now they're going by bus. Or in Rovers! They've got Rovers up there now! Not then. You could hear laughter in the streets and on the hills as they walked. All the walking. And the laughter in the streets because the beer was stronger then. Now you don't hear a sound. It's terrible.

Other sounds, too – like when the hooter would go and the women would run to the mine, and the miners would come out carrying the stretcher, and the women would look at the boots of the man on the stretcher as they stuck out from the blanket and wonder if he was their man, and if he was just injured or dead. But give me them days. We were more together then. It was poor times. I worked hard for my girls but it was my duty, wasn't it? Does it seem a long time ago since I was a girl? – what shall I say about that?

Rough Journey: the Miner and his Wife, aged seventy-six

Jack and Olwyn are in their mid-seventies and live in the house in which Olwyn was born. It is part of a precipitous terrace built near the main pit by the coal-owner in the 1880s. The severe façade of doorsteps, identical front doors, darkly-flashing sashes and blueish slates has architectural integrity, if of a somewhat crushing order. As the barracks of the work-force it was so erected that neither its inhabitants nor the years could fundamentally change or damage it. Into this and similar Victorian industrial street-scapes modern traffic and television aerials still arrive with some intrepidity, as if tempting the wrath of the overseer. It is a semi-vertical canyon through which the precisely timed miners have daily poured ever since the mine itself was dug. It confines the pitched open-air voices of old couples as well as their housed reticence and sedateness. A burst of talk between neighbours is a squall of sentences giving way to a flat silence when the front doors bang shut.

The wife embodies the formality of the street as well as its compulsive communications. She is an elegant, restrained sort of woman who still looks young and who, like her transformed rooms, gives away almost no evidence of what she has come through. For both herself and her husband the last years have been a bit of a treat. How they have managed to clamber to them via the most defeating obstructions in the shape of poverty, toil and illness, they can't think, they say. Now, towards the end, they are eager and hungry for more. Bright carpets fit floors which she sanded when she was in her teens. Her father bought the sand from carts which called once a week. Free coal blazes in the pink and oatmeal tiled surround which has replaced the huge, shining blackleaded grate before which she daily scrubbed her father and her brothers on their return from the pit. Impossible now to imagine such ascrupulously papered interior steaming with their bodies and festooned with their towels. And hardly possible to see in her husband, the comfortable old man on the settee, the young miner injured in the roof-fall, lying on a hard couch in the same room and threatened by starvation.

He has a scarred face, a hand with three fingers and a perpetual cough; his wife a tense dignity and an explosive mixture of reserve, fortitude and candour. The feeling is that, having endured the whole of the twentieth century in coal-valley terms, what the present offers is almost too good to be true. The special dread of their very united old age is that it can't last. They are conscious of not only having earned this rest and comparative ease, but also of a new dimension in their marriage. They are apolitical and are content to attribute the revolution in work and living conditions which they have seen simply to 'progress'. Both have long made a determined effort to keep the pit in its place, which is out of the house.

'He never talked about work when he got home,' she says. 'You see some and all they talk about is their work.' 'You don't hear the old ones talk much about the old days,' maintains her husband. 'They are pleased to be alive in the new days and to have come through, like.'

*

We've had our ups and downs [she says]. We often look back on the old times and think, how did we do it! We don't ask for a lot now. We like our home, we like our holidays and we don't ask for much more. He can't walk much now so the other day he says, 'Why don't *you* go away for a fortnight?' What, I said, and leave you? I'd be worried to death for one thing. But that's the kind of man he is. I could go out all day long and he'd see to himself.

We met in St John's Church one Sunday evening. We were only married eleven months when he had a terrible accident in the colliery. He was under a fall. My baby was born on the Sunday and the following Wednesday he was under the fall. My father came and told me he had broken his leg, not that he was under the fall. He said they had taken him to Cardiff Royal Infirmary, but eventually my aunt told me the truth. He was home for eight months altogether. That February I found my baby dead in bed. Instead of me taking the shock of the pit accident, the baby had taken it through the milk. On another day as I was getting ready to go over to my sister's – I'd left everything ready for him, his dinner and water on the front – he came in and all I could see was his eyes and just his mouth. I said, 'Whatever has happened?' – A heavy haulage rope had hit him full in the face. He's still got the scars and he hasn't no sense of smell. It was continual worry for the women from the time their men got underground until the time they got them back into the house. I watched him. I can remember watching him one holiday-time when he had to bring a pony up to the surface and it was stampeding all over. It was a job to control it. Once he'd brought it up into the daylight the pony didn't know what to do. I was watching him control the pony.

I've never been down the pit, I'm glad to say. *Never.* I didn't want to see it. What I didn't see I couldn't worry about. My husband never talked about it. Oh no, he never talked about work once he got home. I always said that if I had a son he should never go underground. Although they've got everything now – pit-head baths, everything. But I never had a son, I had girls. We're a close family and we've got good children. They come with their cars and they say, 'Mammy, we are going to Porth and you can come with us.' We always go on holidays together.

I have done the worrying for my husband. Always have done, always will. He'd say, 'Can't you leave that till tomorrow?' and I'd say, 'Tomorrow will bring its own work.' But we've always pulled together. He was really looking forward to stopping work, *really* looking forward to it. Some men don't want to retire, do they? We're better off now than we've ever been in our lives. I sometimes think of my parents who had to work so that they couldn't get old. My mother was forty-one when she died and my father fifty-five. We are advancing all the time, let's face it, we are advancing.

I don't think much about old age but sometimes I think about dying. You've got to die, haven't you? You've got to die . . . When our time comes, well, if you're prepared you can't do no more. You've got to die, remember that.

We've had it all ways yet with all the trouble we've had we've been so happy. I do everything now. I tell him I must! He can't do it so I must. We have four tons of free coal a year and I bring it in. He says it breaks his heart to see me doing it, but I must. We have free coal as long as he is alive but once he is dead, I don't. The widows of miners killed in the pit get it, and the widows of those who die from dust get it, but not me. It draws you more together when you've been through the troubles. The other day he said, 'If I had my time over again I'd still marry you. If I had my time over again, it wouldn't be in the colliery I'd go,' he says. But some boys still want to go to the coal-face. The wages draw them to the pit. They say to each other, 'Terry has started in the colliery and look what he's having for a week's money!' But he says, 'If I had my time over again I wouldn't go down no pit. There is easier work to be had.'

*

I got the dust but not enough for the pension. I went to the authorities and they said no, and that was that. Last year I had the last test and again they said no. So I said, that's the last. I won't bother no more. And yet some have got the dust pension 100 per cent and they can get about and I can't move! Can't get over that, see. I don't have pain from the dust; it is just hard to breathe. All the coughing and coughing all the time.

I felt quite strong right up to the last days of my work, to tell you the truth. It was hard work though, particularly the first part. Nowadays it is all pneumatic and the like but there were no machines where I started. In my young time you had a pick and you were digging under it all day long. Easing the coal out. Using your hands. Naked. I can remember first going down the pit as if it were yesterday. We were naked and we were each given a candle, and the men would blow the boys' candles out – as a prank, you know. And they kept you at it with a stick. Digging bare in the dark. My grandson is sixteen and is doing his 'O' levels. I regret that I didn't have such opportunities – yes, yes, yes! And I think often, why didn't I follow in father's footsteps. He was a carpenter. I always regret not doing that. My grandson sometimes says, 'I'm leaving school after Christmas, I'm going underground!' and his father says, *'On my life you will!'* He knew that would get his father going. But years ago there was nothing else unless you left the Valley.

Mum and dad left in 1929. There was work for him in a joinery factory in London. He went up there and I stayed here.

My brothers also left the colliery and did well. But our brothers-in-law didn't because of beer. One of my brothers had cheek as well as brains and he never went down the pit!

I don't worry though. I can remember them at work; 'I wish I was like Jack,' they'd say. 'He doesn't worry.' Well that's the way to be. I am poor. I am completely poor but I'm better off now than I've ever been. I can show a pound note. But now I can't spend it. I have nothing more to buy, you might say. I go with the boys every Saturday night and I have just two pints, and I'm satisfied. What else can I do?

I've been knocked about. I've been through it all, appendix, ribs away, fingers off, this rope mark across my face still and all the coughing now. But I don't know that I think about death. I say, never give in! But believe me, when your time comes to be put away you've got to have a bit of money, haven't you? So I think about that. I spend my day sitting about. I go up the garden now and then, and bend down a bit. I take my time. I've got to take my time. I'm just turned seventy-six and what I can't make out is that I feel like on top of the world – and then, that's it. Nothing more. I can't move as I did. When I go to do something, then I can't. I *can't*! And yet to feel like on top of the world. I look all right, considering I worked so many years underground. I feel I still look all right.

I like seeing sights, you know. What I would dearly love would be a week with Jack Hargreaves, the 'Countryman'. You see him on the TV. I'd like a week with him, poaching, rabbiting, fishing. His life is up my street. There is one young memory I have. I had gone poaching, see, and I had a ferret. But I didn't have a net over the hole, I had a stick, see. And then I'd go fishing. I used to go with the boys on the mountain and enjoy myself. But now I can't walk. I won't be on the mountain again. If it wasn't for my daughter coming to fetch me on a Saturday I wouldn't be going for a pint. I like a game of snooker but I can't walk to the table now. You are very sensitive about it, you know. I should be fishing in the river now, but I can't. They are tidying the river, they tell me. They say they will build factories by it. And they have put grass-seed on the tips. Do you know what everybody says who comes down here now? They say, 'I wouldn't mind having a job down here. I'd love to live down here.'

The Valley has changed. There were no bridges when I started and the horses and carts used to go through the river. I was driving a horse in the second pit I worked, a puller, see. A chain-horse, now. I'd say I was about seventeen/eighteen when I began with the ponies. When they were all mucky from the pit I had to bring them to the river and walk them up and down to clean them. We had a strike in 1921 and it was the best time I had in my life, I think. Because of the glorious summer. We were down at the river the whole time. We'd take food there in the mornings and stay, and I got sunburnt. I got so that I couldn't lay down. I went back to the drift in 1927 after the General Strike and there I stayed until 1963. The job I had wasn't so hard as it was always on the go. All this running about and seeing to the traffic. And now I can't move.

No, if I had my time over again, it wouldn't be in the colliery I'd go. There was a day when I might have left before it all began, like. It happened that I had this job when I was seventeen/eighteen and things weren't going right. They had timber in the trains and it was sticking out. The under-manager came then and I gave him a bit of cheek, and he told me to go out of the pit. Now this was the very day the new manager was starting. When the under-manager told me to go out, I said, 'Right!', got my clothes and was away. When he saw this he shouted, 'Come on back, I didn't mean it!' And there was this full train going up one side and the empty one journeying down, and this endless, endless rope. I jumped on the full one going up and the new manager was coming down in the empty one, and we stopped right opposite. He asked me where I was going. He called me laddie. He was a Scotchman.

'Wheer y'going, laddie?'

'Pincher Martin sent me out, sir.'

'What'd he send ye out for?'

'Cheek, sir.'

'Ach, come on back with me, come on back.'

So back with him into the pit.

'A Comma in your Thinking': the Hill Farmer and his Wife, aged seventy

I am seventy. It is very different to being fifty. I don't take time for granted now. I am lucky that I own the farm and can go on with it, and nobody can say stop. But I like company too and the farm is too remote, too outlandish. We are out of civilization. And yet I am not just wanting to enjoy the pleasures of life now but to be able to keep on working.

I went to the town the other day and the girl clerk said, 'Senior citizen?' I hate the term. Dreadful. I felt the resentment rising inside me.

My best time was when I came to the farm. When I had the farm, I had it! – and that was the moment. I had *something* at last. But there is no achievement in the end. I have a sense of obligation and a sort of respect for the farm, so that I have to go on working it. But although I have been a strong man the work is now getting harder and harder, and we have never been able to get somebody up here for a fortnight – somebody reliable – so that you could leave for a week or two and feel happy.

I was in the mines at first. I had to. I went to work underground with my brother down there where the washer is now. Then I worked in some little levels, as we called them, with the bituminous coal. I'd been on the dole and on the Means Test. I'd got £1 a week for twenty-six weeks, then 7s. Apart from this I've farmed all my life. I came here from the Rhondda Valley. My father was a collier from hill-farming stock, from

Carmarthen. Came out of the *tyddynwyr* [small hill-farmers] as they called them. Came to where the money is, like the people from Cardigan. 'Cardies', they call them. If you're very keen, 'real Cardy', they say. My father was born in 1875, born a hundred years ago. So many of the miners used to be agriculturalists. Lots came from west Wales and Somerset, Devon and from the tin mines in Cornwall. And from the slate quarries in north Wales. All to the Rhondda. And then their sons followed the moving pattern and left the Rhondda to do navvy jobs in London. Thousands went if they could. Some to the Dagenham works. But my father stayed interested in farming, although he had to work in the mine to begin with. I have heard people say that he could work but he didn't know when to stop. His health went in the pit. When he was twenty-eight he had a nervous breakdown. There's a vast difference between a breakdown then and a breakdown now – you didn't have the tablets, you see. His health became better when he started to sing with the Treorchy Choir.

Then he found a little farm for rent. He paid out six-hundred-odd pounds for about twelve cattle, thirty sheep and two horses. He was taken in. I went on working in the little levels. They closed down eventually. I had saved £100 or £120 and when this farm came up for a tenant, my sister and my father said, 'Well come on, you must try for it.' I was about thirty-five years of age. It was part of the Dunraven Estate. The huge estates have gradually diminished, gradually got whittled down, whittled down, until eighty-five per cent of them is now owned by the farmers. We've been offered £28,000 for ours, and it's only fifty-odd acres. Well, you see, it is beyond all reason. They call it marginal farming – between the low and the hill.

I can remember ploughing it with horses in 1940, sowing the seed by hand, cutting it with reaper and binder. In 1940, yes. And then you stacked the corn and the sheaves would be wet inside. You would see me on my own in a four-acre field, turning the sheaves inside out, little specks of thistle in my hands. I don't know how I put up with it. No, they haven't to graft nowadays as I did years ago. I doubt if any industry has progressed like the farmer's has. I honestly believe that the best thing which can happen to this country, and the best way out of this economic mess – the quickest way – is for everybody to work for their living. Work honestly. I'm a Labour man and I'll say it to any Labour man, and they couldn't deny it either.

I will say things now that I wouldn't have done twenty years ago, although they were in my mouth. But now I don't care. I was shy, very shy, as a younger man but now I speak.

I have a sense of respect and obligation for the farm so that I have to go on working it. But I've slowed it down, I've slowed it down, like. I had about ten ton of hay left over from last year, but it doesn't matter. It was clean, it wasn't frowsty, and I sold it for £30 a ton when it could have sold around here for £60 to £70 a ton. To do that for a few tons of hay! I would not exploit the hay. I would *not*. It is immoral.

In some marriages the wife is the worrier. She'll worry for both. We're both worriers ourselves. But we're all right, we manage. I accept getting old. I know there is something supreme. The instincts of animals have taught me this.

*

We are ashamed of being old [says his wife]. When you are in the company of other people you like to think you are the younger. And they say, 'You're looking well!' and you feel so glad and conceited. To the female mind it is entirely different – the appearance, you know. That is where the word resentment can be applied. It's a great resentment, really, not fear. One doesn't understand but sometimes one's thinking matter is barely alive and the ageing frame just does not permit you to do things. Old age is a punishment, I think. I can remember reading, 'Old age was once a privilege but it has now become a condition.' I found that very clever.

Some old people hold their beauty, don't they? Now what you see in my neighbour Mrs Lewis she has always possessed.

Then, on the other hand, she never worried if the kitchen or windows weren't blameless. Those things she did but they didn't *concern* her. She was far cleverer than that – to let them concern her. It would be wrong to say that she left things, because she had a very, very nice home, but it wasn't the end of her life. She was the sort of woman who would wash-up the breakfast things at teatime. But they would be beautiful things she was washing-up whatever time it was. I think it is people like that who stay beautiful themselves. And her husband was a handsome boy always. We were three mus-keteers from Infants to Higher Elementary.

I was the plain one – very much so. I had lots and lots of black hair with a heavy wave, but a bit podgy, the figure. I was plain so I talked my way in everywhere. It sounds terrible now, but I talked my way into life. Otherwise, the door would have been closed. I am a Pisces, you know. We are a floating people, drifting but warm-hearted. We must have a belief in these things, mustn't we. And in the Bible too, of course. We must have a belief in stories. There's Omar Khayyám, now I don't understand him at all, though everybody thinks that he is in my Bible. My favourite is the Book of Ruth. And a long time ago I read *Point Counter Point*. Many years ago it would be. But I never read now. I can't get a book. I belong to the library and you get light fictional things but you can't get what I call a *book*.

My husband and myself, we still get some fun out of life and by fun I don't mean Bingo. Anyway, I couldn't under-stand it – and imagine standing up and shouting something or other! I couldn't. I couldn't join old people's clubs either. I like isolation and can believe whoever it was who said,

> In our earthly temple there's a crowd
> One of us that is humble and the other proud.

I love *lightness*. William is far more dour than I am, which is a good thing, I expect. But I love the artistry of life. There's no lessening of these feelings when you get old but you become

more shy about mentioning them. You don't get less certain
that these feelings are real but of other people understanding
them. They don't understand the way of life which you lived
when you were younger. For instance, years ago when you
were in a lonely spot and you wanted to jump or run, then you
did so. But when you are seventy or more – oh dear! You
could still do it but you don't. You worry that they would
think you were 'around the corner'. This farmhouse is very
lonely and we have got used to dressing and behaving as we
like because nobody can see us, but we have to watch ourselves
when we go out! When William was in hospital I stayed up
here alone and nobody could understand it. It was winter and
so quiet. And nobody could understand that I was all right
alone.

I've always mixed with young people but it was a long time
before I could isolate myself from the fact that if they were
going to Porthcawl and say, 'How about it, next Thursday we
will go to Porthcawl?' it didn't include me! I was an *old*
woman. It wasn't just that they didn't expect me to want to
go but that *I* shouldn't think of it. To be with them, you know.
It is the sort of thing which doesn't revitalize you at all. The
young come here to talk about politics or history, or just mere
talk, but when it comes to Porthcawl . . . You find it hurtful.
Do the young really want to know about the old days? I often
wonder what *are* the old days. When you are over seventy you
can see the end of time. But before that it is just life and the
future is next year. But seventy – well, if it isn't a full stop it is
certainly a comma in your thinking.

I have a feeling of no God. My father was an unbeliever,
although he would never let me knit on Sundays. He was
known to be quite a learned man. He used to sit by the fire
with whisky on one side and asthma powder on the other. He
was an atheist and yet when he was old and very, very ill, he
wanted the minister to know that he hadn't been such a bad
old man. There is fear about God when you are old because
there isn't very long to make your mind up. I would love to

have someone to lean on. I lean on William, although he's not always there because I'm cross with him, or something. Now my mother had an absolute belief. She cherished life. She lived to be ninety-eight and died without a wrinkle in her face. But I have a resentment of all the awfulness of Vietnam and cancer, and a feeling of no God.

Money is different now. William, for instance, was always very careful with money. That's the farmer in him. And when I say careful I mean he would come to something and think, 'I must renew this without spending.' Even if it was only a new milking-bucket there was careful consideration before getting it. Whereas now William says, 'What's in a pound?' It is not that old age has made him reckless but that the quality of his thinking as regards money has become much lighter. Whereas I have become much more careful. I have relied on William. I have thought, he's here, he'll provide. Now I know that there is a limit to what he can provide. We have milking cows but we don't buy more cattle. There can no longer be anything more expected with regard to making a great profit. And so I have become more careful. Immediately William became pensionable I closed all my accounts in the shops. I have since paid outright for everything I have. I had a fear. William, I thought, is now an old man and it is not the time to go on from month to month, but from week to week. William once said, 'I don't think anything of £100 today – I mean it – I don't think anything of it.' So I have become careful.

6 · The Class of '09

I walk through the long schoolroom questioning;
A kind old nun in a white hood replies;
The children learn to cipher and to sing,
To study reading-books and histories,
To cut and sew, be neat in everything
In the best modern way – the children's eyes
In momentary wonder stare upon
A sixty-year-old smiling public man.

W. B. Yeats, 'Among School Children'

A Need to Talk About It:
the Schoolmaster, aged eighty-four

Old age doesn't necessarily mean that one is entirely old – *all* old, if you follow me. It doesn't mean that for many people, which is why it is so very difficult. It is complicated by the retention of a lot of one's youth in an old body. I tend to look upon other old men as *old men* – and not include myself. It is not vanity; it is just that it is still natural for me to be young in some respects. What is generally assumed to have happened to a man in his eighties has not happened to me. The generalizations which go with my age don't apply. Yet I resent it all in some ways, this being very old, yes, I resent it. I have lost most of my physical strength, and once I was strong and loved doing physical work. I am not used to the loss of strength and I object when many tasks show that they are now beyond me. I cannot quite believe that I can't carry this or turn, or hold the other. This old part of me worries the young part of me. It could be that it would be better to be all old. I think that De La Mare's got the confusion in a nutshell.

His poem, 'A Portrait', says it all. I read it often now and find
that the cap fits. Here it is:

Old: yet unchanged; still pottering in his thoughts;
Still eagerly enslaved by books and print;
Less plagued, perhaps, by rigid musts and oughts,
But no less frantic in vain argument;

Punctual at meals; a spendthrift, close as Scot;
Rebellious, tractable, childish – long gone grey!
Impatient, volatile, tongue wearying not –
Loose, too; which, yet, thank heaven, was taught to pray:

'Childish' indeed! a waif on shingle shelf
Fronting the rippled sands, the sun, the sea;
And nought but his marooned precarious self
For questing consciousness and will to be:

Too frail a basket for so many eggs –
Loose-woven; gosling? cygnet? Laugh or weep?
Or is the cup at richest in its dregs?
The actual realest on the verge of sleep?

A foolish, fond old man, his bed-time nigh,
Who still at western window stays to win
A transient respite from the latening sky,
And scarce can bear it when the sun goes in.

King Lear said, 'When the mind's free the body's delicate,'
and that is true. My mind is very free now but it isn't wandering. It is definite and active in all directions. I feel so alive
but my muscles tell me otherwise. I resent it a little and it's
no good pretending I don't. There has been a great loss of
confidence. I'm not certain about anything now. There are
great losses and small gains. I don't think that you grow in
wisdom when you're old but I do think that, in some respects,
you do grow in understanding. The very old are often as
tolerant as the young. The young haven't yet adopted certain

formal codes and the very old have seen through them or no longer need them. I used to think this and believe that but I don't now. I circumscribe my wants. Few are as important as they once were and they tend to lie quiet unless disturbed. They disturb me when I go out of my way to stimulate them – only then.

The young are always talking about being young and the old would sometimes like to talk about being old, but this isn't as permissible, is it? I never thought about age at all until I was really old, now I would like to say things about it, as a matter of course. While it doesn't actually worry me, it is my big subject! Honestly, you don't believe that it is going to happen to you – you really don't. I have heard very little discussion of it in my lifetime. I certainly don't think that young people talk about it, except to say things like, 'You haven't changed a bit!' or 'How well you are looking.' They say these things most of all when one is much altered and rather ill. What they mean, I suppose, is that you are still a recognizable part of their world – still kicking!

They also say that the longest life is short but I wouldn't say that my own life was short in that sense. It seems a very long life indeed and it seems to have proceeded at a steady pace until I was in my seventies, when the years went in sudden rushes. You are hurried along at the end. But it certainly seems a very long time ago when I was a young man, teaching.

Yet I'm fundamentally the same and I know that I am still deeply engrained with my boyhood. My boyhood stays imperishable and is such a great part of me now. I feel it very strongly – more than ever before. There has been a return to it which has allowed me to recover its importance. It is strange that we should think our boyhoods immature; they certainly don't appear so when one is very old. Mine was an incredibly long time ago and I look back on an entirely different person – different in almost every respect, which is why he intrigues me! But for a chance discovery made by mother this person could have been a farm-labourer, instead of a head of English.

My beginnings were like those of a country child in the eighteenth century. The self-containment of the village, its environment, its self-dependence – the whole situation, all were different. And I was different there. We had a little farm which went down, down, down. Communications were non-existent and so long as we held on to our pony and trap it wasn't too difficult, but then it was walk, walk, walk. Countless miles. Walking to school during the lowest possible ebb of farming through fields lying fallow and hedges overgrown, and never seeing anything more than a cart the whole way, that is what I was doing in that faraway boyhood. Things were hard but hard was normal. In any case, I don't think that hard worries the young all that much. I was happy then, I am sure of that. Our poverty was dreadful and extreme, and nobody believed that it would ever go away. Now and then it rose up and struck at me personally and there was absolutely nothing that I could do about it. Or mother, and she had learnt ways of dealing with practically everything.

For instance, the football team was photographed and the enlargements were half a crown. I couldn't possibly afford half a crown and because I knew how we stood at home I would never have thought of asking for it there. So my head-master, a very good man and a tactful man, bought me one of the photographs. Said that the photographer had included a spoilt copy which he couldn't possibly sell and that he would like me to have it. It was a way of including me and it still sticks in my memory. It taught me when I became a teacher to include those who expect to get left out.

Another thing I recall was the worry about clothes. There were no casual clothes. Not even work clothes were casual clothes but were conformist. You couldn't go anywhere or do anything if you didn't have the 'proper' clothes. Or you *could*, but at your peril. Questions such as cricket flannels for me would arise, bringing great anxiety into the house. For school I was equipped with a pair of hand-made boots. They cost a whole guinea. Well, of course, they were very heavy and rather like labourers' boots, and the more sophisticated town boys made great fun of them. For years and years and years! One suffered at that age for things such as this and the pain stays clear over seventy or more years.

On Sundays we sat in the family pew. We all went there in a procession. Not that I enjoyed it particularly. Sometimes I was deputy organ-blower, and there was a mouse on a lead weight which went up and down. My father belonged to a wood-working club run by the parson and he carved the pulpit which you can see there still. He was a much better wood-worker than he was a farmer, really. He was the best of fathers and his chief delight was in woodwork. He was great with his hands but I haven't inherited them.

Our parson was absolutely first-rate. He ruled village life totally. He was sensible. A sensible man. His wife was related to George Frederick Watts and I remember once at a vicarage garden-party that there was a little pastel sketch and that the price was £10. I was about thirteen. We all looked at the pastel by G. F. Watts which cost *ten pounds*. Ten pounds for a little bit of a sketch! We were bewildered by the art and the cost. We didn't know what to make of it. It made the parson's wife mysterious because she was connected with it. We were so limited. Cooped-up in the locality, roughly speaking.

It was mother who found the way out. It was another £10 but in a quite different context. Had she not discovered it my entire life would have been different. I would have left school at twelve or so and become a farm-labourer. Mother heard that an old charity existed in the village which allowed the sum of £10 to educate one boy for one year. One year's edu-cation, of course, was no good to anyone. But this charity had been ignored and neglected for so long that a substantial balance had built up. And so first my brother and then myself got to the grammar school and stayed there, backed by this ancient money. Mother's determination – she would have moved heaven and earth to make the trustees start paying this charity again – altered everything. It made all the difference in the world to my life. It completely re-routed it. Certainly without it I should have been at work on the land and with all the lack of chances which went with such an existence at that time.

The grammar school itself was still stuck in some distant past. It consisted mainly of a seventeenth-century hall with a curtain down the middle to make two classrooms – a very hit-and-miss sort of division with the noise and tensions, and the scrape of two different classes grinding against each other. Half a mile away there was the headmaster's house and another classroom and a gymnasium. There were about twenty boys and two or three teachers. Some of us were boarders and quite a lot of people walked in daily from all the surrounding country villages. One boy rode in on a pony and stabled it at the pub opposite the school. The whole situation was still essentially Tudor. It was surprising what we all managed in such primitive conditions, with no science lab., no specialist teachers bar the headmaster, and a games field which was just a rough meadow. There was only one prize-day all the time I was there and that was thought quite an innovation. In the dinner-hour the day-boys were left in full control of the hall, to behave as they liked. It was riotous, really a very rough do indeed. The whole place was on the tough side. There was no give and take, and much ritual flogging. I remember that once a week we used to have an art teacher and how we all jeered and persecuted him. He never had an earthly chance of controlling the mob. The school thought nothing of art. They didn't want to draw and they worried this poor bloke to death. He was effeminate-looking and he had a hell of a time. Grammar schools and public schools alike were full of tolerated savagery when I was a boy. If you were interested in things like art you kept it quiet. If you were sensitive, you took good care not to let it show. Once something unusual about you 'got out', you'd never hear the last of it. I was a model school-boy! I was pretty strong, pretty good. I'd inherited a good constitution and I've always been pleased that I was born into the English countryside.

I finally left school at the age of eighteen and then I did worry about the future. The headmaster said that he recommended me to give up any idea of teaching. So the choice was between finding work on the farms, from which I thought I had quite escaped, or going into the local solicitor's office, where I might have eventually risen to be an articled clerk. But I stuck to the teaching idea. I knew in my heart that it was what I had to do. I went to work for several years in some second- and third-rate private schools – there were thousands of such places then – and did an external honours degree, gaining second-class honours in English and French. That is how a village boy of my generation got educated! A rough business with all kinds of people warning you and deterring you.

When I was a boy certain things were done and certain things were not done. It was very much Jack and his Master. Everywhere you went, everything you did, it was Jack and his Master. Master told Jack what he should do, and Jack did it. The notion that Jack should do what he *could* do rather broke this rule. But that was how you 'got on'. Once you'd 'got on', people admired you for it. But when you showed the first signs of wanting to get on they were usually very dubious.

I don't know that I was all that keen on getting on, as they called it, I was simply a country boy who had been lifted out of the rut by books. I loved literature, poetry, novels, tales, history. I am in my eighties now and one of the things I still love most is to handle a brand-new book which nobody else has read. This is one of my pleasures now. The others are, driving the car – I enjoy driving the car enormously – reading *The Times*, eating, mucking about with the grass, television and walking. Village churches interest me enormously and I go in search of them as often as possible and it excites me to find one which I have never entered before. My wife and I used to combine our love of country architecture with the long school holidays spent in a caravan. We always settled in one spot and explored the twenty-mile radius all around it. My wife is a first-rate caravaner and nothing ever goes wrong. We started in 1934, in the days when they were novelties.

Old men like to eavesdrop on the work they have left. I have begun to learn how to look at it all from the outside and I can see education rather better now than when I was in the classroom. Many schoolmasters still have a cloistered career. I had so many associations with so many schools that I always saw education in a very broad sense and not in snobbish terms. It occasionally amuses me to park my car under my old classroom windows and to hear a talking shop. A talking and a talking and a talking.

I didn't go away afterwards. It is a mistake to dig up your roots. The business of the seaside bungalow is a catastrophe. No, if you have worked in a place for half a century, as I have, stay there. Stay there, stay there. Hang on to what you have made when you had the strength to make it. None of it can be replaced. As for worrying about not being useful, no old man need be short of a job. Retired teachers are very useful dogsbodies. I have found myself on the governing boards of nearly every school in the town, chairman of the Art Gallery and one of the prime movers of the Arts Club. But I'm moving to the stage now when I am having to retire from the retirement jobs!

What never stops is reading. I read every day and get through five or six books a week. There are scores of things which have become irrelevant. Money doesn't matter any more. If I was told that I could have £50,000 from the pools I should say no – I would! I am surprised and pleased when old boys remember me. Recently a distinguished old boy wrote about me in the *Times Educational Supplement* and in thanking him I wrote, 'I am a bit bewildered when the very homely bread I cast upon the waters returns in the form of a rich cake!'

I never thought of myself as all that great shakes as an

English master. It was clear long ago that I had been given a gift to communicate literature to a boy. Many are academically qualified to do so yet can't do it. It amounts to that. The thing that matters most is to get a boy to read and not worry much about what he reads. To make books as indispensable to him as they are to oneself. That's the ticket.

They come and see me, some of them fifty or more. They come from all sorts of jobs and professions and say, 'You haven't changed a bit.' They have. I can remember the very desk in which they sat, and this always pleases them. They are emotional during our meeting and very kind. I've known better teachers. It is a great thing for me now to have all this long working-life 'investment', as you might say. It is all right to have a handful of silver in the pocket but you need to have a large supply at the bank.

I've got a modest streak of philosophy. I belonged to the classroom and, looking back on what might have been, I now feel very fortunate indeed. It was a lucky stroke that I got an education at all. As I say, I was just a village boy, a Victorian village boy, but I had all the confidence in the world. Confidence and strength. Not like now.

Round the World and Back Again: the Don, aged eighty-six

A few months ago she lost the friend with whom she had lived for more than half a century and she is experiencing feelings of such intensity that they astound her. She is an academic who shared her life with an artist. Still vestigially pretty, elegantly dressed and well made-up, she doesn't look younger than she is but she does succeed in still showing herself as the woman she was, both to herself and to the world. She is truthful and direct, and sees any attempt to mask her personality as pointless as well as tasteless. Her honesty makes her formidable as well as attractive. She is a serious person who seems to exude the type of seriousness in which one can breathe more easily. There is no mistaking what she says.

She is one of those old people whose lives have been briskly and practically rearranged by others with the best intentions. When her great friend died their house and most of its effects were sold, and Miss Llewellyn, plus a few favourite pieces of furniture, came back to the scenes of her girlhood. She now has what is the popularly accepted ideal solution for the aged, a couple of warm, light rooms in familiar surroundings with discreet help on call. Yet, with the best will in the world, neither Miss Llewellyn nor her things have as yet shown much sign of being able to endure in this new-old situation. The fact is that she has been away from the Valley such a long time – nearly seventy years – that her response to it can only be an artificially emotional one, and this she despises. For her, home is not where one comes from, it is where one arrives, and she arrived there in the company of someone who gave her an entire universe of art, travel, literature, love and enthralling work. Among the remnants of her origins she is a displaced person. She blames nobody and sees what has occurred all too clearly and sanely, but her sharp intelligence tells her that she is as much displeased by being brought back to her roots as if she had ended up in some geriatric hotel on the coast with a group of strangers.

Until it actually happened, she believed that self-control, common sense and her Christianity would see her through this final phase. She knew it would be sad and she accepted its disruption, but nothing prepared her for the extent of her suffering and upset. Grief has become the most positive thing in her life. It is too genuine and actual to be exorcized by therapy or drugs. Another bewildering thing is that, immediately after the funeral and the sale, she found herself in a kind of partial metamorphosis. Half of her was her familiar old self, half someone new to her and whom she still cannot quite recognize. She talks without self-absorption and reveals a striking individuality which has been badly mauled by grief and mourning, though scarcely marked by time. Her conversation is not explicit but is full of candid pointers to her life. The rough trick which old age has played on this intellectual woman, in her flat above the collieries, is to have restored her to an ethos from which she long ago escaped in order to be who she is.

*

The eighties are difficult. You wonder how you'll manage them. You do feel a difference. Then, half-way through them, you begin to take them for granted. Everything is infinitely harder, that's all. I spend my day trying to read. At odd times. That magnifying-glass is growing unsuitable but I've got another one coming. I can't read very well and it was the reading which I liked most. I go on crying all the time. That is what I mostly do now, cry. I try to meet things. I think that is what one must do now. You can't say that 'I can't like this' or 'I won't like that.' When you are old you must meet a situation – there is no other alternative. I certainly feel very isolated – I do feel that. It is a strange thing, really. They've all passed away. All the real friends are gone. There are none left of the friends of my lifetime. The greatest friend was the last to go. There are cousins but I don't know these cousins because I was away so long. But there are cousins.

I was born near the Valley, near there, not exactly there. Perhaps nearer the mountain. It doesn't seem a long time since then, not in memory. When one thinks of then one thinks of people, and it is they who are the past. Not oneself. My mother died at my birth and as there were twelve children my grandmother took me two hours after my mother passed away. When my grandmother died and I wasn't of use any more, I went to England. I had a degree and I got a post in a beautiful place. It was the winter of 1916. A little while later I met the girl with whom I lived for fifty-two and a half years. We were together all that time. Together. We went everywhere. We went from post to post. We always went together and shared everything. One was lecturing on one thing, and one on another. Very nice. We motored to the West Country for our holidays and met the artists, and we sailed to New York. We were so perfectly happy.

My day has quite gone. It is over. Quite gone. It is all very different now and difficult to understand. There is nothing I can do here, although everybody is kind. It is too steep to walk to the library and hard to walk anywhere. I need to be somewhere where I can do more things. I certainly want to walk. There is a bus here but I can't manage it. There are no cars to hire. The world belongs to the young.

The world is so different, isn't it? But it is difficult to say whether it is worse or not. Although we find the children very erratic, it could be that they ought to be like that for their times. It is useless complaining about how they behave. We don't know what they'll have to meet when they get older. It will all be very, very different, and we won't know. They must be able to meet what is coming and so it is useless to say whether now they are right or wrong. How can I know what they will have to meet or face? How useless it is for the old to say anything at all about the young. How can I know what they will see or they know what I have seen? It is pointless comment.

As for old age, you are expected to accept it. You know you are a back-number. I don't resent it. I don't expect what I expected when I was young. I don't even think of it. You take a simple thing such as whether somebody likes you or they don't. It doesn't cross your mind when you are very old. I don't expect to be liked or disliked. I don't expect *anything*. I don't expect anyone to do anything for me, but when they do I say, 'How kind they are,' and mean it. It is all so different, you see.

I don't take medicines. People have a way of taking them just to go to sleep! I won't do that. I don't sleep well but one should never do that. It is a very unfortunate thing to do. They are to relieve pain, and that is different. But to take them just because one can't sleep, well really! The doctor says rest. Rest. I was gardening and walking very long distances until her death. I've always been very busy. I was very strong. Then her death and this weakness from grief came in the end suddenly. But my memory stays extremely good and I've never failed mentally in what I've had to do. Which I think is a great boon. I treasure my brain-power. I hoard it. You really must have memories. They are all you have left and if you didn't have them you would think about what is happening now, and it would be fatal. It would not be the wonderful past which would be inside you but the dreadful now.

What I have complete faith in is that there is another life. I've got total faith in that. I don't hesitate at all. So there is a greater experience soon. Everybody is going on the same journey. I think of death but I don't say that I am prepared to die. But I'm prepared to leave. Ever since I got to this place I have been writing out what I want done when I leave. I've got everything arranged. But whether I myself am prepared – that's a very different matter! Towards the end, when one is old, I shouldn't think that many people consider dying. They should prepare for it but not consider it. I've had a lovely life, really. I shouldn't have had the same life at all if I hadn't met my friend. She was a good help. I think there are a lot of wonderful things in life now but whether they are better I don't know. As for myself, I have to say, 'Well, you've had your day and now sit and rest and think about it.' But when I say this I remember that it was *our* day, and then I weep.

Helen,
the Montessori Teacher, aged ninety-one

Frequently, it is some initial weakness or handicap which preserves one from 'cormorant devouring Time'. The strong can be so nonplussed by its first attack that they have neither the power nor the wit to beat it off. But if it has harassed one from the cradle it is a very different matter. So it was, and is, with Helen. For a great teacher to start off from babyhood with a paralysed arm, and from her twenties with little or no formal education, could imply the sort of struggle which burns one out at fifty. Instead, the opposite has occurred and disability has proved to be the preserving factor.

At ninety-one Helen is still very much her old self, alert, radical, amused and the kind of person you would hope to be placed next to at a meal. Her chief difficulty now stems from the contradiction which exists between the rapid senescence of her body and the lasting liveliness of her mind. For her, longevity is full of conflict because flesh and intelligence are not sharing its destruction proportionately. Her head makes it hard for her to accept the assistance which outsiders can see at a glance that her body needs. She knows that 'they are keeping an eye on her' and why they have to – and why she should be grateful – but she also knows she will never reach the stage of geriatric passivity which welcomes it or succumbs to it.

For most of the day she sits reading and glancing out across the hyacinths on the window seat at the quiet avenue. In the afternoons she struggles into outdoor clothes and then struggles along the pavement. It takes ages, this walk and the preparing for it, but each time she does it she achieves a continuation of a normal pattern, and so it is now all a bit of a triumph. She dresses with a hint of earlier severity. The twenties Eton-crop is lint-white and not so much hair as light. Her voice is clear and decisive. Both she and her surroundings reflect an extreme simplicity, an absence of clutter that is both material and intellectual. Having discovered what she needed in both instances long ago, she has never felt the urge to add much more. The plate on the gatepost, 'Montessori School', remains and the full excitement and liberating force of a teaching method which was first used in Rome in 1907, but which carried forward ideas from an even more distant

educational epoch when Itard civilized the wild boy of
Aveyron, has stayed with Helen to strengthen every day of
her existence. She is one of those rare and fortunate people
who, at an early age, discover a truth which exactly fits their
personality and who can turn the application of it into a
satisfying career. She is the good disciple who is not only
loyal to the vision of a past master, but has had no difficulty
in keeping her early enthusiasm.

Old people who have been part of an historic movement and
who retain its ideals into a period where they have either been
forgotten, abandoned or have developed into something more
sophisticated, can be pathetic. They are seen as being stuck
with a philosophy which the world has either discarded or
discredited, and they become tortured by their secret faithful-
ness, like doddering Fascists. In a different way, it is not easy
for progressives to remain true to what made them world-
changers in the first place because progression, being for the
most part the intellectual territory of the young, stretches on
and on every year, bringing constantly fresh vistas into sight.
So that when one meets a woman like Helen, who is in her
nineties, and who without being defensive or reactionary has
somehow managed to stay one of the 'New Women' of 1912,
the contact is rather overwhelming.

To understand and appreciate Helen one needs to have read
her 'Bible', Dr Maria Montessori's *Metodo della Pedagogia
Scientifica* which, translated as *The Montessori Method* just
before the First World War, is as interesting a contribution to
twentieth-century feminism as it is to modern education. 'Like
Pestalozzi and Froebel,' wrote the American educationalist
Henry Holmes, Dr Montessori 'presents her convictions with
an apostolic ardour which commands attention.' These convictions were passed like salvation by Maria Montessori to a
poor English girl only fourteen years her junior who has lived
on to express them far into the age of mass higher education,
and of the comprehensives. Like her teacher, Helen is quite
without that formidable egotism which drove so many of the

women radicals of her day. Maria Montessori created her Method out of a number of other people's methods, and said as much. Her greatest debt was to Edward Seguin whom she watched putting muscle on to the wretched bodies of children in the Roman slums. Seeing these children grow physically but not intellectually, Maria considered St Francis's mistake when he thought that God's command to 'build the church' meant putting up the usual towers, aisles, etc. She also read with fascination Ezekiel's celebrated 'dry bones' prophecy and knew that her work was to awaken the latent intelligence in every child, whether his body was nourished or stunted.

In 1907, when she was thirty-seven – and Helen was twenty-three – Maria opened her first school, the Casa dei Bambini, in the notorious San Lorenzo Quarter, Rome. This Quarter was the seething by-product of a vast and ruthless commercial building development which had taken place in the 1880s, a human warren where few expected to grow up, let alone grow old. Maria's Children's House was opened there partly to provide a sanctuary for innocence and partly to find material on which she could try out her Method. This contained a whole host of ideas which have long since found their way into our contemporary play-schools, adventure playgrounds, educational disciplines and our acceptance of a child's rights. Using equipment which was part-toy, part-instrument, letting small children understand that their classrooms belonged to them and that adults were only guests in their domain, and cutting out all prizes and punishments, she was able to let her pupils develop in a way which challenged the entire school ethos of her day. Her Children's Houses soon sprang up all over Europe and America and, in 1927, Helen, now a convert, heard that Maria was in London and went to sit at her feet. Although the term was now quite an old one, she thought of herself as a New Woman.

'The new woman,' Maria had written, 'like the butterfly come forth from the chrysalis, shall be liberated from all those attributes which once made her desirable to man only as a source of the material blessings of existence. She shall be, like man, an individual, a free human being, a social worker; and, like man, she shall seek blessing and repose within the house, the house which has been reformed and communized.' In each of her Children's Houses Maria had hung a reproduction of Raphael's *Madonna della Seggiola* as an emblem of the divine relationship which should exist between young and old. In her north-midlands town Helen still sits staring at hers, and at the cabinet-size photograph of handsome Maria in her opulent dress, half-smiling like the Virgin. But the Children's House itself is deserted, empty, and the new woman who made it ring with the ideas of Seguin, Pestalozzi, Froebel, Hahn and Neill, is the old woman awaiting death – or meals-on-wheels. When one is ninety it becomes a merely academic matter which arrives first. 'There will be a day [wrote Maria] when the directress herself shall be filled with wonder to see that all the children obey her with gentleness and affection . . . they will look toward her who has made them live . . .'

*

I don't like being called a teacher myself. I've only been on the fringe of things. I don't fall right into the teacher groove, you see. But I've got experience. I've been a form-mistress, I've been a governess – I've been everything under the sun, and without a single bit of paper by way of qualification except my Montessori diploma. A lot of today's teachers are too specialist. But what couldn't I have done in one of these modern play-groups! I was among the forerunners of these more worked-out things. Years ago, teachers would come here from all the surrounding schools – just to watch me! One of them said, 'Why, it's just like a university!' My children chose their own work, of course. This was their learning place and they invited me into it to learn with them. Their ages were between two and nine months, and five. Before 1945 I had them over five. There was a big independent school nearby and the headmaster always used to say that he was going to make my school his intake! Most of my pupils were middle-class, although I would have taught *any* child – and have.

I was always interested in children, and so was my sister who helped me run this school. I've just lost her, in April. She died in April. She didn't take to giving the school up so she died. She just went to pieces when we stopped work. She was eighty-four. Time goes on, oh, how it goes on! Time goes – of that much we can be certain. We don't know, do we? We must just take things as they come, as time goes. My sister couldn't. She became so distressed after our school closed that I have to try not to think of her then. Only now am I able to start getting back into the time when we were happy. I'll say it: her being here with me were the happiest years of my life. Until we had to close and she just went to pieces. I didn't, of course. And won't. We are as different from each other when we are old as we are when we are girls. I must talk about my sister because she is me although she was another person. This school was why she lived. I was looking after her for seven years when she began to stop living, and now that she is dead I can go out again, and even travel a bit. I make myself go out every day; it is a necessary thing to do. I make myself do it. Effort keeps you alive.

My sister was High Church of England and I'm Non-conformist. I couldn't enter into her religion. I couldn't understand it or feel it. But we remained friends together. She walked up the road to her High Church and I walked up the road to the Presbyterians. I never liked fairy-tales when I was at school. When people started 'Once upon a time' I always interrupted, 'Stop – is it true?' Now my sister was devoted to fairy-tales and would get all she could lay her hands on. But me, I'm just one of those women who need the truth. I'm too factual altogether, that's the truth of it!

I have two girls who call on me, girls who visit old women. They arrange for fourteen-year-olds from a local school to come and see us. At first they hardly said a word and just sat in front of me. I had to tell them, 'You've got this visiting thing all wrong, if you don't mind my saying so! *You're* supposed to talk to *me*. I shouldn't be doing all the talking.' So now they're talking. They're educating me, I think. They brought me the book they said they are reading in school – *Dracula* – and showed me a question which said, 'Do children need Dracula?' Well, do I know what they mean? No. I think we must be careful not to make children obsessive. We must keep the truth. They'll be imaginative enough without that kind of help. A little boy at our school used to come along with terrific tall stories – 'We've got a gymnasium on top of the heather' – things like that. Oh, that boy could tell the most amazing stories, and my sister, who loved fairy-tales, would say to him, 'Yes, that's lovely. Now tell me a true story.' She trained him. She always got the truth *and* the story. He's a myth, isn't he – Dracula? He's the sort of person we didn't get in *our* school. There is a fine chapter on the imagination in Dr Montessori's first book, *The Method*, and I do so want to read it all again. I had a copy here but someone has stolen it. She could write. I would like to have been able to write, to have written, I suppose I should say. But I couldn't have written just stories, I'm so factual. As I said, I'm just one of those women in need of the truth.

I found that old age came to me through the physical, not through the mental. Old age for me, who started off with a withered arm at eighteen months, is just a progressive crippling. I am able to do less and less and less daily. I have arthritis in both knees and both arms and it is this which has made me realize that I am very old. Otherwise I can't say that I know what old age means. I don't feel one scrap different to what I felt when I was talking to the parents fifty years ago. Of course I can't walk very far but the inside person who can't walk very far is still the same young woman who rambled for miles and miles. And another thing. I can still learn things off by heart as I used to at the beginning. Perhaps it is because I am experienced in fighting the physical that I have lived long and stayed young. I have to keep on telling myself, 'You can't do it. You must realize that you cannot-do-it, so stop trying to! You are *old*, that is what you are!' I'm nearly ninety-two and I'm arthritic from the top of my head to my toes, and I can't keep my head in any one position for long. But I won't make this an excuse for not reading. My sight is still good. The oculist just laughs when he looks into my eyes. There's a cataract advancing but it isn't ripe. I see well so I read. Thankfully, I read. Oh, books, how I love you!

I see the past well, too. The tiny ones doing their movement exercises. I see a child brushing crumbs together and it is the prettiest sight you could wish for – the intent look on his face. I see him opening and closing the door, the discovering action of his hand and eye. We never touched the children. They put on their own things, moved their own way. Of course, if they said, 'Will you help me?' we'd help. But I persuaded their parents to have the pegs put down low so that they could hang up their own clothes. So many people like children to be dolls to fuss and pet and manipulate. When one mother said, 'I've come to the conclusion that I'm here to live with Harry and Harry's here to live with me,' I knew that she had learnt the secret. I had a father who brought his son to the school each day, and the boy would be running up with joy when he would be called back in a furious voice and to a finger pointing to a place on the man's face where a kiss was demanded, and I soon showed him that he couldn't go on doing things like that. The little one knew that it was the time to hurry towards his work and not the time for kisses. I used to go for the parents and not for the children. The children, I always told the parents, were people to live with, not creatures they owned. Most parents had no idea what they had got. When they got to the school I would tell them that it was their children's 'office' and that when you go in, don't disturb anything. They were never allowed to interfere or talk to them. They were treading on holy ground.

Children love the old. They love grandparents with a special love because they are immovable. Mother isn't. Father is always disappearing. But Grandpa is stationary. It is very satisfying when a child finds out that Grandpa is there and that he doesn't move.

I think I was wise to close the school when I did. It was getting so that I couldn't compete with television. The children would run out of our parties – and they were the most favourite thing in the entire neighbourhood at one time! – so as not to miss *Doctor Who*. Perhaps I'm exaggerating. I don't like television. I have it put in and I have it taken out. I call television a tragedy for a child.

I don't feel left behind, you know – left behind because of so many deaths. It could be because I believe they are not dead. They can't just finish off like that, can they, because of the waste? Oh, the waste of it all if that were so. Yet we can't know and we shouldn't expect to. A little child doesn't know its father's business. We were a family of ten and we've all gone now except one sister. So many deaths and all of them so close. Just one sister left. One of those girls who has taken it on herself to visit old women said to me, 'Miss Macnamara, do you think all this violence in the world is because Adam disobeyed God?' and I answered, 'Yes, perhaps it is. Perhaps it is our making the wrong use of his laws.' These girls do ask me the most extraordinary questions. I suppose they know that I am really listening. The young come to the old to be listened to. Although I'm not really on the older child's platform, that's not my place. I'm in at the beginning with the first talk and the first movements. I'm looking for the man in the youngest boy. Dr Montessori taught me how to do this.

I came to her because of my dead arm. It kept me at home when my brothers and sisters went out to work. So I gathered up any of the poor children round about and gave them lessons on the things which interested them. I would find out why they weren't doing well at the village school, or why they couldn't talk or read or sing, and soon it would all flow along. I called them my cases. It was a sort of job and the local people got to know me and they'd send along their 'stuck' child and

I'd free him. The ignorance in the schools then was amazing and it would often be some teacher who'd object when I got a child on too quickly. One Christmas, my oldest brother gave me *The Montessori Method*, Book I. It had just been published for the first time in England and it gripped me. I had it by my bedside and I'd read and re-read it. Then its author came to London and my life began. What she said all hung together and was wonderful. People say, 'What do you think of her system *now*?' They say, 'It's a nice teacher's aid for you, but it hardly comes into our way of doing things *now*.' But I answer, 'It all hangs together still and it is wonderful.'

Maria Montessori was a very beautiful woman – very pretty. When I first met her she was dressed in black veils and things, but we soon Englishified her! I'm very grateful to her now. She made me a little part of the system which brought the good changes into education and made children happy.

My sister also took the course when Montessori came to Manchester. She had been a Norland nurse, so that was useful when she came to help me run the school. Yet it was a great grief to me to have someone besides myself with the pupils, good though she was. She cared for the very little ones. And she took over things such as the cooking because of my withered arm. Now she's gone and it's difficult. I know how to cook but I can hardly do it. To stir something on the gas-stove I have to throw my good arm forward to seize the sauce-pan and to bring it down low on a chair or stool so that I can let my not-so-good hand hang over it. I can't move one arm and I can only move the other by throwing it forward and up. Dressing is hard – but wonderful therapy. It takes me hours. I am very limited and if that is old age, then I am old, very, very old. I open tins and things. Meals-on-wheels came – and went! Most people like them but I didn't. There was too much on the plate. Too thick, too much. I couldn't look at these heaped plates. I'm sorry because they were kind who brought them. So now it's tins and things. A home-help has her eye on me and I suppose there are some risks. But what can I do, except go on? I'm a problem for someone if I stay here, and I'll be a problem to myself if I leave. An old people's home, what is it really? Just somewhere to die in. My friend went to one and she was bitterly lost. They just dumped her there. My heart aches for her. I think it is terrible what they will do *to* the old when they say that they are doing something *for* them. They lost my friend in a home.

As long as I can go on, I'll go on, and they'll have to let me go on. I was once told I was a high priority for an old person's bungalow but now that I'm ninety I must have gone past the priority, because I never hear anything! That's what happens to you when you get very old, you go past the priority. It would be best to stay in this house until the very end. I hope so. It would be very nice. Do you know what that old artist Michelangelo said, 'I'm so old that death often pulls me by the cape, and bids me go with him. Some day I shall go out like the lamp, and the light of the world will be extinguished.' And that is how I ought to think, I suppose, yet I can't say that I do. More likely I think of all the children. Their books and models and things are all in that big room, as good as new.

7 · Getting About

The old absorb the familiar streets for as long as they possibly can. Where planners haven't muddled their ancient sequence, the buildings and pavements become very special. They are a measure for what can still be achieved each day, for how far one can go and for how often one will be recognized. 'I must get out,' the old will say, and they do, although often there is nowhere to go. But the shops and crowds tug them back into mainstream living, they exhaust them though at the same time they fill them with buoyancy. The effort to get dressed for outdoors and to leave the house is enormous but soon, when the crossing-lights, the swing-doors, the reading-room's muted bustle, the dodging children, the roaring traffic, the shouting advertisements, the town-hall flags and the snatches of other people's talk are accepted as being as much for them as for everybody else, whatever their age, they begin to feel good. They feel legitimate. They are in the thick of the ordinariness of things in a ticking-over, not a ticking-away world. They buy little bits of meat and fish for their sparrow-sized meals in huge shops which have no greeting. If they are lucky they will bump into a contemporary and swiftly size-up his condition. 'So you still manage to get out, then?' they say to each other, meaning, 'So we are still a part of all this!'

But just to be able to look out is something. To spy on a street, no matter how minuscule the action it provides. All

streets are theatres. Before television anybody, whether local
or foreigner, knew that to walk through a street was to walk
into the range of interested old eyes. Such watching, which the
aged brought to a fine art, is not what it was, although one still
finds many old countrywomen who contrive to combine a fair
amount of small-screen viewing with plenty of what goes on
the other side of their window-pane. It is not nosiness but
nourishment. The old woman left alone in her four walls is
starved and parched, and what goes on on her set, however
sensational, is never going to be as interesting as a neighbour
taking a short cut, or a stranger entering number eight without
knocking. The old become their own novelists when they fall
into abstract street-watching.

To walk in the streets themselves puts them back into the
story. The currents of activity are so inclusive that even the
fact that much of what stirs them is future-orientated far
beyond what is possible for them – a scheme for a new theatre
or by-pass, building society investment, etc. – there is still a
feeling that they are helping to create the excitement which
keeps communities vital, and not mere spectators of it. Being
able to get about in a town, particularly if it is your own
town, when you are very old forces you back into the swim.
The crowds and distances may batter you and make you weary
but they also underline your right to be there, which is ener-
gizing. Those who are able should do their own shopping,
fetch their own library-books and walk to church or friends for
as long as it is humanly possible. It is better to get tired than
to get torpid. Also, as with the glimpse of a child naturally
and unaffectedly demonstrating his childhood in the multi-
farious scene, so the glimpse of an aged man or woman simply
living his or her life at the centre of things is part of the enrich-
ing process. What is clearly needed in every city centre, and
particularly in the vast new shops and public buildings, is
many more seats. Supermarkets especially are barbarously
indifferent to the needs of the old; their assistants should be
trained to have a word of greeting for them, particularly if

they are regular customers, and there should be a place for them to sit and organize their purchases.

Different places create different out-of-doors elderly customs and attitudes. On the south coast they are sea-watchers. Every fine day, winter or summer, finds them on the esplanade looking at water and allowing the mesmeric effect of its sound and movement to wash through them until nothing matters any more. There is a unique calm to be found on the front at Eastbourne on a fine Sunday morning as the ancient sea-watchers take up their positions and, three or four thousand strong, begin their day's staring. Debussy's sea is caught in their grey gaze from one meal to the next and there is an oceanic contemplation which is soothing and which is, at the same time, wide awake. These old people are uncertain why they watch the sea. They talk vaguely of its being healthy, or they intimate that it is what they are paying for with their pensions and with the effort of leaving their inland homes. But they do not admit to its being a powerful drug to the over-seventy-fives, which it mysteriously is. It seems to extend life by exercising the intelligence outside all the factors which formed it. Those at the tail-end of life are dragged into its pull and immersed in life's origins. Its amorphousness and monotony devitalizes them, but the draining can be exquisite. The novels slip on the pastel laps and the gold ornaments on the tanned wrists glitter. White shoes are stock-still. The deck-chairs touch but everybody is alone. The old who have drifted to the seaside resorts are the great idlers. They spend every hour the climate allows looking away from their own element, the land, and into the depths. In the big hotels they pay the piper and call the tune, careful Spanish waiters and palm court numbers. In the retirement bungalow and the discreet 'residence' they recall the regular old faces they have left a hundred miles away, their children's, the postman's, Mrs Edwards their neighbour since 1934. It is a quiet way to go – via the coastal route. 'Do you know, I could look at the sea for ever!' they say. 'It gets a hold of you.'

In Cambridge the old and the young appear to assert themselves with equal confidence and vigour. Looking for the aged in places identified with youth turns all the generalizations upside-down. An Australian, returning to London after a month in Amsterdam, said, 'But this is an *old* place' – meaning the inhabitants, not the architecture. Cambridge too is an old place once one has adjusted one's vision to notice such things. The old, though not as swarming as the young, are still abundant. The exuberant, annually topped-up flood of students, with its ritual display and antics, is complemented with a remarkable number of old people who seem to be unusually determined and mobile. Cambridge parades old age almost as much as it parades youth. So many septuagenarian and even octogenarian academics speeding through the streets on bikes, whatever the traffic, is a startling sight. Not only have they preserved flexibility and movement but an alertness in the face. The run-down of mobility is too early accepted by many aged people. The contrast between these elderly Cambridge cyclists and the cumbersome, heavily-dressed old men lugging shopping-bags along the pavements is striking. In the last years, as in the first, there is a mounting exhaustion which comes from inactivity, from nervelessness and stolidity. Many old people are slowed to a shuffle in their seventies because they lost their élan in their forties, or even earlier. Agility should be accepted as a longer lasting thing.

In Cambridge, too, one sees much human clinging-together, young lovers and old couples. In the new shopping precinct the old couples break-up as the husband takes a bench to which his wife can return with vegetables, groceries and sometimes with a garment which is measured against him. These aged women repeat what they did fifty years before when they parked a small boy on a bentwood chair at the counter with instructions not to move. They return to base like faithful birds, straightening ties and turning out pocket-flaps, and saying briskly reassuring things. Nearly all the old men have boxy, ill-fitting clothes which weigh them down, and which are the result of their believing that if you have a fifteen-and-a-half collar and eight-and-a-half shoes you will have them for life. While most of them are clean and tidy, almost none of them attempts anything more. Many are over-dressed, waistcoat and pullover, plastic mack and overcoat. So they sit, oddly shrunken here, broad as the bench itself there, encased and awkward, their monumental faces faintly glistening from sweat and silver stubble, massively-torsoed creatures with thin legs doing exactly what they were told, which was not to move, not to go away. They are the husband-children of the old bird-wives. To the old people on bikes they are as far from them as are the undergraduates. Ancient female academics shop in the Market Place, calling stallholders Charlie and Terry. They wear tweeds and flatties, carry satchel-bags and have large snakes of grey and saffron hair. They are lean and grimly cheerful, with clever old faces, arthritic hips and fighting eyes. Aged scholars of immense celebrity pass through confident posses of students like crows through flower-beds, apparently indifferent to the contrast, full of their own subject and impervious to all else. The youth–age time game is played out to the very last move here, and in the street. E. M. Forster used to warn anyone who wasn't young or old to steer clear of the place.

A village funeral is a great coming-out occasion for the old. The deceased was eighty and had a finger in every pie from local politics to the flower festivals. She was commanding and splendid with a tally-ho voice and an immeasurable kindness. She died one May morning after a good breakfast and without a hint of illness. At her funeral the church was filled to the doors with old people, gentlefolk, as they still privately thought of themselves, all of them decorous to a fault and each of them displaying a perfect ritualistic response to the occasion and not a tremor of grief. Mourning for the aged members of a rural society can be a very repetitive business and the newish growth of the memorial service can mean even more such dutiful turn-outs.

Turn-out is a phrase much used by this group. It is applied to Armistice Day, Holy Communion and funerals. The group knows exactly what and whom to turn-out for. Its composite years on this occasion run into millennia; hardly anyone present in the packed building is under seventy and nearly all have known each other for a lifetime. Its catchment area is what used to be called the 'county', meaning not the whole of Norfolk but a socially viable stretch of it. There is a superb quiet and simplicity, a knowing where to sit in somebody else's church, a knowing who is present without moving one's head, a knowing what to wear and how long to pray. Cars stretch for a mile outside. The coffin is trundled along on a hand-bier, the widower refusing the undertaker's transport. Everybody sings Crimond with the minimum of voice, yet touchingly. She was having dinner with them on Saturday and here is her coffin. She had a full, long life, the young clergyman tells them, but so have they. Afterwards he climbs into the hearse with her for the crematorium twenty miles away. He waves everybody towards the house and tells the widower, 'I'll see that everything is all right.' He is like a good best man.

The mourners pack the house for sherry and talk of gardens, and say, 'How are you getting back?' to friends. The very old faces look fine and healthy with no trace of fear or tear. There is no hint of loss until, grotesquely, the deliberately flat, controlled talk turns to plastic bags instead of dustbins, which makes the octogenarian widower think of Christmas boxes for tradespeople and say, 'Eleanor looked after all that, of course,' bringing home to him his remorselessly alone situation in the future. He looks from face to face – how on earth will he manage? The mourners all drive away saying, 'Take care' and 'Come and see us – later, you know . . .' Suddenly he and they look tired and glad to break away and get home. A month later he announces the memorial service and they all return, polite, dutiful, feeling little or nothing. 'They blame me for not weeping,' the old man says, 'but I can't. I am too old to weep, too old to cry.' Nobody has blamed him for not weeping; it is not something they would blame anyone for not doing.

The outside old are conspicuous rail-travellers. They have half-price tickets and are using the trains more and more. They keep their cars for short journeys and book at the station for longer ones. A train is such perfect transport for the elderly that it could have been designed for them especially. It has the right kind of seat, an attendant, food, heating and a lavatory, and usually good-natured youngsters to give a hand. Best of all, it has a certain drama, a sense of occasion which is restorative. The late twentieth century is only just finding out that it is one of the most agreeable ways to get about. Seventy- and eighty-year-olds are able to recall its heyday. There is a continuity in rail travel for them which cars and planes do not possess. The train, however advanced the model, is their vehicle because it was there at the beginning. It is powerful and dream-inducing. The old married couples sit very quietly in them, communicating without words. They are both vacant and absorbed, and unembarrassed by taciturnity. Old women often dress very elegantly for trains, as for parties. They wear all their best outdoor clothes and lots of make-up and rings, and their hair looks as though it has been done especially for the tea-car. They have gloves and novels, and they scarcely move for a hundred miles. Their spectacles glitter and they hold their heads in the position in which they were once told they looked beautiful. Many of these old novel-reading women are handsome and cool; they understand all about cosseting themselves. Very old men, in contrast, often look weary and lost, tired to death as station name-plate after name-plate lurches by. They look like Hardy's 'journeying boy' decades hence who is 'bewrapt past knowing to what he was going, or whence he came'.

Outdoors, the aged are making their way to the basic amenities, the park seat, the public library, the allotment shed, the deck-chair, the municipal lavatory, the pew, the pensions counter, the pub, the shop. They pause to watch things yet are little seen. Some shutter falls across our vision to distance them from us. Some adult version of don't stare, it's rude, which, in this case, means don't look, it is myself – it is all of us. There is an unspoken and quickly dismissed, though recurring, wish that when the senescent reach a certain stage they should be withdrawn from such circulation. Although there are times when the sight is heartening and when it is actually heady to realize that we are in it together, this business which we call the flight of time. It is then that we notice that the old often have amused eyes and are not necessarily desperate. Serviced with dentures, lenses, tiny loudspeakers, sticks and hip-pins, the flesh has become absurd and can no longer be taken seriously. The body has become a boneshaker which might just about get you there, if you are lucky.

It has got Lily – and Ted and a few others – to their cavernous East End pub on a wild February morning. The pub has a muddled double entrance which turns out to be blackout arrangements from the last war. The bar is enormous with smoked *putti* holding up a filthy ceiling and with a fitted carpet covered with ginger roses. The counter is backed with mahogany shelves covered with curling silver doilies and glass fawns. Lily and Ted and the others have been coming here since the twenties. They are all in their late seventies or early eighties. They are raucous, defiant. They talk against the sound of demolition going on across the street. They are soaking wet from the rain and they are all smoking. Lily shakes ash and moisture from a bunch of paper chrysanths. Her hands continue to shake incessantly.

''ow much?'

'Forty-five p.'

'Christ!'

'I've brought the two pumps I 'ave to use to 'elp me breathe. She stopped me breathin' tablets. She said they made me shake too much. They took me to the 'ospital and got me down from twelve to ten. There was a time when I could throw 'em over me shoulder – you know that, don't you, gel? Now they're

like two fried eggs! [To Ted] Why don't you get a drop
of whisky? Go on, get a drop of whisky. I'm tellin' Ted,
why don't he get himself a drop of whisky to warm him
up.'

'Warm him up?'

Shrieks.

Ted: 'I never needed no whisky to warm me up.'

Lily: 'It's his birthday. Eighty-one, yes eighty-one.
Though he say he don't want the whole world to know.'

Friend: 'Yes, you have a whisky to warm you up.'

Ted: 'Warm me up . . .'

Lily, sipping Guinness: 'I'd sooner see a church fall down
than waste a drop o' this.'

Friend: 'There's no Guinness up there, gel!'

Lily: 'Oh, I don't know. Anyway, I'll have another.'

Friend: 'Yes, gel, you have a bit of life, your mother won't
know. Not now.'

Lily: 'Bobby's gone.'

Ted: 'Yes, Bobby's gone.'

Friend: 'Bobby gone?'

Ted: 'Poor bloody Bobby.'

Lily: 'All my family died now and me left. 'Ere – I 'adn't
thought of that. Did you 'ear, Ted, all my f –'

'Yes I 'eard.'

Friend: 'It's the cold. Since we heard o' them people dyin'
we keep the gas-fire on all night. But how can you pay? It
cost me ten bob a day old money and then the bloody place
isn't warm.'

Ted: 'As you get old you haven't got the blood.'

Lily: 'Fancy my Ted eighty-one! 'Ere, get him some
whisky, somebody. Take this an' get him some whisky. To
warm him up.'

Friend: 'You watch it, gel, he might spark.'

Lily: 'Ah, my Ted!'

Friend: 'You chose a good 'un, gel – I'll say that.'

Ted, looking around: 'This is comin' down. That's

why they ain't doin' it up. It's all comin' down on this corner.'

Lily: 'One more. Let's 'ave one more an' bugger the fare. We can walk. I'll say this much, me and Ted, we can still walk!'

8 · The Vanished References

*Although I constantly talk aloud, never letting an observation
or an idea enter my head without proclaiming it to the
trees or clouds, I note with every day that passes the collapse
of whole sectors of that citadel within which our
thought dwells and moves, like a mole in its network of
tunnels. Those fixed points which thought uses for
its progression, like crossing a river on stepping-stones, are
crumbling and vanishing beneath the surface.*

Michel Tournier, *Friday, or The Other Island*

Frank,
the Civil Engineer, aged seventy-five

*One advantage in keeping a diary is that you become aware
with reassuring clarity of the changes which you constantly
suffer and which in a general way are naturally believed,
surmised, and admitted by you, but which you'll unconsciously
deny when it comes to the point of gaining hope or peace
from such an admission. In the diary you find proof that in
situations which today would seem unbearable, you lived,
looked around and wrote observations, that this right hand
moved then as it does today, when we may be wiser because
we are able to look back upon our former condition, and for
that very reason have got to admit the courage of our earlier
striving in which we persisted even in sheer ignorance.*

Franz Kafka, *Diaries*

I am not who I was and there's no mistake about it, because
the young man I was is plain to see in my diaries. I started
keeping a diary in 1918 when I was fifteen, and I kept it until
the day I was married. The day after I was married I found I

couldn't write in it. And never again did I write in it because it was too embarrassing to put things down once I had begun to share my life with another. I have just re-read these young, pre-marriage diaries and all the letters and bits of paper from those private days, and I find that they are all about a person I recognize, but also about a man who went away a long time ago to leave room for the present one.

I am rather amazed that I have survived. My eldest brother was such a terribly fit person that it was he who should have survived, yet he got cancer a few months ago and went. He was famously fit, the active, charming, kindly one, the handsome one, the popular one. And now he has died and it has shaken me. It has been a most shattering experience for me. I saw him as always well but during his last illness the doctor and all sorts of people talked of his being 'a good age', and things like that. If *he* was a good age, and popular and strong, as I thought, then what am I? I am not a good age, *I* am old. That's the truth of the matter. And this thought has changed me. All at once I have an awful lot to do and must do it quickly. It is as though my brother was saying, 'If I can go, who was so perfect and popular, then how much longer can it be for you?' So I am systematically working my way through everything because I am now the head of the family and I must.

I don't know what mother would have said if she had known that I would become the head of the family! I had such a very dominant mother, a dear person, but very dominating. I have this stammer and she would shout, 'Come on, come on! Hurry up. Get it out, get it out!' She made me worse. I started stammering at six and then I got worse and worse because I could never measure up to mother's standards. And my dead brother was so charming and strong, so that there was no measuring up to him either. When I went to the engineering college the stammering was a great disadvantage. I would never take part in anything and I would never go out to see people because I could never be sure of what would happen. This was a terrible predicament for me. It affected my character. It altered my whole life. It made me inferior and intro-spective. Nobody, however hard they tried, ever succeeded in making me believe that it was anything less than it was. It was a big difficulty for me, and it stayed big. Many people have these beautiful words, these easy ways of talking, which makes others listen to them and so see them with attraction and interest, but I have never had them. Only those with an impediment know how much life depends on speech. I with-drew into myself many years ago; it seemed the best and only thing to do.

But I also did something else. I forced my body to be athletic and shapely. I wanted to attract people to myself without words, and sometimes I did. Rowing and running was what I did to catch the eye. The effort I put into making myself physically attractive, well, it was incredible! I was not up to my brother but I knew by people's reactions that I looked good on the river. It wasn't vanity, or it wasn't *all* vanity; it was a kind of communication I made with my body because I couldn't get a sentence out. That all went a long time ago and my stutter stays on. So I'm not only an old man, I'm a stut-tering old man! 'Get it out! Get it out!' as mother used to say. A dear woman but very dominant. She shook me some-times. Once she had a migraine in church and was so self-conscious of perhaps making an exhibition of herself, as she would have called it, that she never went again. Never.

The young man in my diaries seems to have had a better time of it, generally speaking, than what I have had since. I know that the things he did were the things which I did, but yet he himself doesn't seem to be me at all. I have got cut off from him somehow. For one thing, I notice that he doesn't so much as mention his stutter! And then, after his wedding night, to be unable to say anything.

Death is a funny thing. It can make you get up and go, as they say. It pulls you together. I had another brother. He was mother's starry-eyed boy. He went off to France in the last war and got killed in the retreat from Dunkirk. I was at the meeting of mother and his widow afterwards. Immediately afterwards I applied for a commission – and got it. His death made me lively and confident. Or grateful to be living. So there you are then, such deaths change things. Death comes and off you go in another direction. It hurries you up.

I've always had to *make* myself take part in life. My brothers were never associated with ageing or death in my eyes. Now both are gone and I'm still here. I know I am different some-how because they have gone. My brain has got better and better at early memories. They are a great part of this new vividness and the one who died this year is nearer and plainer to me than at any time since we were boys. I love continuity. I'm a great traditionalist. My brother's death has awakened me to my place in my family's continuity. I feel very responsible for my family now.

Energy's the thing, of course. I wake up fresh as a daisy and I intend to do so much, but there is a general decline soon afterwards. Lunch and rest revive me, but only for a little while. Whatever it is, the fresh morning, the new interest, there is always this quick decline. The spaces in the day when I am alert and busy get shorter. I got out of my difficulties long ago by working harder, and I certainly intend to work myself out of sadness for just as long as I can. Now that my brother is dead, who is going to see to family matters if I don't? There's a lot to be done. I still enjoy meeting people I can learn from, though this gets harder and harder as one gets old. I am not happy with the young; they assume too much and they are irritating.

I was in on the early days of telephony, telecommuni-cations, etc. I had an engineering degree and I was very up-to-date with everything that came along. But I can't keep abreast now or understand what is happening in these fields. I am a layman where I used to be a professional – that is what old age does to technocrats!

The Senior Consultant, aged seventy-nine

I am seventy-nine and would like to go on. It is still good to be alive, and I appreciate it every day. I am still curious about life and I want to know how things will work out. It frustrates me to think that my death will come long before all kinds of interesting ideas now being formulated will be carried out. I remember that I went to Russia to see what was happening there in the thirties on behalf of the Rockefeller Foundation, and that I've always wanted to go back and look again. But I won't now, will I? Russia mightn't allow it and life – what is left of it – won't allow it.

Some people don't have this race-against-oblivion feeling. My father didn't, for example. He was a devout Scot. But I don't understand religion, I don't understand it at all, although it isn't this which is making me uneasy or despairing about the end. On the contrary, I think I have an easier outlook because I can't understand these things. I don't get violently depressed but I do get depressed. I was depressed at the thought of retiring because I wasn't quite sure what would happen to me. You see, I had had my position for so long – my specialist work, my hospital, my staff, my professional travels, my teaching. All these things which I had were what I *was*, and to have to give them up at sixty-five left me with something quite unrecognizable. Old age for me has been the recognition of what was left when all that I was was taken away from me.

But it was just. Some people get radical changes in the brain when they are old, and they are the geriatric tragedies. I have remained wonderfully well in this respect but I have to admit that there comes a moment in research work when you simply can't do it, no matter how brilliantly you did it once. You have to tell yourself, No, you cannot do this work because you are old. You must not deceive yourself in these matters. Being old is the reason why you cannot take things in as you used to. It is difficult to remain creative. The common way in

which to estimate the decline of creativity is from the menopause, which is round about forty-five, although some people
will happily carry on their full creativity well enough until
they are sixty, and a few to seventy, even. But creativity is rare
at eighty, though perfectly possible, as the absorption and
vitality seen in certain brilliant old men proves. But, generally
speaking, if you look back at the work done by old men, you
will see that it is not creative. Originality at eighty? No, no,
no! All you can do is to be useful without being original, and
taking a long time to learn things which once took only a short
time, and this is what you must accept. You must step down,
and that can mean quite a step, egotistically speaking. The
only thing is that the world expects you to take this step quite
matter-of-factly – to clear your desk and to drop everything
you have earned by your creativity just because it happens to
be your sixty-fifth birthday. It is a great shock to relinquish it
all and terrible to have to behave as if there were no shock.

I'd read a paper when I was young and get the guts out of
it in an hour or less. Now I would have to read it three or four
times and take days. My ability to acquire new knowledge is
small or impossible, and I get into a remarkable mess over
what I could do, and what I now cannot do. But I continue to
work. There is a tendency to underestimate the energies of
old age, which are considerable. You won't do what you could
do, but yet you find that you need to do far more than society
allows you to do. I fill the emptiness now by saying to myself,
'I wonder what I should do tomorrow?'

I was an empire-builder in my own sphere of neurology and
knowing what I accomplished keeps me going now. Also, I
know that I have been lucky in having been able to show what
talent I had. I went out and I did something in the world. I
was able to improve things. I know I didn't have all the
answers, but I had some. I helped. My contemporaries say
that I must write it all down, but I can't write. Some old men
need to put things down, but I don't. Anyway, where would I
begin? When I went off to fight the Kaiser? For it was then

that I really began to learn. I learned more about human nature in that war than I ever did since. But I cannot really remember its amazing atmosphere – and I doubt if few can. Imagining that war is like imagining pain or fear when they are past – impossible.

I find the world a more peaceful place than when I was young – which might sound strange. But we were preoccupied with romantic militarism. Armies, armies, armies, we talked with shining eyes. Our talk wasn't peaceful.

My end is near. Comparatively speaking, I mean – I'm not quite on my deathbed. But I have angina attacks and they can be a damned painful thing. I know how to control them but, as a doctor, I also know that I won't always be able to control them. A doctor has difficulties about his own ageing because he knows too much. His old age is rather too much of an open book for his comfort! I make a great effort to be detached. If I feel sick I say as calmly as I can to myself, 'I wonder what it is, let me see . . .' and try not to be damned silly. When I was at Bethesda, the Institute of Medical Surgery, I would be asked every now and then to see some dying man. 'Would I let him have a quarter of morphia every four hours?' Or something like that. 'He's obviously got to die and his friends are so distressed to see his suffering. If only he had a quarter of morphia it would be such a kindness . . .' You must never kill a person but you must make death very easy when it could be very hard. I am sorry that death is the end, not that I want further life after this life, but because I now fancy another look at the world.

I am lucky. There aren't many old people in my circle who have lost their reality or identity. Like mine, their bodies are aged but recognizably what they were when I first met them. I used to amuse my ward sister when I spoiled the elaborate make-up which some of my old women patients hid under. It is so important to accept old skin and bones. Anyway, you don't necessarily have to have a nasty skin when you are eighty. In fact, you often don't. Nor do you look so bad to others as you do to yourself – and that's worth thinking about!

Alfred, aged eighty-three, Gets to India

'The day of small nations has long passed away. The day of Empires has come,' declared Joseph Chamberlain at Birmingham in May 1904. Alfred thrilled that *the* Empire had come and that he, the poorest of village boys, was by virtue of being English superior to the most superior native in it, but he has never been able to accept that it has gone. How could the British Empire go? It is a question silently posed by countless aged people. To have to listen to its rational answer is like being torn down themselves, lowered in their self-estimation like the flag, like having their hearts filled with dust and their mythology erased. All of today's old were fed with Empire fervour. In comparison with its internationalist nutritional value the advantages and historic worth of the E.E.C. are a bag of chips. When Alfred was in standard three, singing,

> 'What is the meaning of Empire Day,
> Why do the cannons roar,
> Why does the cry, "God save the King"
> Echo from shore to shore?'

every old man now alive knew the answer. It was that his little island ruled close on 500 million people. And, knowing this, the masses in their poverty and semi-literacy felt a personal glory. Its everlastingness was never in doubt. Keeping the Empire was, indeed, a high trust. Getting it had been sheer dash and haphazardry. Alfred was taught a romance about the getting and a religion about the keeping. The most fabulous tale of all was the tale of India. Lying on his deathbed he tells his fragment of it.

*

After the war I was demobbed from the East Kents. It was 1919. They marked me out A.1. although I had six/seven/eight wounds. But I'd got over my wounds and I thought to myself, 'Well, I've had some of the bad and some of the rough, and now, if I can get back into the army again, perhaps I can have some of the smooth. So I joined up in the 1st battalion of the Suffolk Regiment for seven-and-five. I prayed that this regiment would take me to India. That is why I joined it, and many another beside me. India was all our glory then.

I had to do my training all over again in spite of the trenches. Then I was sent to the Curragh, where the trouble was. And from the Curragh there were all these drafts which kept a-going off to India. India! Of course, I set my sights on these drafts but I couldn't get going towards India because I had such a bad set of teeth. Chucked out every time. I know there was three drafts went straight to India and I know my mates were going and going and going until it looked mighty like no mates left! No mates, no India for me. So then I said to myself, push forward! Push forward to India. Came the doctor. This doctor, he said to me,

'Do you *want* to go to India?'

'I *do*,' I say. 'My mates have gone and I must go.'

'To India?' he say.

'To India,' I say.

He looked at me hard. 'So you shall,' he say.

I couldn't speak. It was happening.

'You'll promise me faithful to do somethin' if I let you get to India?'

'I promise you faithful.'

'You've got a terrible set of teeth, terrible! You'll promise me that you'll have them all out when you get there?'

'Promise,' I say.

'Then – to India!' he say and he marked me for the draft.

I had fifteen out. Good gracious! what a time. It was up at Wellington, a lovely hill station in Madras. Half the regiment was down at Calicut and I said that when I had got over this lot, it would be me for Calicut too! It was a lovely seaside place. How I liked India! It was marvellous to be an Englishman there. Why, you were more somebody there than you were in Suffolk. True. Of course, I took good care of myself –

though many didn't! They'd get out there and they'd not wear the helmet, or they'd go out and encourage a snake, and all such tricks as that. But I took care of myself. But, oh, the loveliness of Calicut and the palm trees down there, the all sorts of spices down there in Calicut, and the ginger factories. How can I describe it all!

But we had to return to Wellington, where we had the hell of a do. There was a lot of rats about and a chap got bitten. I knew the man who was bitten by the rat. Oh, then – the to-do! Everybody in the cantonment for a three-mile radius had to be inoculated – and where do you think? Yes, there, in the groin. It swelled up mighty and afore long the whole regiment was bent over. Bowed low. We was all moachin' about in India bent over. They'd given us the plague – blacks and all. A touch of the plague *there*. None of us could stand upright because it pulled the lump in our groin tight. After a while, when we could get about a little bit better, we all had to shift out and march to Malabar Hill and live in tents while the barracks were fumigated. It rained and rained, and was wretched. It was the monsoon. Before this, we'd had to dig the rats out, long-tailed ol' rats like they cawpues in the Broad. So I saw India and brushed with the Black Death, they reckon. But it was only one bad thing and the others were fine, fine. Soldiering in India was good.

After three-year we came back to Gibraltar and we stopped there for a time. I couldn't swim when I left the village for the army. I learnt at Gib. I swam all the year round. Soon we came home. My time was gettin' short and then my time was finished. They said to me, 'Would you like to take on Class A Army Reserve?' and I said, 'Yes.' I didn't know what it was but I took it on. I then got a job in Essex and had done no more than a week when there was trouble in China. So off to Bury St Edmunds to get my uniform and off to China. They gave me seven bob a week.

I often think of the army and our Empire. They got us all about. Travelling on troop-ships across the wide world to

everywhere British. You see, I was different. When I was in
the army, I liked it. I liked it all the time. I didn't mind it a
mite, I enjoyed it. I always wanted to do everything they said
right. And so I got on. I liked it and so it was easy for me.
Some disliked it and it was hard for them. But I liked it. It's
a long time away now but I can't stop thinking about India.
Not now.

Michael, the Character-Actor and Fabian, aged eighty-three

> *The theatrical system to which the stock company belonged
> decomposed and broke up; and when I came to London it
> seemed to recede into a remote past. I hastened to the famous
> little theatre off the Tottenham Court Road . . . The play I hit
> on was* Ours; *and in it I saw Ellen Terry for the first time. She
> left on me an impression of waywardness: of not quite fitting
> into her part and not wanting to; and she gave no indication
> of her full power, for which the part afforded no scope . . . It
> was not until I saw her in* New Men and Old Acres, *which
> was made a success by her performance as* The Two Roses
> *had been made a success by Irving's, that I was completely
> conquered and convinced that here was the woman for the
> new drama which was still in the womb of Time, waiting for
> Ibsen to impregnate it. If ever there were two artists appar-
> ently marked out by Nature to make a clean break with an
> outworn past and create a new stage world they were Ellen
> Terry and Henry Irving.*
>
> George Bernard Shaw

The irony of being given small parts in television documentaries about the celebrities from whom he learnt his craft as a
child and as a youth has not occurred to Michael. The continuity of his working life from about five to his mid-eighties

is maintained because he has never thought in terms of clean ·breaks. He knew Ellen Terry and was rehearsed by Shaw. He travelled the Atlantic by himself at an age when most small boys trudged no further than school. He threw up his Catholicism for Fabian social justice and his saints were Olivier (Sydney), Besant, Wells and the Webbs. Now he travels from the country to the television studio to put on the kind of clothes he bought when he was twenty and to act in the reconstruction of the life of someone he used to act with. The past is a tangle and he unravels it with difficulty. It has never been his area of contemplation and having to concentrate on it gives him a kind of vertigo. It is an enormous relief when he can click back into the Now. The past's references are so strong that recalling them seems to put years on him.

*

I'm perfectly fit but all my senses are a little bit down. I don't think about being in my eighties – I don't think about it ever! I might say, 'Good God, eighty-three!' but I don't feel what this is supposed to mean. How do you feel eighty-three? What do they mean by 'feeling' your age? I feel nothing. I can do a day's work with anybody, only all my senses are a little bit down.

I can't say that I'm grateful for my life; that would be going too far! But I admit that I've had a reasonable life; yes, I'll admit that. I've done a lot of things. I've travelled the world. I've been to China, to India and to the States umpteen times. I've never thought of success, only of living. I haven't got the typical actor's temperament, although I'm a bit egotistical. You must have a modicum of egotism to act at all. I've never stopped working and I don't think that one should. Why stop eating or making love? Working is just as good. Keep it up! I started to work at the age of five and so I've acted for well-nigh eighty years. It is only strange when you begin to think about it. I don't think about it myself, or I try not to. I'm in a telly play about Louis Pasteur at the moment.

I'm his father. But I was in a play with Ellen Terry in 1905, and so maybe it is strange when you come to think about it. Only don't think about it!

My father intended me to be an actor. He'd got mixed up with the theatre himself, so that is what he wanted for me. I started off at the age of five at the Olympic Theatre, which is now the Adelphi. I was understudy to a girl and all I had to do was to cling to my mother's skirts. I was smiled at. The play I was in with Ellen Terry was called *The Good Hope* by Christabel St John. The Americans couldn't take it and so it was a flop, so the management gave me my fare back to England. I was only a little boy of eleven and I had to make my way back home. But really, I'd been on my own from the very beginning, so I didn't worry. I went right down to New Orleans, with men giving me lifts and putting me up, then I picked up a boat. It took me many weeks to reach England because the boat put in at Vigo in Spain and made all sorts of calls to discharge cargo. I helped the men. There were no passengers and I went what they called 'super cargo'. It cost less than a quarter of the conventional fare. Everybody was good to me. It was risky – but there you are! Anyway, times weren't as fierce as they are today and there was more innocence about. There were many innocent men. There was more friendliness generally. It would be impossible to do today what I did when I was eleven. America itself was different; so much quieter, so delightful, so kind. A travelling boy just travelled like any other traveller.

During this time I was more or less at school, a convent to start with and then a Catholic grammar school. I was actually entered for Stonyhurst, but never went. I lived with an aunt who was connected with the order of Sts Vincent and Paul, and who took Mass every day. Every day. And when I was with her I had to serve Mass every day at St Charles's, Ogle Street. I had to be up by six every morning and sometimes I had to serve three Masses. It became absolutely intolerable. I won't say that I got fed up with religion just because of all this serving, but when a man in the company told me about Mrs Besant and Theosophy he began my desertion from the Church. Gradually it began to slip. It feels like freedom even after all these years. Catholicism is murder, so negative. It is an appalling religion and it is still wonderful to wake up in the morning and feel emancipated from it. Thrilling.

When I was going to be married, my religious aunt cut me off completely. My knowledge now tells me that she was a bit in love with me. Yes, that was it, she saw me as more than a nephew – a son. And then more than a son. Yes, that was it. There is one thing about being very old, you can see what happened.

I became very involved with all the new movements directly after the First War, both in the theatre and in politics. I came to know Gordon Craig quite well. He had invented a peculiar system of scenery – screens – but they were never used because to use them you would have had to invent a new kind of stage-hand. They were all made like roller-blinds and you just put them into any shape you wanted. At that time the theatre was dreadfully elaborate and just to have screens bewildered people. Gordon Craig's screens eventually became buried at the White City – stored there. They were about sixteen feet tall and in huge rolls – massive. They weren't used because Gordon Craig was before his time. And I was also influenced by Shaw's politics. I knew Shaw very well indeed and he was always kind to me. But this would have been about 1910. Old men carry young marks, don't they? You make up your mind about a lot of things before you are twenty and time isn't necessarily going to alter them.

Just before the First War was a marvellous time. Things were boiling up, things were beginning to change, things were on the move. We were like young revolutionaries. I was a Fabian and the excitement was intense. But the war destroyed that fantastic atmosphere, the war and the slump which came after it. But I still feel marked by what happened in 1910. We knew so little about the background of anything. We were

patriotic and ignorant. I was patriotic and primitive – as well
as a revolutionary. Everybody was so much more self-centred
in those days and the modern idea of an all-embracing world
didn't exist when I was young. Also, you learnt how not to
look, how not to see things for your own comfort's sake. So if
there was all this terrible poverty about, then I didn't see it.
It didn't impinge on me. My politics were made in lecture-
rooms by thrilling speakers.

I loved touring more than anything else. Touring was the
happiest time I ever had and when all I possessed was a
basketful of costumes. And I also loved the nice Heath
Robinsonish way all the great things got going, like the very
early talkies at the Gaumont Film Parlour. These were the
talkies before there were talkies, if you follow me, in which
you synchronized your film acting with the words on a record.
But of course there was no amplification, so in order to hear
the talkies every theatre-seat had to be fitted with a little
receiver. The London Pavilion was fitted this way. *And*, the
machinery was so bad that it couldn't record naturally spoken
words and we all had to t-a-l-k l-i-k-e t-h-a-t, mouthing
every word. We once rehearsed one of these early talkies in
Paris for six months! It was a far cry from Louis Pasteur in
colour. The years hurry along and the equipment gets better,
and you get worse! That's the way it is. I began with declaiming
and now it is all naturalistic. I was never type-cast, I was
always a character-actor. It is the most lasting thing you
can be.

Walter, aged seventy-eight, Lets the Side Down

Bow, bow, ye lower middle classes!
Bow, bow, ye tradesmen, bow, ye masses.
W. S. Gilbert, Iolanthe

I'm getting on for eighty and the most tedious thing in my life now is being expected to denigrate the young. It seems that the young have fallen from some state of grace which was the usual state of the world sixty years ago. Have they? How would I know? I don't see enough of the young to know things like that. What I think is that a lot of old people are secretly enthralled by the young but daren't say nice things about them because they don't want people to see how much they attract them. People who go on about certain groups often fancy them. Using a framework of morals and manners is a way of talking openly about young bodies.

In my opinion, many people under forty – and that is young to me – have far better manners than those which I saw as a child, because their manners aren't just class manners. I don't quite know what you would call their manners, and I certainly haven't any idea where they get them from, but they're good manners of a sort. Not our sort, of course, and there's the rub! If only old men would understand that manners aren't a fixed code, they'd find life much easier.

Our manners were class manners. I was brought up in the country near Cambridge in a world of such ghastly awful snobbery as you couldn't imagine today. Everybody from high to low knew how it worked and everybody contributed to it and kept it on the go for all they were worth. My dear mother, God bless her, played her part. She brainwashed all her children into their class-reaction from the minute they could crawl about and be seen. She was kind, she was just, but she looked on most people as lower-class and had nothing whatever to do with them. A lower-class person could never cross her boundaries – *never*. Class was the first thing which mother saw in a person. She saw it before she noticed anything else, and usually she saw it accurately. Having seen it and recognized it, she then spoke and behaved accordingly.

It was because of women like my mother that so many people tried to conceal their class. It was a waste of time, of course. Mother being not *quite* middle-class, was a genius on class and even when she couldn't quite 'place' someone, she'd patiently listen and watch, knowing that eventually she would. A movement, a vowel, the way a cake was taken off the plate, a reference would suddenly reveal All, and her guest would be ticketed 'common'. Or worse than common because they'd had the cheek to try and hide their commonness!

Mind you, a lot of life then was common with a vengeance. Raw. The crudeness of the masses was such a long way from the least kind of refinement that it allowed anyone with a bit of good taste to feel as if they belonged to another order of creation. It wasn't because you despised the poor that you kept your distance from them, it was simply that they were too dirty and ignorant and rough to allow you to get anywhere near them. There's nothing like it nowadays, nothing. You'd get some poor girl from a backstreet being house-trained like a dog before she was thought fit to be a skivvy to the family of some clerk or local shopkeeper. And there were pubs all round here which catered for the different classes of working-class men. Work that one out. Like mother, the publican would know at a glance in which of his little rooms a customer should be – or whether he should be in his pub at all! You got to be top working-class mainly by being respectable. It was quite a high position – higher sometimes than lower middle-class, unless you could show something tangible to back up your claim, such as being a small tradesman with your own card, or having a double-fronted house.

Mother knew more about all this than a lady should! The

sad thing about mother, and thousands of women like her, was that they had next to no education and they'd never been anywhere. Mother's life-long study was of Ladies and of perfecting their way of talking, and doing quite ordinary things such as eating. Mother also believed that Ladies had to give orders and that to be an order-giver was really a great privilege which was given to you by the Almighty, so you always had to remember this and Be Fair. If mother could convince herself (she always could) that she was being unselfish and polite, she could give her orders. She gave orders all day long. To the servants, to the children, to the tradespeople and, just before she went to sleep, to God. 'Send down thy blessings on this house,' she ordered.

The funny thing, or should I say the sad thing, was that mother wasn't a lady. Not a real lady. Yet she wasn't playing at being one, and she certainly wasn't pretending to be one. She was just sincerely doing her level best to be one because she sincerely believed that it was the best thing a woman and a mother could be. All this meant no end to me as a boy. But soon it meant nothing to me at all. I don't know when or why it stopped, but it did. It may have had something to do with my natural unorthodoxy.

But it hasn't stopped with lots of people, has it? It's deep in the system of my generation – working away inside them and a constant irritant. I suppose they want to give orders and they can't. They daren't say all the things they would like to say because they would sound nasty and silly. When they go about they get very bothered inside when younger people ignore the class situation. I've seen it on the bus and in the post office. How it would have upset mother! Being a lady was her profession and her faith. When she died the village said, 'She was such a *lady*, wasn't she.' Dear mother, she worked hard to keep society unequal and they all loved her for it. And they knew that they'd all helped her in their way.

Coming Down in the World:
Lady Thelma, aged ninety

She is a tall, gaunt, upright woman who, after having lived most of her life in country-houses, has retired to a little bungalow on a modern housing estate. Her furniture, her pictures and her manner are all much too large for its rooms, which she likes but considers rather a joke. She wears trouser-suits, jewelled clips and head-scarves. Retainers from the country-house, a middle-aged couple now living in a near-by village, drive over every Thursday and give her what she describes as a good do, cleaning the bungalow and straightening its patch of garden. Framed photographs show her leading in race-horses and wearing big gauzy hats at garden-parties. There is a littered table where she moulds horses' heads in plaster and some of her paintings are either portraits of winners or pictures of apocalyptic steeds, roseate and high-stepping, and bursting from the clouds. Her drawing-room is hot and heady with the scent of hyacinths, tea and chypre. Through the netted windows another life goes on which to her is a kind of shadow-play, young marrieds with their cars and cries and children, tall coloured airmen from the American base, aubrieta and concrete, TV rental vans and ice-cream music. 'It's all really very nice,' she says doubtfully.

She still does all her own shopping, trailing languorously round the little town with a wheeled basket, each slow step of her skeletal feet not without its old elegance. What she misses most is her car, a big brown Rover with its silver vase fixed to the inside of the windscreen and holding a carnation or a rose. Her eyes light up with a ferocious interest at the mere mention of it. But no more driving – ever, ever. 'I drove all through the Kaiser's war!' She confesses to a history of successive enthusiasms and her liking for 'a bit of a dash', for lost causes, moving house, for laying out gardens, for painting, writing and for 'making a bit of money'. She still wakes each morning full of plans, then she remembers how old she is and says to herself, 'Be sensible.' She remembers that her brothers used to call her 'scatterbrain', though she has never been quite that. She is both impetuous and astute, trying anything once but rarely losing her footing in the attempt. She is a tough mixture of the romantic and the worldling and she trusts in the Hereafter as vehemently as she trusts in the Stock Exchange. The old English gentlewoman, in fact. She laughs a good deal, revealing all her own teeth, discoloured but strong and well-formed. Her days now alternate between brief periods of energy,when she manages to get through an enormous amount of work connected with her passion of the moment, and steadily increasing stretches of profound weariness. She wakes up each morning giving herself orders, prodding herself into action. 'Up, up! Go out and get the tomatoes. Do something *today* about Patsy [her dog] so that she'll be all right when you've gone. Don't say when you've gone, say when you're dead. Dead – say it.'

'So you think about death?'

'Well, naturally. You have to when there's a dog, don't you? I tell myself I'm thinking about death but what I'm really thinking about is the dog. Death – dog, that's the way my mind goes now. I'm so old, you see. Terrifically old. Even so, there are still things that I have to do; a lot more things. Are you listening up there? I'm saying that I haven't finished, not by a long chalk! And I don't mean just getting ready for death, which I call the Other Side. Of course, the more time you have, the more you need. Not that I'm frightened by death, oh no. Dear death, how I look forward to it. I look forward to it because I am so tired. So weary, you know. This tiredness just falls on top of me like a dead weight. Such utter, utter weariness – you have no idea. It's worth talking about because it is quite something. I mean I've known what it is to be really tired, like everybody else, but never a tiredness like this. If I tell you that it is too important a tiredness simply to sleep through, you'll know what I mean. It keeps me wide awake so that I can feel every bit of it. I lie on the sofa – or even get the tea – in this huge, huge tiredness. It's not exactly unpleasant but it is becoming rather a nuisance. I wouldn't mind if I could just doze off and wake up and find it gone, but I can't. That's not its little game. Being so old is a very funny business. To tell you the truth, I can't make head or tail of it! If I get ga-ga, take no notice, it will be this tiredness. What did they used to say – tell me if I snore – well I'll have to tell you when this tiredness starts its pranks.

'Let's be serious. This weariness is death. Don't you realize what death is? It is a lovely mist which takes us away. Did I once tell you about an experience I had in my twenties and the doctor thought I was dying? He had to be sent for to help me about ten o'clock one night. The children were small and sleeping in the nursery, and my husband was away somewhere. The doctor, apparently, suddenly called out to nanny, "Nurse, come quickly, she'll be gone in a moment! She's unconscious!" And so I was as far as they were concerned. I, the real me, was alert and waiting to hop out of my body at any minute. And I could feel this mist coming towards me, a sort of swirling bank of marvellous love, love such as you'd never guess it in this world. And I could hear myself saying, "Oh, take me, take me. Quick – take me!" And the mist started to go back slowly and it was most disappointing, and I came back to life. Sixty or more years of it! Later on the nanny told me that the doctor said, "Open the window, nurse. Quickly! She'll be gone any minute." I'm so looking forward to this bank of mist coming again to fetch me. It can hardly go back without me this time, can it!

'I believe that we are more alive when people say we are dead than we are now. So I'm looking forward to being more alive. Who wouldn't at ninety! I don't want this carcass I'm living in at present – who would? Don't be polite. It's seen better days. Oh, I'll be glad, glad, when I'm free of it. And then I have all these people to meet, my father and mother, my brothers and sisters, and my little daughter who was

killed in the war. A Halifax bomber, of all things. She was a
meteorologist and flew when she shouldn't have flown,
though most of us have done that, if you get me. There isn't a
soul left on this side. It's uncanny when you are old, the space
and the silence which are left by all the people who used to
be in your life. Believe me, there is nothing of the least
importance left on this side when you get to my age. So, in
other words, nearer, nearer, nearer God.

'Of course you get worried stiff in case of pain. I don't have
pain so far and I mightn't have it at all. Everybody doesn't
have pain, do they?

'Talking of the dead, I'd like some of the people I used to
know to see me in my new bungalow. See their faces, you
know. They'd look around and say, "Thelma – *dear!*" '

Peals of laughter.

9 · Prayer-Route

*It is not, I confess, an unlawful Prayer to desire to surpass the
days of our Saviour, or wish to outlive that age wherein
he thought fittest to die; yet if (as Divinity affirms) there shall
be no grey hairs in Heaven, but all shall rise in the perfect
state of men, we do but outlive those perfections in this World,
to be recalled unto them by a greater Miracle in the next,
and run on here but to be retrograde hereafter. Were there any
hopes to outlive vice, or a point to be super-annuated
from sin, it were worthy our knees to implore the days of
Methuselah. But age doth not rectify, but incurvate our
natures, turning bad dispositions into worser habits . . .*

*He who thus ordereth the purposes of this Life will never be
far from the next, and is in some manner already in it,
by a happy conformity, and close apprehension of it. And if
any have been so happy as personally to understand
Christian Annihilation, Ecstasy, Exolution, Transformation,
the Kiss of the Spouse, and Ingression into the Divine
Shadow . . . they have already had an handsome Anticipation
of Heaven; the World is in a manner over, and the
Earth in Ashes unto them.*

*In seventy or eighty years a Man may have a deep Gust of
the World. Know what it is, what it can afford, and
what 'tis to have been a Man. Such a latitude of years may
hold a considerable corner in the general Map of Time;
and a Man may have a curt Epitome of the whole course
thereof . . .*

Sir Thomas Browne, *Religio Medici* and *Christian Morals*

Charles de Montalembert, the nineteenth-century French
Catholic apologist, in his *Monks of the West*, believed that the
genuine religious enjoyed benefits in old age which the more

earth-bound personality could scarcely imagine. For, besides possessing a vocation which usually allowed him special access to the wonder of the world, life for him 'was prolonged without being saddened'. The religious, he said, could take pleasure in and propagate *benignitas*, which he describes as a purified benevolence. *Benignitas* was the legitimate last stage of their religious vocation. They continued to exist in order to display *benignitas*; it was their senescent function. *Benignitas*, he added, had to take its place alongside the earlier monastic virtues of *simplicitas* and *hilaritas*, 'thus creating the special fragrance and significance' of the old man of prayer.

The aged members of the Society of Saint John the Evangelist at Oxford, the 'Cowley Fathers', although the last people to claim any spiritual achievement during their seventies and eighties, are strikingly unlike most old men. Bodies fail and time closes in, yet often as much as sixty years' observance of their religious rules has clearly separated their experience of decline from that of the majority. They are not an enclosed order, physically or intellectually. Most of them have travelled extensively and many of them study incessantly, so that their Christian argument is lively in the extreme when compared with that of many a parish priest. Their journal, *New Fire*, must be one of the best written of modern religious periodicals and it contrasts strongly with the limitation and unexcitingness of some of the Christian press.

Something about which the old Cowley father can congratulate himself is his security. Severe bodily or mental hospital treatment excepted, nothing can remove him from the community until he dies. An old priest can retire from certain duties which are becoming unmanageable but never from his cell, his seat in the garden, his stall in chapel, his place at table, his corner in the library, his turn at the sink or from the concern of his brothers. To appreciate the traumas of modern retirement one only has to stay a few days where they do not exist. Similarly, to recognize what is bad in the huge busy industry devoted to geriatric care in the late twentieth century, one needs only to glance at a group which doesn't talk about the 'problem of old age', has a system which doesn't have to allow for most of the emotional and economic difficulties of the ordinary aged man, and – above all – tries to look at life as a natural entity, whatever its length. The latter part of the entity is accepted as as legitimate, even if obviously not as enjoyable, as the former part. As *differently* enjoyable, perhaps. But to live in community until the last, and whenever this last should be, thirty or ninety, goes without saying.

The rule of the S.S.J.E. and of all other religious orders has nothing to say on what to do with or for the old. The aged religious is expected to face up to the end of life with philosophy and metaphor, extracting something positive from it. Unlike the majority of professional people, he is never cut off from the special language of his profession and driven out into a lay wilderness. He can even employ *hilaritas* to his becoming an old crock and remark, like Maud Royden, 'They say we are going downhill – but they are wrong. We are going *up*hill, which is why it is such heavy going!' Being part of an institution which ignores the popular ploys of the generation game tends to make one not think about age much at all. The Cowley Fathers see themselves as figures strung-out along a path and at various distances from a pre-determined destination, and one can hardly expect to ask for pity or show regret simply because one is within sight of home. Death is not their great worry and they are remarkably buoyant when confronted by geriatric diseases. What disturbs them most about age is the decay of spiritual passion. Prayer is not what it was. Although they try to re-ignite its flame with every technique known to them, it barely sparks. As one of them said, so often having nothing to offer, he offers Nothing. For increasing stretches of time, it is all he has now, and he offers his all – Nothing. Cowper summed it up when he wrote of the toil

> Of dropping buckets into empty wells,
> And growing old in drawing nothing up.

In another poem Rochester calls Nothing his elder brother because he had 'a being ere the world was made', but Keats, a very young man, would not allow beauty to pass into nothingness. Making the acquaintance of nothingness is among the shocks of old age. In this sense 'having nothing, and yet possessing all things', as St Paul wrote, is not a comforting notion. But it must be added that the best and most attractive religious is self-dismissive, and the nothingness of the old Cowley Fathers is not apparent to the outsider or to his younger colleagues.

Some sixty years ago Father Congreve, during the last months of a very long life, wrote a study of his experience of old age as a member of the S.S.J.E. It was conceived when attention was fixed upon the slaughter of the young in the grounded armies of the Western Front and at the suggestion of an old friend, the Mother Superior of the Convent of St Mary the Virgin at Wantage. Father Congreve was eighty-two. He was a boy when the vicar of Cowley, Richard Benson, had founded the Society in 1866 and thus he was among the first people to grow old in an English religious community since the Reformation. He wrote his *Treasures of Hope*, his Gerontian confession, when almost completely deaf, in constant pain and failing. A scrap of the Vulgate version of the eighty-third Psalm – *Ascensiones in corde suo disposuit* ('He hath set ascensions, aspirations, in his heart') kept him going. He fed on the phrase. He told a friend, 'One feels instinctively that the Christian's last stage of the journey on earth should enjoy some special happiness.' To a ninety-year-old companion he stated:

> 'If I find no home any longer in this world, it is because God has been withdrawing me, my love, my treasures, my remembrances, my hopes, from a place where the frost-wind of death touched every precious thing, where no good can last, but night falls, and only icy solitude and silence remain. This is no home, this is but a lodging . . . God is making all things dark and silent around me . . . I

must begin to long for home. I seem almost asleep, but my heart is awake . . . Memory sleeps, action sleeps, thought sleeps, but love is awake. It does not think, or plan or labour to remember, but it loves; it is withdrawn from the surface of life to the centre . . . My God, I would not die as the unconscious things, the frozen sparrow under the hedge, the dead leaf whirled away before the night wind . . .'

Father Congreve's anxiety not to perish simply as a perishable part of the natural order was shared by agnostic Victorian intellectuals. In the brilliant scene in *A Pair of Blue Eyes*, Hardy's novel based on his Cornish courtship, the Man of Letters clinging to the cliff-face above the boiling sea, and gradually slipping, observes in his Darwinian way that the crumbling shale before his eyes contains a fossil. 'Separated by millions of years in their lives, Knight and this underling seemed to have met in their place of death. It was the single instance within reach of his vision of anything that had ever been alive and had had a body to save . . . He was to be with the small in his death.' Richard Jefferies in *The Story of My Heart* denied the remotest companionship between men and nature.

There is nothing human in Nature. The earth would let me perish on the ground . . . Burning in the sky the great sun, of whose company I had been so fond, would merely burn on and make no motion to assist me. The trees care nothing for us; the hill I visited so often in days gone by has not missed me. This very thyme which scents my fingers did not grow for that purpose, but its own . . . By night it is the same as day; the stars care not, and we are nothing to them . . . *If the entire human race perished at this hour, what difference would it make to the earth?*

Terror for the old religious comes when he drifts into areas where he can no longer hear, feel, see or taste Christ, when the ascensions and aspirations originally set in his heart, though still subjected to all the familiar and beautiful disciplines, fail to lift it.

St John, the Cowley Fathers' protector, had himself lived to be very old. Escaping execution, he had, Father Congreve believed, been kept on earth 'not as a mere working out of a penal sentence, a purgative exercise, but as an opportunity to advance to a higher experience of communion with God'. In his Gospel, John reports Jesus chillingly telling Peter, 'When you were young you fastened your belt about you and walked where you chose; but when you are old you will stretch out your arms, and a stranger will bind you fast, and carry you where you have no wish to go.' The reference is usually accepted as being that to Peter's execution although it is vividly applicable to the old generally and the way they are pushed around regardless of their own mind. Peter had looked round at John, then very young, and had asked what would happen to *him*, knowing of Jesus' special love for him. The answer was enigmatic and even rough. 'If it should be my will that he wait until I come, what is it to you?' said Jesus. Peter and the others took this to mean that John would never die, although the saying could refer to the ultimate spiritual reunion of friends who die many years apart. The dilemma of long out-living the only really important person in one's life is often not reconciled by and certainly not healed by it. This is the chief theme of Tennyson's 'In Memoriam'. Jesus' saying, 'When you are old you will stretch out your arms, and a stranger will bind you fast, and carry you where you have no wish to go,' is his only possible reference to old age. He made it during an emotional breakfast meeting near the Tiberian Sea after he had returned from the dead.

Although people had besought him to cure all kinds of physical and mental illness, and he had constantly restored life to those who had died young, there is no similarly specific incident in which Christ had returned life to an old person or had been asked by an old man or woman to turn back the clock and make them young again. Old age seems to have intruded itself most upon Jesus during his childhood in the figures of his cousin John's parents, Zechariah and Elizabeth, both surprisingly ancient to have a little son, and in two old religious, Simeon and Anna, the latter aged eighty-four, whose sole purpose in hanging on to life for so long was to see the Messiah before they died. And it was a man in his sixties, then a great age, Herod the Great, who had tried to exterminate him as a child. Herod had been given the Kingdom of Judea by Mark Antony from as long ago as thirty years before Jesus' birth. Thus both benign and dreadful old people waited his coming. But it was to be primarily to the young that the God of Love and the revolutionary disturber of the individual heart, the Jewish radical and idealist, and the tragic thirty-three-year-old victim was to communicate with the most overwhelming immediacy.

Commenting on his wife's at first indignation and then partial understanding of the condition of her grandfather – 'What happens to the true spirit, where does it go in old age? *Why* must people one loves suffer these intolerable miseries? And yet even as I write I see a kind of beauty in it – a starred kind of light' – Laurence Whistler wrote:

> It occurs to me that it might almost have been necessary for Christ to die in the prime of his beauty and vigour, for to have experienced old age without impoverishment would have been not to be fully human. Perhaps heaven exists for living in the prime, enriched in some simultaneous way by the other selves we have been between life and death. Andrew Young suggests in *Out of the World and Back* that 'a changing Proteus' will arise for each of us.

St John was forced by old age to reduce the sublime message to a single sentence. In Jerome's commentary on Galatians there is a startling little picture of him as a very old man being carried to church daily. His assistants are awed and bored by him in equal parts. Awed that he actually walked and talked and ate with Jesus, bored that all they can get out of him now is 'Little children, love one another.' That is all he can say. They challenged him on its adequacy and he replied, 'If you perform it, it suffices.'

Having to reduce the elaborate intellectual and ethical structure upon which their lives have been built to a formula which can satisfy both themselves and others is the none-too-easy task of the aged, particularly if they have been connected with some great spiritual or political movement. An old, bed-ridden and lonely woman achieved this when, in answer to a question on how she managed to pass the sleepless nights, she said, 'I mostly sing.' Writing about John's pruned-down beliefs, Cornelius said that he was like all old men and lovers who can think and speak of nothing else but what they love and have loved. Father George Congreve describes the 'thinning of the scene of life by loss of objects and interests' and of personal littleness being no longer chilling. His horror of shrivelling up as inconsequentially as a leaf passes and he sees 'that small faculty of love, our personality itself, begins to grow as it begins to contemplate the infinite Love' and he breathes again as 'the abyss of Deity is no longer a fearful solitude and a desert where baffled thought is lost'.

Old men who have never had to think in terms of retirement are confused by the slow coming to a halt. Father Benson, the Society's founder, was baffled by being 'utterly incapable of joining in anything that is being done'. Half-blind – 'It is impossible for me to read ordinary printed books' – and so deaf that every service except the Mass is 'of little avail', he sits by the fire in resentful inaction, glad that he knows the Psalms by heart and grateful for the community's prayers on his behalf, but scarcely able to accept that he will never really be able to join in again. Someone told him that 'One must try in one's last years not to be a hindrance to anything that is good.' And not to be able to summon up the usual intellectual energy to comprehend the new ideas that will produce the new good is further frustration. But he does his best – 'The tem per in which one accepts change at a time when one is more than ever attached to the past, and longs for quietness' has to be cultivated. What one must never do is to stop – until one was stopped, that is. 'It would be nothing less than a heinous sin in me to become superannuated!' wrote the Unitarian minister James Martineau when he was ninety-two.

Aged religious are to be comforted, said Father Congreve, by constantly reminding themselves that the world to which they belong is not that of any one generation but the eternal world and they are to make a positive effort to concern themselves with it for as long as they are part of it. Just because they can no longer put their shoulder to the wheel they are not to 'care little whether the wheel moves or stands still'. Creeping indifference is a large factor in the self-hate of the aged. The old religious has less excuse for it because, never having to step out of the ambience of his vocation, as the majority of men have to do, he retains the comfort of a familiar role and its status. When the famous surgeon Sir James Paget had to give up at seventy-nine, his son wrote:

> In this period he learned the full hardship of retirement – the inevitable time when the callers are none of them patients, and the letters are all of them advertisements, and other men do all the science, and get all the practice. The more success a man has enjoyed in our profession, the more he dreads the loss of all work, all influence, all engagements – the mornings without a patient, the afternoons blank, the evenings without anything that *must* be done. And consider how much he must give up, who loves work passionately, and has a keen delight in his own energy and influence, and in social life. But Paget had to give up everything: the companionship of his wife, and the sight of his friends; the very power to stand, or to write his own name, or to speak above a whisper. These last two years of his life are nothing short of a miracle; they cannot easily be reconciled with any natural interpretation of things . . . he

surrendered every vestige of his old life with a sort of courteous, half-humorous gentleness. So long as he could hear a note of it, he delighted in music; so long as he could see a word of them he read his books of devotion . . . the longer he lived, the higher he went.

So there are geriatric distresses connected with ambition, marriage and worldliness generally from which the religious can count himself free. All the same, when the assault comes it is neither less amazing nor less painful. 'Age seldom arrives smoothly or quickly,' says the novelist Jean Rhys. 'It's more often a series of jerks. After the first you slowly recover. You "learn to live with the consequences". Then comes another and another. At last you realize that you'll never feel perfectly well again, never be able to move easily, or see or hear well.' And Father Congreve agrees that the sickness of the old is not generally a single blow:

> It is more often a process of gradual destruction; day and night I have to deal with this siege, as it were, which is ever silently going on, the enemy at work out of sight and sapping my defences. I can deal with every turn of his weary process of destruction only in one way – the Name of Jesus . . . I look up out of all the ruin to God. Nature in its loveliest and tenderest moods does not heal or help me. I can see its peace but I cannot make it my own. Nature sends me back to myself, unhealed, uncomforted, an alien . . .

He denounces the philosophical acceptance of suffering which has a 'capacity for drinking-in ruin and death, and which can accept dullness, solitude, uselessness, because Christ has opened a door which lets one through all this . . .' More should be aimed for than just 'a happy release'. He believed that if one looked for it, and could accept the sort of thing it was when one found it, that there was a particular happiness which specifically belonged to old age. 'All the way to Heaven is Heaven,' is what St Catherine of Siena maintained.

Jean Rhys describes the emergent pleasures of an old woman's day as she gets up when it is still dark:

I used to keep a book handy, put the light on and read, but now I've decided to save my eyes I get up instead, and without looking at myself, stumble along the passage, switching lights on as I go. Then I am filling the kettle, taking the blue cup off its hook (careful, now, don't drop it), getting a saucer, spoon, sugar. From then on it's routine. After tea and cigarettes it gets lighter and I am happier. Perhaps the real deep feeling is of joy, even triumph, that one has survived the night. Once more darkness has been conquered and, however dreary, day will soon be here. Of course you could die during the day, but it's not likely, not even possible, is it? This year, next year, sometime, again becomes never.

The first motor bicycle passes, the sun rises, cold and watery, perhaps, but sun. It is then that time stretches, time that you're free to spend exactly as you wish. You can eat what you like when you like, drink what you like when you like, or not at all . . . you can spend a couple of hours dressing or slop around, not bothering to dress at all, reading passages from *King Solomon's Mines* or *Lady Audley's Secret*. Or wander about in what passes for a garden. There's time for everything. The intoxicating feeling of freedom repays you a thousand times for any loneliness you may have endured . . .

The other compensation is the calm that often comes with age. If you've often tried in the past to put yourself to sleep by repeating, 'nothing matters, nothing matters at all', it's a relief when few things really do matter any longer. This indifference or calm, whatever you like to call it, is like a cave at the back of your mind where you can retire and be alone and safe. The outside world is very far away. If you sometimes long for a fierce dog to guard your cave, that's only on bad days . . .

The daily routine and the general régime of the religious life could be said to be therapeutic for ageing people, although some orders are tough and austere to a degree. The Cistercians of Caldey Island rise at 3.15 a.m. and go to bed at 8 p.m. Their day is divinely spaced out with seven services and, when the Pembrokeshire weather allows, garden meditations. Worship apart, they obey St Benedict's injunction to farm the land excellently and to be practical and self-supporting. On Caldey this has led to the famous perfume industry. This delightful variation on St Benedict's agrarian theme was actually the invention of an old man, Walter Poucher, the distinguished perfumier who, on his retirement in the 1950s, helped the monks to extract oil from the local gorse. The monks were in great financial difficulties after the last war when an elderly oblate, Brother Teilo, suggested selling bunches of dried herbs and everlasting flowers to bring in a little money. This was sufficiently successful to make the community think of selling lavender-water, and from this enterprise there developed the now splendid Caldey scent factory. The monks smilingly give scriptural authority for their unlikely trade. Perfume, they explain, comes from *per fumum* – 'from smoke'. And this was the aromatic wood-smoke of the frankincense tree once used to help stifle the stench of burning flesh of the old sacrifices. Caldey is a mixture of the contemplative, the imaginative and the strenuous, ecumenically outward-looking and a somewhat devastating situation to find oneself growing old in.

The Anglican Cowley Fathers' régime contains far less manual labour and perhaps more study. Their house is warm, bright and roomy, and their Conventual Church a handsome achievement by Bodley and Comper. A beautiful walled town garden winds its way round refectory, library and common rooms. The community eats very simply, spends a lot of time in comfortable individual book-piled cells, gathers seven times a day to sing the office, walks to the centre of Oxford to visit colleges and bookshops, and keeps its Rule not so much by some obvious strictness as by a very English kind of duty expressed gently. The members of the S.S.J.E. are aged from early twenties to mid-ninety. Everybody works, everybody dreams, everybody sings and nearly everybody seems to have travelled a lot. The atmosphere is one of reflection deflecting drive and of open generosity. The Fathers quote Acts to sum up their corporate life: 'Now the company of those who believed were of one heart and soul, and no one said that any of the things which he possessed was his own, but they had everything in common.'

The Society's emblem is the eagle, St John's bird of keen sight and Milton's creature 'mewing her mighty youth'. It soars, metaphorically, above the white head bowed over the sink, the book, the prie-dieu, the bee-hive, the altar. For the religious Time is a mortal interregnum. But although, in Father Congreve's moving phrase, he realizes that unspeakable solemnities are being enacted just out of his sight, the actual *flight* of time 'which is little observed and has little significance for others, becomes sometimes to those who are growing old, a terror. The weeks, the months, the years, that used to seem interminable, because so full of hourly interest, hope and result, now in their emptiness impress one as might the rush of vast machinery at full work without any material to work on.' Time-scarred and timeless, he has to consciously prepare for death.

The Flight of Fervour:
Father Michael, aged seventy-seven

It astonishes me very much to be old. I was born in the Diamond Jubilee year of Queen Victoria, and so I have seen six reigns and all the changes. I remember running to see a motor-car pass, and the soft, pretty light of oil-lamps in all the rooms.

I am under the weather a bit now and only this morning I was attended by a surgeon and was told that I must have a prostatectomy in a month's time. I am anxious, of course, though not *worried*. Any operation is a serious matter at seventy-seven. I told the surgeon – he was rather amused – 'It doesn't make much difference if you're stumped at seventy-seven, or caught or bowled at eighty-three!' What I pray is that my body will not outlive my mind, but otherwise I'm ready and I've rather laughed for a long time now at people who've wished me 'Many happy returns of the day'. I think about death; it must happen. My sister's recent death has brought it home to me these last few weeks. I also think of what an aunt of mine said to me – she knew that she didn't deserve salvation and she knew that she'd get it! So there it is. Death. Although constantly reading the Bible and going to chapel has been telling me about it for many years, life and death, death and life. Death and life – near now. Surprisingly near. So there it is.

There is one thing about old age and that is, you are likely to find yourself spending a lot of time *on* yourself! You see, you're slower. Slower and slower. It is surprising when you have been quick by nature. Everything takes longer and longer. With my prostate I have been getting up six or more times a night and getting back to bed again. It is better to have it out, it is so uncomfortable at present. Whatever I do now is very leisurely. For instance, ever since I fainted I have had to take a hot drink with glucose first thing in the morning which means starting to go to bed at half past eight in order to get it ready. I go to the kitchen and have a cup of stuff called Complan and do my coffee for the morning, and in the morning I have it with glucose, do a little reading and rise by degrees. I'm getting into a new little rhythm but looking after yourself in a new way takes a lot of time when you are old.

I am very lucky to be in this Community now that I am growing old. Luckier than my sister's poor husband, now that he is left. I think widowers are more to be pitied than widows these days. They are lost. He will feel lost. Whatever happens, you cannot be lost in the Community. You don't even retire because if you only go to chapel you continue to give and take your share there. A few days ago I returned to choir-practice. I'd given it up because the choir-school was so dreadfully cold – it has an outside wall! I'm not much good at the singing now but every voice contributes something. In a community one is always useful. There is no one here who is not useful. We stay useful and see that we are kept useful and we know that death alone can end our usefulness. It has to do with keeping the Christian pattern. Most Christians have a pattern of prayer and know that to keep it when you are old is a great help generally. It is harder – *hard* – if you are on your own, of course, and not in community.

I haven't really found a new pattern for my day since I gave up being the librarian. I have lived in communities of men since I was eight years old. School, army, university, then the Cambridge Brotherhood in Delhi, and then, when I decided that I wanted a stricter rule, the Cowley Fathers. I've enjoyed the society of men all my life. I came here as a postulant in 1936 and was professed in 1939. Then I returned to India for seven years. I see my vocation as my outlook and gifts being focused in a particular direction. I think that the same qualities which make a good husband and father probably make a good religious. Faith itself is bound to be a leap and we must face up to this. The concept of the cosmic Christ has always been more real to me than the personal-saviour aspect. I believe that Christ has saved me because he has saved the world. A salvationist would, of course, say that Christ saved the world because he saved him personally. But the cosmic Christ is what gives us our social gospel. I feel him very personally, too, of course – although I now could wish it were more so. I was a rather late starter. I did try to learn the truth as a boy but I couldn't. And all the time I was in India I don't think that the Indian approach to spirituality influenced me much because my own prayer is discursive and I don't seem to be called to their form of contemplative prayer. I have to believe in reason, right reason, and some Indian men of prayer are called to cut themselves away from that. When I was in the Indian Army I got to know Indians intimately, but in what would now be called a 'father-paternalistic role'! Later I taught at the English College, Delhi, as a lay-missionary. It was a college in the very best liberal tradition and the first ever to have an Indian principal.

But reason must obviously be transcended – particularly in old age!

The Flight of Certainty:
Father Edmund, aged seventy-five

I'm old but I don't think that I've changed my life very much because of it. I got back from India seven years ago, became an archdeacon in charge of parishes and things, then came to the Community, where I am Assistant Father Superior. Also the librarian. But I'm still doing all the same kind of things, taking services and retreats outside, being warden to a sister-hood and hearing confessions at a lot of convents. But no actual parish work; that part of life has changed to some extent. Apart from this, I'm almost as busy as I have ever been.

We have our timetable, as you know, getting up at six, the morning office, then Mass, then breakfast, then an hour's prayer and, after all this, anything you like, really. Study or chores or administration. In the afternoons I garden. I look after the bees. I'm very fond of nature and that kind of thing. I was very interested in bees in India – wild bees – and made a very intense study of them, and I was allowed to keep up this study here. I'm partly a naturalist and I generally spend the evening between supper and Compline doing something with my bee studies. I have written various papers on bees. They have been one of my great interests in life and they have led me to some of the modern poets who are interested in nature. Before I die I would like to settle and publish all the work which I did on Indian bees, information about their nests and many other things about them which may be entirely new to naturalists. The bees from our hive collect honey from all the Oxford gardens within a mile or so radius and from the beautiful lime trees hereabout.

I'm a deeply sceptical person. I carry no certainties. An American writer named John Dunne says that we ought to give up certainty and any hankering after certainties. I've never hankered after certainty! And at the same time, I would say that I've deeply valued failure. I could never say with certainty that I know God exists, but I've always arranged myself on the side of the people who believe. This is the human way to live – the proper way to live. I do feel certain that doing this gives one a more satisfactory life. Now that I am old I have a deepening faith but my certitude is less than when I was young. There are different kinds of doubt, of course. Dunne's doubt is much more attractive to me than Cowper's doubt, which horrifies me. I lived with doubt as a young man and at seventy-five I still do. That's not changed with me.

The one writer who has undoubtedly influenced me is von Hügel, who wrote during my undergraduate days. The whole of my outlook was influenced by him. Still to me he offers the ideal approach. His outlook on life was a very unobtrusive thing and had no kind of narrowness about it. He taught the intellectual, emotional and ethical approach in such a manner that they affected you strongly from within. He also thought that religion could not do without the institutional or structural side. But as a Christian gets old even his most influential authors fade in significance compared with that of his Lord. Parts of my 'theology' are much less important to me now than the Gospels themselves. My favourite Gospel is St John. I don't think that it has much historical value but I love it very much and I think its spiritual insight is wonderful. What is tremendous for me is the way it is able to directly penetrate into things. It is curious, really, because the picture of Christ in it is not very human at all. He is the intellectualized Christ. For the actual Jesus I would go to the other Gospels. St John has this absolutely dazzling beginning. There is something quite extraordinary about it.

I was interested in religion from the age of twelve onwards. But I was always interested in science too, an interest which I have always kept up to some extent. You can have a 'natural' religious just as you can have a 'natural' artist or writer. Such people have a natural wish to live apart to some extent. They are cut out for the religious life and they don't have a natural drawing towards the family. They don't 'give up' the ordinary family expectation because they have never felt that they possessed it. All the same, when one becomes a religious, there is often an element of romance at the beginning of one's vocation which has to be lived through – shed. This is all quite natural too.

I don't think that I lean heavily on what one might call the religious aspect of old age. I accept the naturalness of it. I very rarely think of coming to an end, even though I'm getting on for eighty, because it is a fruitless preoccupation. And I can quite well imagine that old age needn't worry an entirely non-religious person – a humanist for example. I think there are many humanists with no belief at all who don't worry about old age because they are rational and because, to tell you the truth, they have very much taken up the attitude which I have taken up myself. What happens is that you have certain beliefs when you are trying to live by faith and, in old age, as in every human stress, these support and help you.

I think more about death than I did years ago. I think about how little time I have left, ten years, five years. And, looking back ten years, I think, 'yesterday!' Just yesterday. So looking forward to even ten years is only looking foward to tomorrow. Tomorrow it will end. I accept death as a natural thing, even a rather nice and beautiful thing! I think of death and zoology. God has been so good to me, so extremely good. I've enjoyed living so much, so very much. Life is such a gift but I can quite see that it can't go on. It can't go on. But what a share of it I've had!

I was in India for thirty-three years and I think that that land's habits of prayer have touched me. Yes, I think that they may have had a big effect. Gandhi's teaching, for instance, his non-violence has entered into me. And the tolerance of spiritual India. But the present enthusiasm for comparative theology doesn't interest me much. I'm in the Christian tradition and that's where my path lies. I wouldn't claim the exclusive truth of Christianity but it seems to me the most satisfactory path. I feel very repelled by the attitudes of Karl Barth and people of that kind, who simply rule out any non-Christian religion. Barth used to talk about 'religions' – meaning everything except Christianity. 'Religions' were a bad thing. Christianity was *the* good thing. Some of the new insights into theology irritate me very much. They are so shallow. God is dead, that kind of thing. On the other hand, there are theologians who are now going much deeper into the idea of God than ever they used to. I get upset by young theologians who can advocate violence and make it a legitimate protest against injustice. I am a pacifist myself and maintain that the Crucifixion was the ideal answer to evil.

I love the physical world. I appreciate it. It is said that when you are old all this should decline and I do think about this. But I find that I can't leave the body behind when it is still with me! I don't think that I can say more than that. It's odd to be old – odd to know that you are old when your body doesn't remind you. I've been the most fortunate person and although I now notice that I get a bit tired I really don't feel all that different to when I was forty. I sleep well and I work. Music is still one of my great joys. I don't pray more – though I think I should! This does get much more difficult, especially when you're beginning to fail and need prayer badly. I don't ever expect a voice telling me to do something. The voice of God has always come to me as a pointer to where my best and deepest part is journeying, and not as a kind of command. I'm waiting not listening. Listening is Pentecostalist, and I find it very hard to do. I am well and strong and busy and happy – and old! So there you are!

Having Nothing:
Father Luke, aged seventy-five

All I feel now is that I give him what I have to give and he gives me what he has to give, and that I am thankful. Sometimes it's nothing. What one has to learn is to use 'the nothing'. You spend a whole hour in prayer and at the end there is nothing at all. But St Paul says, 'Give ye thanks for all things' – and so you learn how to use nothingness. And this is what I often have to do now that I am old. I have to be honest and tell myself that often I hear and feel *nothing*. Then I have to make it something by acknowledging its nothingness. My nothing. The alternative is despair and I would never choose that. There is nothing in despair either, but nothing *without* despair is an emptiness into which you just might manage to put something. This is what an old man like me says to himself.

One of the best things which all these new changes have brought about is this notion of waiting upon God. We used to chatter to him all the time, never giving him a chance to say anything. Or, when we had said our Office, we would say to ourselves, 'It is done, it is done!' The idea of waiting was hardly understood when I was young. It is so necessary, not only for us here but for the world too. We have tried to bring this sense of waiting into this house. Lots of us began by being taught by our mothers to say prayers, then shown by our teachers how to say more prayers and so on we went, talking, talking, talking! But *praying*? Old ffrench-Betagh, who was so brave in Johannesburg, he wrote, 'It is no longer a question of "Speak, Lord, for thy servant heareth" but "Hear, Lord, for thy servant speaketh".'

I sleep very well, you know, but I don't read much. I'm a very bad reader, very slow. In fact, I'm not what you would call a reader at all, which isn't good, but there it is. I pour out such a lot but don't have a sufficient taking-in. I go back to Gore's days. I was brought up on a few books, Dr Waterlow on Meditation, old A. J. Mason on the Catholic faith, and I find these are good still. They are old-fashioned, I daresay, but the truth is still in them, and I can turn them round a bit to help with today's tune! Everything has altered so much lately and I'm not able to go along with all these alterations. Can't keep up, although I know that if I could they would help me a lot. I see things which I thought were essential being put on one side and it makes me look at life differently. But whether this is because I am actually being carried along by modern change or because I am getting old, I don't know.

I care less. I feel now that I am tempted to hand everything over to God and to leave it at that. I don't really care two hoots about lots of things now. They make no impact on me at all. In fact I'm just about to fly out to South Africa and I don't much mind whether the aeroplane crashes or it doesn't. For myself, I mean – not for the others; that hardly needs adding. I'm unafraid of death, in other words. But there again, I may have to worry because I may not be ready for death. It is these sort of things which come into the minds of old men.

I live with a little doubt. But it would not be fair to say this of all aged people. I was brought up in my Leeds parish to say, 'This is the Faith, take it,' and I am not sure that this was not a good thing. Although there is nothing wrong with doubting. In fact it is very healthy; if you didn't sometimes doubt you'd go all over the place. Having been given a firm background I now feel that I can doubt what I like. But as I grow old I find that the background stays firm. You see, I was a missionary for all these years and I simply said, 'This, this, this and this is so.' The European wouldn't have taken it but the African could. I am not ashamed of this. I believe that I laid a foundation and now he can go building upon it. He can go his own good African way towards the truth. But when I came home I found it very difficult talking to teenagers – school-leavers mostly. They'd got all this odd television stuff in them which I hadn't heard, and so they made rings round me. About *nothing* could or would they say, 'This is the truth.' They accepted nothing except what was said or written by the popular myth-mongers which they watched or read daily. But I loved talking to these children and seeing the truthfulness in them which they refused to say they had! I have never wanted to be apart from the world and I have always talked to everybody. The fathers here think of themselves as not of the world but never as *out* of the world. Most of us here are great travellers. We have been about and we go about. And when we are outside we wear our habit. I don't think it is fair to be in disguise when you are a priest or a religious, or both. In our American house they hardly ever go out in a habit. I hope I never take off my collar. Some people think that they are very off-putting but I have never found it so. I always have a wonderful time when I go travelling. Father Superior lets me do this because in Africa I'd been on a horse for thirty years, travelling around, and he knew that it would be hard for me to stay put.

I was ordained just fifty years ago and came here as a novice in 1933. A vocation is both a natural and a supernatural thing to me and I see my long life as all of a piece. Very much so. I went to Sedbergh and was known as 'Parson' Luke from the day I arrived. My father was a priest and my grandfather was a priest, and when somebody asked this new boy, 'What are you going to do?' – that was that! A tremendous help to have decided from the start. But I never imagined that I would end up here. I thought that only brainy people got to Cowley but when a friend of mine who hadn't even got a degree was received, I thought, 'If he can go, perhaps I can go.' So here I am. As many as are called are received. It emphasizes the

question of responsibility, of course. It is remarkable what
privileges we enjoy here and I've never wanted to simply live
in the Community and take all that is offered, so I return
what I can. If there is a broken chair and it has to be done, it
is Father Luke every time. Any mending job. But my real
work is providing addresses for retreats. I visit four other
communities to help. I do whatever I can and whatever it is.
Of course there is a security about our life which some may
envy. They might even say that we are running away to be
secure, and I can quite see that side of the argument. After
all, we know that we are going to be looked after until the very
end. You can't get away from it. But we didn't come here,
long ago, for that. And we have no retirement in view.

The clock regulates us along until the end. Very much so.
If the timetable became lax the whole thing would collapse.
When I was in Africa or when I am careering down to Sussex,
I know what is happening at home here to the very minute and
because of its trustworthy regularity I am 'there' and 'with it',
and in my place at Terce or Evensong in Oxford even when I
am separated by distance. Of course you don't notice time
being regulated when you are here. You don't feel tied to time.
You feel freed by having to keep to time – if that doesn't
sound paradoxical. Old people particularly who no longer have
a time-pattern are in bondage. They often lose the time-
pattern when they retire. Perfectly true. The religious life
stays disciplined and even a bit strenuous whatever your age.
Things like getting up early don't bother me. Getting up
early keeps you healthy. And young! There is a lot of walking
about each day, long walks which you'd never get in the little
private house. We don't smoke or drink. We eat good plain
food regularly. You get your leg pulled a bit by your friends
and there's always a joke. You have plenty of company and
plenty of opportunities for escaping it! When you are having
to be solitary you know that soon you will have to be sociable.
It's ideal in its way.

But there is a changed atmosphere and one that is very

noticeable to an old priest. I prefer the holy mysteries in the far distance – and now we have brought the altar down! My Christ was Christ the King and now my Christ has to be Christ the Carpenter.

The Flight of Energy:
Father Stephen, aged seventy-nine

Now it is very different. I used to be hurtling all round the map, Lenten courses, retreats – everything. Now I'm less mobile having slipped and wrenched my foot, taking the muscle off the bone. And so I can say Anno Domini and have laziness as catalyst. Now it is more letters and less movement. Letters because almost every day one hears of a death and one must write. It is non-stop, the dying of friends and acquaintances, when you are eighty. It is one of the hazards of being a clergyman to make a large acquaintance! Having been an idler here for so long I have had the time to keep in touch with all those I knew in my first parish fifty-five years ago. I arrange reunions and I never miss writing to each one that is left at Christmas. Now we are all white-haired penfriends. They were boys when I went away and now they are old men.

It was an extraordinary church such as one would never see now. It was in East London. East London was thrilling, absolutely thrilling. I went there with desperate quickness after the trenches and Oxford. The church itself was a huge kind of preaching-box built at the time of the French Revolution and we always used to have just on 2,000 people for Evensong! It was a lovely sight. It was in 1922. Marvellous. And well over 1,000 communicants. There were 1,100 children in the Sunday Schools and we had to lay on two special trains from Hackney Down Station to take them on their summer outing. I didn't build all this up, I inherited it. It was an inheritance. We fielded seven football teams on a Saturday.

There were between three and four dozen choirboys. It's nearly all quite unimaginable now, and it's a pity. It was charming, the great *esprit de corps* among us, the goodness and kindness of everybody. I was young and it was a young church. I shall never forget it. Now what it gave me I must hand on. As Bunyan said, 'My sword I'll leave to him that followeth.' The inheritors, the generation now coming on, are very wonderful people.

My beloved boys from the East London church are dying-off. Dozens of them have died already – the boys from my communicants' guild. They are old men really, of course, who are dying off. Old men with my old boys' faces and names. People you've loved don't age if you don't see them.

I've belonged to the Community for forty years. I spent a quarter of a century at our London House, where I was in charge of all the children's work and the schools in London. I still take retreats for schoolchildren. I think of my own boy-hood now, of being taken by my mother to a Lent course at St Mary Abbots and the preacher hanging over the pulpit in his spectacles and saying, 'The peace, the *peace* of God . . .' and the war just about being to begin! I still think of this when I walk along Honey Street and Church Street, Kensington. Little absurd things seen from the threshold of eighty, and so clearly.

I rose to the solemn heights of a captain in the war. I was with the regulars and I was thankful for this because they knew their job and made it much more comfortable. I was com-missioned straight from school and that terrible mêlée had as much an effect on me as all the sermons.

Later I went to be chaplain at Cuddesdon and that, of course, was paradise on earth. Simply wonderful. I was there for about five years when everybody was coming through, including Michael Ramsey, the recent Archbishop of Canter-bury. He's living near here now and he always greets me. Then I became chaplain to the Bishop of London, Dr Winnington Ingram, and that again was simply fantastically wonderful.

You couldn't imagine anybody a more complete personification of charity. Nobody could say anything horrid about anybody when he was around! And happy! Then I came here. So there it is, all rather uneventful, yet wonderful.

I read – and have read – incessantly. One has read almost everything. Such a lot. So many. Good books by quiet, clever, unexcited men who lived what they were saying. Reading – another job!

We accept Thomas à Kempis's 'Don't desire to live long but to live well' here – and it doesn't mean pork chops for breakfast! But I have lived long. And things don't get brighter. They are as Keats described them in his 'The Human Seasons':

> ... quiet coves
> His soul has in its Autumn, when his wings
> He furleth close; contented so to look
> On mists in idleness – to let fair things
> Pass by unheeded as a threshold brook.
> He has his Winter too of pale misfeature,
> Or else he would forego his mortal nature.

I think there are some very big lessons for the old. Some old people trundle along, some old people stay alert. I feel about twelve! And the lesson I must learn is, what does it mean not to be able to do things? Everybody screams – and I include myself – 'I can't do this and I can't do that!', and 'I used to do this and I used to do that! – and *baaah*!' The lesson to be learnt is to understand the promotion from plum-easy doing to the surprisingly difficult non-activity of just *being*. Be patient, be gentle, be *nothing*. Somebody said that the real vocation of old age was to give out love. So no more doing, but being. I told an old lady in a home this and she said, 'What a lot of rot. Never heard such a lot of rot!' But within a fortnight she'd begun to get the hang of it and it made all the difference to her. She stopped grousing and fussing, and doing things so badly that they worried her. Do nothing.

One seems to have no worries here. Days and weeks simply

whiz by. Even the young fathers say the same. All gone so fast. For the first time in my life I don't care a hang if I miss seeing the Boat Race on TV. It all goes on, it will all go on. On and on. But one will not. Not in this context.

Going Out Good:
Colonel Hardy, s.a., aged seventy-five

The Salvationists' religion incorporates much that conflicts with the normal experiences of old age, mental and physical. It advocates a strident sunniness, positive action, and a dramatic interpretation of, and obedience to, orders. The orders either filter down from the Army's own High Command or are given directly to a soldier by God himself, and a lot of the excitement of life devolves from the receipt and operation of these instructions. But life – even the most kindly understood life – being what it is, the year arrives when the orders officially cease and, since one has never smoked, drunk, or had much money, or much liberty to worry about one's own affairs, and is thus likely to be exceptionally healthy at seventy, one has a problem.

The traditional virtue of elderly Christians, *benignitas*, a sort of exuding of long-amassed prayer, is more likely to be the reward of the religious introvert than the average Salvationist during the interim between his being relieved of his command and his being 'promoted to glory', as the obituaries in *The War Cry* put it. For the average Salvationist is a person of stir and movement, a spiritual *possibliste* for whom inaction is unnatural and uncaring. Of course, like all religious organizations, the Salvation Army says that there is no real retirement from its ranks and that its members soldier-on until the end. Yet when the day comes when '(R)' has to be placed after one's name in the List, no amount of lip-service to careers which only death can halt is able to conceal the fact that it produces a shock in many a life geared to action and selfless involvement. When the involvement is checked and curtailed, energy becomes deflected into channels unaccustomed to receive it, those of the self when brought to a standstill. This unfamiliar and usually unattractive self hypnotizes the old man or woman. It is something they have not had much of a chance to see in themselves before because of the clarion uproar caused by battle orders and being in the thick of things. 'There is no retirement for the Salvationist,' repeats Colonel Hardy, even as his entire personality, at seventy-five, witnesses to the unique effect which his stepping-down from Active Service has had on him.

The notion that the old should either avoid or be shielded from dramatic change might seem sensible to those for whom change is a problem at forty, but it has no general validity. The Colonel's life was all change. When change did not threaten him, he grew anxious and even took measures to precipitate it. Like all Salvationists, he loves to describe his own great moments of transition. Life for him is not a steady uneventfulness gradually leading up to the thrilling climax when the spirit is released from the flesh, it is a series of colourful upsets along the Damascus road. The first and most important upset remains inexplicable even to this day, if one is impervious to the lure of bands and the brave music of drums, far or near. The Colonel was never impervious to either. When he was in his twenties and a guardsman in the Regulars, he heard the throbbing sound beneath the barracks window, rushed downstairs and pursued it through the town. When the band marched, still playing, into the citadel, he marched in too. When it mounted the platform, he threw himself before it, at the Mercy Seat. He was entranced. After a few minutes a young bandsman joined him, kneeling beside him, holding his hand. Not a word passed. The Colonel had had no religious instruction of any sort but faith passed to him via touch and music. As soon as he could he transferred commands, was retrained, commissioned and told to set up

the Salvation Army in one of the African colonies. He arrived
there, like Mother Theresa in Calcutta, without a stick of
equipment but with high expectation of some amazing orders
from above. If one acts on principle, believing the principle
to be God's, one acts astonishingly and frequently in imitation
of the divine restlessness. In between his tasks of polyglot
welfare officer, missionary, educationalist and chief executive,
the Colonel learnt to paint.

His hot African oils, flowers, veldt, huts, heads with
brilliant eyes and hands with bibles, surround him in the flat
in the Home for Aged Christians. He cannot see them. He is
blind. Like his conversion, his blindness was not some end
result of what was long endemic to him, but again the Pauline
bolt from the blue sent to deflect him from one path to
another. The path he was trudging down, uncomplaining
enough, was that of the old widower contemplating a companionate re-marriage and of an old letter-writer holding
together for as long as he could the rapidly snapping strands
of his wide acquaintanceship. His sudden blindness altered
all this. He could no longer write or read, and he felt that he
could no longer offer companionship or anything less than
love. His blind renaissance supports – of all people – John
Webster, when he asked, 'Is not old wine wholesomest, old
pippins toothsomest, old wood burn brightest, old linen wash
whitest? Old soldiers, sweethearts, are surest, and old lovers
are soundest.'

When the Colonel was struck blind he offered to release his
fiancée, another widowed Colonel who, like himself, had once
governed for the Salvation Army a territory the size of half a
dozen dioceses but who, entirely unlike him, had sunk into
abject self-pity in her old age, but she would have none of it.
His blindness was to be her geriatric reformation too. She had
become a recluse in a bungalow after her husband's death and
a bore to her children. She was morbidly intrigued by grief,
smelling it out around her and 'weeping with them that wept'.
God was fed up with her because she had turned down all his

sensible solutions. She then had a crisis of faith. As God was
telling her what she did not feel like doing, was he there? God
then said, 'There are a lot of dreary old women like you. Go
and do some work, you are as strong as a horse still. How
about reading to the blind? Something like that? Only leave
your misery behind – they've got enough to put up with
without that.' Mrs Colonel Hardy then obeyed God to the
letter – it was just like the old days – and in her mid-seventies
finds herself 'deeply in love'. Both she and her husband
decline to see their marriage in 'companionate' terms. They
are, they both stress, 'passionately and deeply in love'.

They are large, commanding figures, both enormously
handsome with beautiful skin and fine eyes. The Colonel's
blind gaze is focused and blue, and without clouding or
stigma. He is not in blackness, he says, he is in an object-less
light, opalescent and restful. He has no intention of ever
reading Braille because he has no intention of ever reading or
writing again. That is the joy of it. And he is quite pleased to
no longer see his paintings because the African pictures in his
mind have been sharpened by his sightlessness into an iri-
descence which has retrieved every sight and sound he
experienced while working there.

*

I was there for half a century. When I first arrived I saw the
smile of the Africans still open and quite undefensive in places
where the colonialists had not yet penetrated, and then
becoming narrow and watchful as time passed. It was while
I was there in 1930 that I managed to establish a link with a
great personal hero, David Livingstone, through friendship
with an old, old man who had helped to carry his body to the
coast on its last journey. He and his friends carried Livingstone
as carefully as the old Christians in the Middle Ages used to
carry the bodies of their saints to shrines. This old, old man
had been Livingstone's servant Matthew Wellington. There's
a big blow-up picture of him at Blantyre. I visited him every

year until he died. He'd been a slave in the old days and then he got into Livingstone's service. He was from the West Coast, had been liberated in Liberia and then taken up by David Livingstone. The old African is so frail and so respected in old age. The name for Jomo Kenyatta all over Kenya is M'zee – the Old Man. M'zee is a word full of respect and reverence. But old age in England is just a social nuisance. I saw some boys talking about an old man when he was struggling onto a bus, saying they thought he should be shot! The old man turned to the lads and said, 'Be careful, you could be when *you* get to seventy.'

I have to admit that I don't feel old and I do feel profoundly happy, but that's the way life has gone. I've led the religious life and it seems to have worked. Though it's not for me to say. Ours is an experimental faith, not just an intellectual one. Our religion is far more experimental than credal. I have had to apply it to such a succession of social changes in my lifetime that it had to be flexible. It should be flexible. Love is flexible. It winds round everything. I don't think that I ever thought about being old when I was being young! And I wouldn't want it – life – all over again. Once is enough. Young people often say, 'Would you like to be young again?' and don't really like it when you say no. I soften the blow. I say, 'Just think of all the years I should have been done out of heaven!' Though that doesn't please them much either. When you are young you think it is better to be young than in heaven. It was dreadful for many to be old in my boyhood. For working people there was still the fear of the workhouse, the last remnant of which didn't go out until 1949. Dreadful it was. And working women of forty-five were 'old' when I was a child. I knew what I was doing when I got out of the Regulars and got into the Army, you know. That band was part of the sound made by all kinds of thinking people to bring the wicked old walls tumbling down! The action is over, so far as I am concerned, but I hope that now I am an old man there is something written into me, or on me – an epistle which people who encounter me can read. I mean, I hope that what I've done has left some sort of a mark. If the mark shows, then my ministry continues. Old men are heavily marked and can be read. Good things, bad things, are in their marks.

Death wipes them off, of course. The best and the worst people, when they are old, leave the world not looking a bit like their old selves. I've seen a lot of it. I knew a remittance man in Kenya, a grandson of the general manager of the Great Western Railway. And there he was, swashbuckling about with a revolver in his belt because of Mau-Mau, and with his ten-gallon hat and his imperial beard. And towards the end he looked terrible. Heavy and debauched, pendulous jowls. A dark man through and through. And the African woman came over and said, 'John's ill, John's sick.' He fell back dead as I opened his chalet door. It was blood-poisoning. And all the blackness and grossness drained from him as I watched, and he lay there handsome and refined again. All the filth of the years ran out of him and he had his young Cambridge face to take to the grave.

My wife, too. We had been married for forty-five years. If she had a fault it was a fault to which I was blind. I never saw her fault. When she came to the end I came to her in the Anglesea Ward with my arms full of flowers at the visiting hour. On the day of her death her face was very stricken and it was hard to look at. She had double pneumonia after an operation. Her change panicked me and I called people and nurses and doctors. She couldn't communicate but needed to. And she suddenly sat up, smiled, put out her arms and died. Her last words were a gesture. I thought I was seeing things when I saw her face. Even her hair glowed. When I looked in to see my lady after her death she had the face of a girl. That is how we enter the presence of Christ – at our best. In full revelation.

I suppose I am part of the old Salvation Army. Yes, I think I am. You see, in the beginning we were an army of twice-born men and women. Now we are, in large part, merely the descendants of twice-born men and women. There is a different type now – men and women who have never seen the work-houses and the poverty wages and the old people of forty-five. They read about them, of course, and their grandmothers tell them about them. But to see them when they were just *normal* – that was quite another matter. We older Salvationists grew out of it and voluntarily marched back into it, for Jesus' sake. But now we have a large sprinkling of university people and so on. Sophisticated charity workers – and very useful too. The decline of church membership in the Salvation Army is rather less than most. I think that is true. But we share the same cycle of the apostolic, then the respectable and then the modernist of the other churches. Our youngsters, like Soper, question the Virgin Birth and the Resurrection. I tell my friends, 'If this goes on in our second century – it's the Army's second century now – one of two things will happen. Either the Salvation Army will go on the scrapheap, or a man and a voice will arise from within the movement and will bring back the rich red original wine.' The emphasis will return to the evangel, even if much of what we do continues to be the social-welfare thing. The world honours us – myself – for being social-welfare workers, not evangels.

My blindness has been astonishing. I remember everything about it. I remember vividly it was the 20th May and I was at a holiday home, where there were forty of us, to say morning prayers. I read the passage for the day and my sight was as clear as it had ever been. Two days later I met my wife. Three days after that I proposed to her and she accepted me. A week later, and I could not have read that same passage. I was frightened when it completely happened. It was one Saturday – we were engaged now but living apart and alone. That day I had typed six foolscap pages to friends in Canada. My fiancée rang that evening and asked how I was and I said, 'I'm fine. I've brought my correspondence right up to date – single spacing!' And we were so happy, both of us. And in that night it went, my sight. I was asleep. I noticed it when I woke. I

rang my fiancée, who came immediately and then I rang
Moorfields. They gave me an interview the next day. And from
that time I have neither typed nor written, nor read. I said to
her, 'I'm blind. It is not the same. I'm blind. You may withdraw, you could withdraw.' But she knew then that my blindness was within God's plan for her and she said, '*Withdraw?*'
From the day of my blindness I haven't felt the urge for
nearly everything that absorbed me before the blindness. I go
down Memory Lane and it's often better now than when it
was taking place. More pleasurable. Recollections of years and
years spent in God's service. It was ordered. We both felt
that it was ordered. Our marriage was ordered. I think that
old, widowed people should try and marry again. I think so.
If they share something, some background such as we do,
then they should share each other. We do. We are not just an
old couple, we are deeply in love.

It would be nice if we could go out on the crest of the wave
and not via the geriatric ward! To go out *good*. Pray God lets
us do that, go out good.

Is there Anybody There?
The Spiritual Healer, aged seventy-nine

I discovered when I was still young that you don't have to
just imagine any human experience – you can try it. So I've
tried a surprising number of things in my long life. So have
most people, only they won't admit it. When I go on, via
death, I believe that I shall go on being human in another
place. Being superhuman is really inhuman, and I wouldn't
want that. All I know is what has happened to this body and
to this intelligence, and with a bit of luck it should determine
my position in the spirit world. I shall feel comfortable there
with my humanity. Since none of us can think outside of his
humanity, you may as well give up heavenly notions, because

what isn't human is beyond human involvement. My old brother – he's eighty-one – says, 'When you're dead, you're dead,' and this seems to cheer him up no end. 'Curtains, boy,' he says, patting his old dog.

Spiritualism gives you a sensible interest in your old age. It stops that petering-out feeling. It even makes you care for your body because, as the vehicle of your personality, you know you will be recognized by it on the next plane. I find my body very pleasant still; it's done me proud. It's quite nice still, if I say it myself. It all works. I shall be quite pleased to have it in its spirit version and it will remind me of my earthly humanity – which I've so enjoyed.

Of course, I've had to work at it, this spiritual development, but I haven't minded that. It's stopped me being selfish and it's made me experimental. I do absent healing. It's prayerful concentration on somebody who is ill. It's nicer to know who they are, of course – more helpful – because it gives you a familiar body to concentrate on. But all I have of many people is just their name and the information that they are somebody's son or friend. It doesn't matter where the healing is concerned. Nearly all my absent-healing patients are strangers. I started absent healing when I was fourteen, and without knowing what I was doing.

There was a girl in our village who was dying of galloping consumption – a common thing then – and although I'd had nothing whatever to do with this girl, I couldn't stop myself thinking about her lying up there in her little cottage bedroom and being rapidly consumed by disease. She filled my head morning, noon and night. It was pathetic, a girl being consumed by disease. I imagined her as hard as I could and said prayers for her all day long. My mother was a Protestant and my father was a Catholic but they didn't go in for any religious practice, and neither did I, although I sometimes went to the village church to hear the lovely music. Anyway, it got so that I could think of nothing else except this dying girl whom everybody was discussing so morbidly. Then I stopped

316 · *The View in Winter*

thinking about her and it was quite a long time afterwards that I suddenly asked about her funeral. When had it taken place?

'Funeral?' they said. 'What are you talking about, old chap? She got better, didn't she? Didn't that monkey take her sickness for her?' Now there was this pet monkey in the village and as this girl got well, the monkey grew ill, and when she was healed, the monkey died. Or that is what they said. I never saw her and I never had anything to do with the poor monkey. All I did was concentrate on her for days and days and days, holding her back from being consumed by her tuberculosis. I knew that she was only a girl and that she should have more of this beautiful world. All the boys and girls, then, being carried from the cottages in their white coffins! Common sight, common business. So that is why I began to do my private spirit healing, to give young people time and strength enough to enjoy the world and their humanity, and to put a stop to their pain.

Our son was only ten and three-quarters when he went. It was meningitis. And it was then that our friends said that we should get in touch with a good medium. So this was how it started, my spiritualism, and this is how it usually starts. We got a bit hot and bothered at first, then we settled down to it. I got very easy about it all in mind and heart. I've stayed close to our David. I'm very old and the earth has been my school. Soon I shall have to leave this school and live in another place in accordance with all I have learnt in it. Many of the effects of earth-experience are tragic, but in general they aren't, and it's up to each of us to control tragic effects when they come to others whenever we can.

The trouble is that, when you are old, you know exactly what to do and say, because everything imaginable under the sun has happened to you, but then you find that you haven't got the mental brightness any more, so you can't help others with what you've learnt. Or your authority has gone, perhaps. Because when you retire your authority is taken away from you, though you still feel your authority even when it isn't there. It is like amputees feeling pain in their sawn-off leg. So although you may see somebody young going through all the misery and muddle which you went through yourself, and you know what to do about it, *you can't do it.* Your brightness has gone. So you write a letter to the newspaper instead! Half the letters you read in the newspapers are written by old men whose brightness has gone and who are still trying to show their authority. I concentrate my old dimness into my spiritual healing. I don't get hurt that way and, who knows, somebody young might get strong enough to live to be old.

It Can't Go On: the Clergyman's Widow, aged ninety-two

I say to people, 'Don't give me presents, don't give me presents! I'm trying to get rid of things.' I don't want to accumulate any more. Often now I have a tidy-up, getting ready for when I go. It's just like moving, no better and no worse. Having a clear-out. What I dread isn't death but all the nuisance I shall be at the end. I've always hated being a nuisance. So I'm organizing myself a bit so that I shall be as little a nuisance as possible when the time comes. I dread having a stroke because that is the most ghastly nuisance which will go on for months and months, and when I finally manage to go my daily woman will say, 'Oh, what a nuisance she was, poor thing!'

Except she won't because she is so good. Come to think of it, I could afford to be a bit of a nuisance with her. She wouldn't even notice it, I daresay. She has become my closest and most trusted friend now. She lets me rely on her, and anyone who will let you do that is worth their weight in gold. And the woman who does my shopping would come to me at once if I needed her. I see them both as part of the goodness of God, you know. All the same, I don't see why they should be put to a lot of mess and muddle when my time comes and so I shall be so pleased to just go off quietly in my sleep, or something like that. It must come fairly soon although I feel as right as rain!

I don't actually feel so old, now I come to think about it. I have sons and grandchildren and great-grandchildren, and they all troop in to see me, and none of them treats me like an old woman, and that helps. I forget their names, naturally, but not their pretty faces. They're very casual. The young are so casual. But charming. They are very careless, well, of acknowledging things. There, I've said it. It's no good, I shall never get used to it. Had *I* forgotten to send thanks by return of post I should never have heard the end of it! Oh, but they're charming, my young people! They are so kind to me and they show their love for me. You get things back, don't you? Friendship is one's own responsibility. Old age shouldn't make one less friendly or interested in getting new friends. All my old friends are in the graveyard and if I hadn't made some new ones, where would I be? I think a lot of old people just aren't very sensible. They only have old friends and then they live to be ninety or something, like me, and then they start moaning because their friends have gone before, as they say.

My advice to the aged woman is find some young people. Don't go to these dreadful old folks' clubs but find some young people. Put up with their casualness because it's worth it. *Why*, I should like to know, are they so casual, I wonder?

I'm lame because I've got arthritis and it is *the* most perfect nuisance. When I was seventy I was having this most awful pain and my sister said, 'Look here, it can't go on,' and my cousin, Lady Eileen, who has just died, aged ninety-seven, said, 'Look here, it can't go on,' and so they took me to London to an orthopaedic surgeon for the hip operation. I said, 'Operate on both at once, if you can, because if I once get out of here I'll never come back!' So he did both at once. I knew nothing about it and just had a lovely sleep. I was seventy-four. When you are ninety-two and you say, 'When I was seventy-four,' it is almost like saying, 'When I was young!' The surgeon said, 'Your heart is a girl of eighteen's.' He was quite a flirt.

I am exceedingly glad that I was brought up without the wireless and on Thackeray, Dickens and Thomas Hardy. I still love Hardy. My son said to me recently, 'You never taught me poetry.' So accusing! I said, 'My darling, did I ever have the *time*? You went to prep school when you were eight and in the holidays I spent my energies making the days jolly for you. If I'd started teaching you poetry you'd have thought I'd gone off my head.' He found poetry for himself. That is what one has to do.

A woman comes every day to do my shopping for me since I've been lame. This woman who is now my friend. And I don't go out unless I go in the car. About once a week I go out in the car, and that is enough. I don't do any housework – I don't bother about that! The daily does it. How well she does it! But I love cooking. How I cook! And I love warmth. When you're old and you can't take exercise and your blood is thin, you do feel so cold. How cold we get, we old souls. Being old is very chilly, I assure you. Cooking keeps you warm inside and out. As for sleep, I sleep very well indeed.

I don't dread dying in my sleep but I do dread dying any other way. Mostly for the nuisance, you know. And I don't dread being dead. My heavenly Father has looked after me from the cradle and he won't stop at the grave. Through all my life he has taken care of me. Even if I just went out like a candle, what is there to dread?

My husband was a clergyman and we were in our Huntingdon parish for seventeen years and then in the Isle of Ely. They were very unsophisticated people there. It was 1925. They were almost like foreign people, so elementary. But kind hearts, I'll give them that. My sons loved them and they all went wildfowling together. The village had lost so many boys in the war that it loved my boys. It's all ages and ages ago, of course, years and years ago.

BIBLIOGRAPHY

A Happier Old Age, H.M.S.O., 1977.
AGATE, J., and MEACHER, M., *The Care of the Old*, Fabian Society, 1969.
The Attitudes of the Retired and Elderly, Age Concern, 1977.
BARON, BARCLAY, *In Flanders Fields*, Toc-H, 1935.
BLUNDEN, EDMUND, *Undertones of War*, Cobden Sanderson, 1929.
BRYANT, CHRISTOPHER, *New Fire* and various pamphlets, S.S.J.E. Publications, 1965–75.
CHAUCER, GEOFFREY, *Canterbury Tales*, tr. D. Wright, Barrie & Jenkins, 1964.
CHOWN, SHEILA M. (ed.), *Human Ageing*, Penguin Books, 1972.
CICERO, *De Senectute*.
COMFORT, ALEX, *The Process of Ageing*, Weidenfeld & Nicolson, 1965.
CONGREVE, GEORGE, *Treasures of Hope*, Longman, 1918.
CURTIN, SHARON, *Nobody Ever Died of Old Age*, Little Brown, Boston, Mass., 1977.
DE BEAUVOIR, SIMONE, *Old Age*, André Deutsch and Weidenfeld & Nicolson, 1972.
DE LA MARE, WALTER, *Early One Morning*, Faber & Faber, 1935.
ELLIS, HAVELOCK, *From Rousseau to Proust*, Houghton-Mifflin, Boston, Mass., 1935.
FISHLOCK, TREVOR, *Wales and the Welsh*, Cassell, 1972.
GORER, GEOFFREY, *Death, Grief and Mourning in Contemporary Britain*, Cresset Press, 1965.
GREEN, PETER, *Kenneth Grahame*, John Murray, 1959.
GROTJAHN, M., *Some Analytic Observations about the Process of Growing Old*, International Universities Press, New York, 1951, pp. 301–12.
HIGHAM, T. F. and BOWRA, C. M., *The Oxford Book of Greek Verse*, Oxford University Press, 1938.
HINTON, JOHN, *Dying*, Penguin Books, 1967.
HOWELLS, ROSCOE, *Total Community*, H. E. Walter, 1976.
LARKIN, PHILIP (ed.), *Oxford Book of Twentieth-Century English Verse*, Oxford University Press, 1973.
LEA, F. A., *John Middleton Murry*, Methuen, 1959.

LIVINGSTONE, R. W., *The Greek Genius and its Meaning to Us*, Oxford University Press, 1915.

MCCABE, JOSEPH, *Edward Clodd*, Bodley Head, 1932.

MEACHER, MICHAEL, *Taken for a Ride*, Longman, 1972.

MELINSKY, HUGH, *On Dying Well: An Anglican Contribution to the Debate on Euthanasia*, Church Information Office, 1975.

MÉRIMÉE, PROSPER, *An Author's Love*, Macmillan, 1889.

MONTESSORI, MARIA, *The Montessori Method*, Heinemann, 1912.

New Deal for the Elderly, Fabian Society, 1978.

POWYS, JOHN COWPER, *The Art of Growing Old*, Cape, 1944.

POWYS, JOHN COWPER, *In Defence of Sensuality*, Gollancz, 1930.

RENN, LUDWIG, *War*, Martin Secker, 1929.

Report on the Aged Homosexual, Campaign for Homosexual Equality, 1974.

RHYS, JEAN, 'Whatever Became of Old Mrs Pearce?', *The Times*, 21 May 1975.

SCOTT-MAXWELL, FLORIDA, *The Measure of My Days*, Knopf, New York, 1968.

SEARLE, CHRIS (compiler), *Elders*, Reality Press, 1973.

THOMAS, GWYN, *A Welsh Eye*, Hutchinson, 1964.

Toc-H Journal.

TOURNIER, PAUL, *Learning to Grow Old*, S.C.M. Press, 1972.

VISCHER, A. L., *On Growing Old*, Allen & Unwin, 1966.

WADE, AUBREY, *Gunner on the Western Front*, Batsford, 1959.

WHISTLER, LAURENCE, *The Initials in the Heart*, Hart-Davis, 1956.

WILLIAMSON, HENRY, *It was the Nightingale*, Macdonald, 1962

ZINBERG, NORMAN E., and KAUFMAN, IRVING, *Normal Psychology of the Ageing Process*, International Universities Press, New York, 1963.